JOHN J. WRIGHT LIBRARY
LA ROCHE COLLEGE
9000 BABCOCK BLVD.
PITTSBURGH, PA 15237

PENGUIN BOOKS

FRUITFUL

Anne Roiphe is the author of seven novels, including the ac-
claimed *Up the Sandbox* and *Lovingkindness*. Her articles and
reviews have appeared in *The New York Times*, *Vogue*, *Redbook*,
Glamour, *Working Woman*, *Family Circle*, and elsewhere, and
she writes a biweekly column for the *New York Observer*. She
lives with her husband, Dr. Herman Roiphe, in New York
City, where she raised her children.

D1125467

THE JOHN J. WRIGHT LIBRARY
LA ROCHE COLLEGE
9000 BABCOCK BLVD.
PITTSBURGH, PA 15237

FRUITFUL

Living the Contradictions:
A Memoir of Modern Motherhood

ANNE ROIPHE

306.8743
R64f
1997

PENGUIN BOOKS

PENGUIN BOOKS

Published by the Penguin Group

Penguin Putnam Inc., 375 Hudson Street,
New York, New York 10014, U.S.A.
Penguin Books Ltd, 27 Wrights Lane, London W8 5TZ, England
Penguin Books Australia Ltd, Ringwood, Victoria, Australia
Penguin Books Canada Ltd, 10 Alcorn Avenue,
Toronto, Ontario, Canada M4V 3B2
Penguin Books (N.Z.) Ltd, 182–190 Wairau Road,
Auckland 10, New Zealand

Penguin Books Ltd, Registered Offices:
Harmondsworth, Middlesex, England

First published in the United States of America
by Houghton Mifflin Company 1996
Reprinted by arrangement with Houghton Mifflin Company
Published in Penguin Books 1997

1   3   5   7   9   10   8   6   4   2

Copyright © Anne Roiphe, 1996
All rights reserved

"Disobedience" from *When We Were Very Young* by A. A. Milne.
Copyright E. P. Dutton, 1924. Copyright renewed A. A. Milne, 1952.
Used by permission of Dutton Children's Books, a division of Penguin Books USA Inc.

The verse by Sharon Olds is used by permission of the publisher.

THE LIBRARY OF CONGRESS HAS CATALOGUED THE HARDCOVER AS FOLLOWS:
Roiphe, Anne Richardson, date.
Fruitful: A real mother in the modern world/Anne Roiphe
p.   cm.
ISBN 0-395-73531-9 (hc.)
ISBN 0 14 02.6672 0 (pbk.)
1. Motherhood.   2. Feminism.   3. Family.   I. Title.
HQ759.R636   1996   306.874'3—dc20   96-17459

Printed in the United States of America
Set in Monotype Bulmer
Designed by Anne Chalmers

Except in the United States of America, this book is sold subject to the condition
that it shall not, by way of trade or otherwise, be lent, re-sold, hired out, or otherwise
circulated without the publisher's prior consent in any form of binding or cover other
than that in which it is published and without a similar condition including this
condition being imposed on the subsequent purchaser.

To

HERMAN ROIPHE, M.D.

My fisherman

CONTENTS

PREFACE

NOW THAT MY CHILDREN no longer wake me in the middle of the night, hungry or wet, with bad dreams or sudden stomachaches, I should, returned to myself, sleep soundly. But I don't. They are adults and still I am not myself. I remain a mother linked — or is it chained — by a thousand thoughts to her children. It is clear to me that feminism, despite its vast accomplishments, has not cured me of motherhood.

Born in the late nineteen thirties I came to feminism just in time. There will be no return to the way it was when I was a girl with a poodle on my skirt, afraid of my own desires, pretending to be weak where I was strong, strong where I was weak. I am profoundly grateful for the political movement that insisted that the fullness of life was mine to grasp and that gender was a glory not a prison.

However, we don't live our lives by the rhetoric of the most conspicuous feminists. We don't experience ourselves the way politicians would have it. They no more speak for us than Michael Jackson's surgical mask reflects his real face. Feminist politics may be personal but the personal always slips out of the grasp of the political. It seethes and squirms, it bites and soothes in ways that make all rhetoric seem like baby talk, while real life is experienced in the parentheses, in the subclause, in the ironies.

When it comes to motherhood we shrug, we blush, we look at our feet and we attempt private solutions, we worry whatever we do. At the place where feminism and motherhood intersect the fires still burn. We thought we could wish the conflict away. We thought we could ignore it. We couldn't. So when I started this book, I wanted to see what mothering does to women, what price it exacts, what mothering does to our souls, to our ambitions. I read feminist scholars and feminist politicians. I read psychoanalysts and psychologists. I saw that in order to address the questions in my mind I would have to talk about my own experiences. My stories are personal and in the details unique but they belong to this time, to this place. They reflect the way history runs through all of us digging craters in our hearts. Just as political puzzles are half-understood clues to private life, so private life, with its ever moving currents, carries the answers to political puzzles. When I write about mothers and mothering I am not talking about every mother across the land. No two women will have exactly the same experience, and when we acknowledge the differences in life and health, in worldview, that come with class and region, country versus city, any conclusions about mothers will have multiple exceptions and remain somewhat particular and eccentric. I am describing a narrow band of middle- and upper-class mothers who have education and professions, who have been exposed to the ideas and fashions of the last forty years and have taken them to heart for better or worse. Race, religion, and ethnicity are enormous factors in our lives, but for the purposes of this book I am putting them on the back burner and focusing on the common shared experiences of bearing and raising children in these fragmented times. I want my daughters to understand that their easy, natural, assumed feminism, the careers that they are launched on, will be impinged on by their emotional lives. I want them to find better ways of being both mothers and working women. I'm frightened they might sacrifice one for the other. I want to warn them that the feminism I preached needs to be tempered with connection and love, for partner and child. I want them to understand that life is not a gaggle of political slogans, however stylish, smart, politically correct they might be.

I have been thinking about ways to design our families so that the pain we know could be lessened and the pleasure we find there enhanced. How sad it would be if feminism ended on the rock pile of tarnished visions, like the other "isms" of this benighted century, born of idealism and buried in mockery.

PART I

FEMINISM AND MOTHERHOOD:
A COLLISION COURSE

The clean new snow is piled high against the cars. The streets are impassable as the plows push and scrape, back and forth, like ancient mammals in a mating dance. The lights turn red and green, the wind blows cold, snow falls in thick clouds, in bursts, in flashes. It is December dark and the city lights blink like conversation interrupted. I am nine months pregnant with my first child. I am carrying my first husband's typewriter home from the repair shop. He is at a neighborhood bar drinking straight scotch — that's what male writers did in 1960 when feminism was no more than a faded photograph of a suffragette with black buttoned boots and a placard in her hand, when feminism was a mummy wrapped in old wishes waiting for Betty Friedan to burst open the wall of its sealed cave. As my water broke I leaned against a snow bank to rest the heavy typewriter. I held back panic, the urge to scream for help. Explain to me again how this baby is going to get out of my body. I felt a moment's mourning. This was the end of self as I had always known it. This was the beginning of my destiny. There was no amniocentesis in those days. I was afraid that the baby might be retarded or a hole had opened in its spine. I was afraid of giving birth to a monster. There were no sonograms to show me arms, legs, head. The thing that moved in my belly was invisible. There were no Lamaze classes in those days. There were no fathers holding your hand and breathing deeply with you. I was like a blind person moving toward the edge of a cliff. The species may have been forcing itself into renewal down the dark hall of my vaginal canal, but I was without glory, scared, alone, holding a typewriter that was not mine.

Ah, ah, I said when I saw the baby eighteen hours later, and those early moments as I counted the fingers and the toes, and looked at the lashes and felt the soft indentation on the scalp, touched the black wisps of hair, were my first and possibly last moments of wordless joy, of lifting up like the Eastern religions a promise of transcendence and peace. Temporarily I was blissed. So blissed I hardly noticed that I had lost my place on Huck's raft, would soon lose my indifferent husband, my time for myself, my ambition, my freedom to go wherever the mood took me and stay as long as I liked. I was no longer the subject of my own days. Now I was the soil, damp, dank, wormy, from which someone else might grow. If I did badly I would never forgive myself. Judgment hung in the closet where the dark creatures of my childhood had once lurked. I had given up my boundary, the wall of self, and in return had received obligation and love, a love mingled with its opposite, a love that grabbed me by the throat and has still not let me go.

Whatever I had once been, center forward on the field hockey team, poet of the fifth grade, winner of the long-distance swim contest, collector of tiny glass animals, traveler, wearer of corsets, girdles, garter belts, supporter of lost causes, kicker-up of heels, slow-dancer, biter of nails, thumb sucker, prone to earaches, I was now someone else. I had dreamt of becoming an artist, an escapee from the rules and regulations, a flyer of fancies, a romantic figure in a blue beret, a resistance fighter, a planter of trees in the Galilee, a poet in the garrets of Montmartre. Instead I became, like a moth to its flame, like a snake curling out of its basket, like the fleck of fertile human matter I most certainly was, a disciple of Darwin, proceeding as if pulled by a magnet, pushed by a great wind down the road of my DNA: a mother. I was in love with my child, not sanely, not calmly, not rationally but wholly and completely, the way people get on an airplane and give control to the pilot, to the currents of wind, and let themselves be lifted up, taken away. This love is not so simple, it is certainly not pure or unselfish. It is indecent both in its proportions and in its motives. Deep embedded in this love was the story of my life, both the past and the future, my handprint on the universe, so to speak. My love so ordinary, so commonplace, so usual was not romantic. I might have known it was bad for my mind, fatal for my freedom, but I didn't. However, when the milk came in and the nipples stopped aching and the baby lay against my side, I took refuge in the moment, not thinking ahead or behind.

My own mother read mystery stories, romance novels, and smoked three packs of Camels a day. She had no work in life other than the beauty parlor, the shopping lists, the decorating of the house. She played a high-stakes game of canasta, two, three after-noons a week. She blew smoke rings across the card table. She lay for hours soaking in the bathtub, a glass of scotch balanced on the rim. She had servants for the real work of the home. She cried herself to sleep most nights. She yearned and did not know what she yearned for. She wanted me to be different and the same. She wanted me to be safe, protected. She believed in princes and witches and diet doctors. She wouldn't open an umbrella in the house for fear of supernatural repercussions. She spit if she saw a nun on the street. She was afraid the disappointment was catching. She took me to the tarot card reader at a fashionable Midtown restaurant. "You will marry a tall dark and handsome man," said the seer. I did but it wasn't such a good idea.

I have written it many times. I can't seem to stop. I come back to it in novels, in stories, in articles. I started writing my first novel with the picture of a child waiting outside a closed door. The child was me. I would lie on the carpet outside her room, my face pressed to the crack under the door through which I could see the blankets on her bed rising and falling. I didn't play. I didn't move. I waited, my back pressed to the wall so nothing could grab me. She was there but I couldn't reach her. My legs would go numb and with my hands I would rub them again and again. I learned patience. I learned how to sit in the center of a pool of time and float without flailing about, without shouting out loud, with the calmness of a lizard on a rock. In the dark corridor a child was learning that all love is not requited, at least not in equal quantities. When I was sick for long periods throughout the year with the earaches that would take me in those pre-antibiotic days, my mother would not come into my room. The governess would sit by my bed, solid, functional, unwanted by me, fussing with steam kettles, hot-water bottles, soft-boiled eggs. I would wait for a glimpse of my mother, a flash of a gold bracelet, a black hat with a net veil, pausing at the door. She would send me books. She was afraid of illness and would enter the room only when the fever was gone.

I had always felt some contempt for my mother as she lay in bed throughout the morning, curtains pulled closed to block the day, ice packs on her eyes to bring the swelling down, the swelling produced night after night by tears that flowed from exhausted ducts, after long screaming fights with my father. I knew that as she lay there, empty scotch glass on the night table, on satin monogrammed sheets, in lacy lingerie, there was a smell of rot in the room that wasn't just the smell of powder, perfume, stale nicotine-stained air. Feminism showed me that the fault was not hers alone. Timing is everything. Sometime late in the morning she would ring for the maid to bring in her breakfast and then I was allowed to follow.

My mother's lipstick always ran onto her teeth. Her nails were always chipped, although she tried to keep herself perfect. Beauty she said has to be maintained. Pain is necessary she said, hair dye stings, shoes pinch, corsets leave red marks in the skin. She was always repairing herself but the erosion was constant, roots grew out, hairs straggled, legs needed waxing, the days passed and she considered taking a flower arranging course. She didn't. She was nearsighted. "Men don't make passes," she quoted Dorothy Parker, "at girls who wear glasses," therefore she was always bumping into things, tripping and falling. Her glasses were worn on top of her head. Sometimes they fell in her lap. Once at a party she put her cigarette out in a caviar bowl thinking it was an ashtray. When she ran for the bus on her Cuban heels all her gold jewelry rattled. In winter she wrapped herself up in her long mink coat and looked like a creature wandered in from the woods. In summer she covered her dyed hair with a scarf so it wouldn't turn green in the sun. She had freckles on her arms. She applied vanishing cream but they never vanished. She sighed, the sigh of a woman whose husband plays around and who has forgotten still another birthday, the sigh of a woman who isn't sure how to take a train to Philadelphia, who wants to have an adventure but can't imagine how and doesn't dare: coward, my beloved mother, who did the crossword puzzles in pen, read mystery stories, and loved Chinese food and pastrami sandwiches, a terrible coward. She was afraid of thunder and elevators, cats and dogs, tunnels and bridges, poverty and betrayal and the evil eye. She never became poor. She made her psychiatrist's appointments after noon, otherwise she slept through them. She played the stock market, calling her broker from phones in department stores, ladies' rooms, doctors' offices where she spent hours in waiting rooms checking out pains in the chest, the toes, the belly.

All the boys I knew while I was in college in the late fifties joked about marriage as a trap, a female plot to end their adventure. Meanwhile the women were knitting argyle socks for the fellows they hoped to trap. In addition there were mother jokes, and mother-in-law jokes everywhere. The *New Yorker* ran the Helen Hokinson cartoons of women, sexless, always peering at paintings they didn't quite get or setting aside their gardening shears to exchange recipes. It got under our skin, we didn't want to be those kinds of women, each of us wanted to be something other than a mother. At the same time, most of us also wanted to be mothers. It was one of those contradictions that was lived out by women: womb by womb, period by period.

Now we can talk about self-fulfillment, career or profession, now we can have ambitions, disappointments, economic responsibility, lust, love. Then we had only vicarious accomplishments, vicarious triumphs and failures. We had limits on our growth, limits on our potential, limits everywhere. I had married a writer and was working as a receptionist when the success of his first play made it possible for me to bear a child. Like many other women of my time I was humble, eager to please. My only power depended on my body leaning forward, bending back, moving across the room, leaving a burning trace like a falling star, holding the eye, sparking a wish. I didn't know if I had that power, was I pretty, pretty enough? I laughed, patted, cajoled, comforted, supported, listened, served. I typed my husband's manuscripts late at night after a full day's work as a receptionist. I was grateful to be my husband's muse, I had chosen the position, auditioned for it, but in the first days after my daughter's birth a new sadness came over me. She would have limits on her too. I was twenty-four. I intended to keep my daughter by my side, to hold her head when she threw up, to read stories when she was tired, to do with my own hands the work of the mother. Maybe that way the longing for the Mama kiss (Proust wasn't the only one) would stop. At least that was my original plan. I didn't know that change was just over the horizon.

I did know that Flaubert's Mme. Bovary had grieved over her child's female sex. The literary allusion was not comforting. God help my baby, she was female like me.

FEMINISM ARRIVES: TOO LATE FOR SOME

My mother knew all the odds. She was a card counter. Finally her luck ran out. She lay dying of a melanoma as my first child approached her second birthday. The year was 1962. In my mother's bedroom the curtains were pulled. I sat on the satin coverlet among the beads, pearls, rhinestones, charm bracelets that I had turned over onto the bed covers for my daughter to play with. The child draped herself in baubles. She put them into the box and took them out. I looked at my mother, who had lost the power of speech. "You look better today," I said. I lied. She looked at me and I saw in her eyes that she despised my evasion. I saw that it was over and she didn't care anymore. I saw that I had disappointed her. I saw that she didn't love me anymore, nor anyone, what had mattered no longer mattered. Her eyes were empty, emptier than those of any character in a Beckett play. My daughter bounced on the bed and I tried to keep her still. My mother's wedding ring slipped down her finger. She had at last lost the ten pounds that had plagued her the past thirty years. Always a small woman, not quite four foot ten, in the bed she was shrunken, diminished, blind in one eye, paralyzed on one side.

My daughter reached across me and, seeing a figurine, a French porcelain shepherdess with little red flowers on her china apron and a small sheep nuzzling against her skirts, on the night table she grabbed for it. It slipped out of her small hand hitting the side of the bed and fell into a thousand pieces on the carpet. My daughter wept in fright. Pearls and ropes of beads rolled over the satin bed cover. My mother's good arm was waving in the air. There was a smell of urine in the room. My daughter was shaking on my lap. I could feel the tremor in her thighs. I took my mother's hand.

Whatever the word freedom means, I knew I did not have it. Responsibility weighed on me. Was I a good enough mother? Would I drive my child neurotic, psychotic, phobic? Would I make her creative, bold, or obsessive and timid? How she would grow would be the mirror of my faults, the mirror of my soul. My patience varied, my own flaws beyond count and most of them beyond cure. It was my work to make my daughter's life good and rich and safe, to teach her about the books I loved, the music I listened to, the politics I believed in, to give her the universe, to bind her to me and my world, to make her brave, to give her myself, to give her herself, to never drop her, to never forget her, to hold on to her as long as she needed me.

As my mother was dying my marriage was ending. It was about time.

My husband was a man whose language, fake English accent, dazzled. He could weave Kierkegaard into Joyce and logical positivism into Picasso all without pausing for breath. His lean tall body, the shock of black hair that fell over his brow brought images of the French Resistance, of foreign correspondents, of cafes in Montmartre, of gunrunning in North Africa. He had been a poor boy supported by a grandmother who sold lingerie. He had shared her bedroom in Jackson Heights, Queens. He had a dancer's sense of physical grace and his long-fingered hands fluttered in a continual panic. He wanted to be Keats or Byron. I knew, however, that he stayed in the closet for hours on end, shaking his hands back and forth in front of his eyes in some futile attempt to soothe the excitement that raged within. I knew that he needed a few drinks before he could leave the house, that he was nervous as a racehorse, that sometimes he was cruel, and that he believed that a writer owed all his loyalty to his art. Nevertheless, I was willing to serve as his muse. I thought my love could calm him. He told me I wasn't his ideal of a woman. He told me that if he didn't drink he would die. He told me that he wanted to die. I was a romantic and his words did not serve as warning, they served instead to link me to him. When I thought of bearing his child I thought of his intelligence, his beauty. I did not think of his drinking, of his vulnerability, of the way he moved through the night from bar to bar, like an alarmed stork with a broken wing. I will always feel for him a gasp of sorrow, a taste of early love that burns on in the mind, a wish for his well-being, a sadness for his glory that wasn't to be, a sadness for the errors of our lives.

When I became a mother to my first child I stopped believing in art as the only good in the world. I thought my baby was good. I thought my responsibility to my baby was good. In the early hours of the morning as I held the baby and watched out the window for the return of his taxi, I knew what mattered. I didn't believe that motherhood would lead me to freedom or wisdom, but I knew that the urgency of my life was my child. This was the beginning of my feminism and I don't care that that was an odd way to find it, a weird way to express it. I think many women know that their motherhood was the beginning of their determination to stand strong against the currents that would carry them away.

Shortly after my mother's funeral as the sixties began its Punch and Judy show, the this-time-around feminist movement rose from behind the curtain. You could virtually hear the whoop of relief that rolled over the country. The first and most important message was that you didn't have to, you didn't need to, you had other choices, whether this was a turn against marriage, a turn against cooking, a turn against babies as destiny, it was all about not having to, not being coerced into, about not polishing the furniture till it shone, about searching for meaning outside the home. What wonderful fresh air this feminist wind brought to the choking lady in the apron holding her cookies on a hot baking tray. Now she could see her children, her always needing to be chauffeured children, with tennis rackets and piano lessons, with Little League and skating competitions and play dates, as sucking the life out of her, as draining her of her own dreams, as eating at the promise that had been. Now she could see that always giving and never getting were not divinely ordained. She was not just a Mrs., someone's wife, and not just a mom, someone's mother. She breathed her own desires, expressed her own anger, and suddenly everything was changed. All over America consciousness raised its own rooftops and fled the house. Women remembered that they had once run like crazy, climbed trees, planned to visit Istanbul, intended to ride a motorbike or go to graduate school. Women took courses, learned karate, let their body hair grow as nature intended. They became aware of all the denigrating images in the culture, all the insults to their brains and bravery that blared at them from magazines, books, movies, children's readers, billboards. Seeing the insult defused its power. The madwomen in the attic gave up their delusions, depressions, hypochondria and made plans to become potters or neurosurgeons. By the end of the nineteen sixties if a woman put her head to her own pillow she could hear the band playing, the coming of freedom, the hope of power returned, of self-expression, of self-fulfillment, of her intelligence newly awake, in love again with life.

This from the short-lived feminist magazine *Witch*. This is your real challenge:

> Renounce your martyrdom
> Become a liberated mother
> A woman, not a mom.

This loosening of the tie to the baby was exactly the nightmare in the head, the worst fear of the now galvanized traditional forces opposed to feminism. It always had been. In the 1912 film, *A Cure of Suffragettes,* women who wanted the vote were seen abandoning their infants in prams on the streets to total strangers — in this case a policeman, a representative of the state. What kind of horrible woman would do such a thing? A suffragette of course. The scene in the film reflected the widely held belief that a woman who loved her children would not want the vote: in other words, to have interests outside the home the woman must abandon her children, literally or emotionally.

"Just a housewife" became as dirty and derogatory a term as "spinster" had once been. In certain hip circles "barren" was replaced by "cow," "old maid" was linguistically lost, children were no longer proof of goodness, justification for the earthly space you occupied. The common omnipresent fifties absurd idealizations of wife and mother were quickly replaced by a loud and occasionally vituperative conversation across the culture about the very real dispiriting problems of motherhood, marriage, and home. The Madonna view of motherhood (Thackeray said, "The mother is God") was debunked by every feminist writer worth her salt. In some feminist circles children were plucked from their place of honor in their mothers' lives and seen as albatrosses hanging from the neck. The new focus on the demands of job, self-fulfillment, female dignity, and progress caused a divide through the country, separating women from one another and causing cracks to run deep in each of our hearts and all of our minds.

Shulamith Firestone said giving birth was like "shitting a pumpkin." Other feminists were indignantly pointing out that TV commercials, soap operas, magazine ads presented endless positive views of child care, encouraging conception. A lot of us, however, didn't believe that the media were the agents of our conception. We were listening to inner voices, and motherhood seemed to be something more complicated, more essential, more primal than a capitalist scheme to sell baby clothes. As I woke each morning and answered questions, prepared food, washed clothes, tied shoelaces, I was forging a thing inside myself that would become my character, my story, and it would include, for better or worse, in sickness and in health, in pride and in shame, in fear and in peace, the child who was growing beside me, because of me, with me.

I would have marched in Selma. I would have worked with SNCC. I would have joined CORE. I cared, I wanted to change the world and make it just. But I had a small child who had only me. When the Cuban missile crisis came I thought about carrying her out of the city to a safe haven. I didn't know where. I didn't have the money. I sat with her in our kitchen and watched the sky. Was it turning pink? Would we die? My husband had gone. I had to rise early to feed our child. He came home at dawn. I was domestic by obligation. He was a prowler by nature. I went to Tijuana to get a divorce. I took my child. We stayed in a hotel on the border. At night I heard the prostitutes making deals in the courtyard. I heard screaming in the halls. In the open patio of the hotel, suspended from a palm tree, a large parrot hopped about its cage. My two-year-old child put her hand through the wire bars and pulled out an ear of corn and put it in her mouth. I was afraid she would die, a parasite, a tropical virus.

I was twenty-seven years old. In those days a woman approaching thirty was considered close to the end of her childbearing years, an old maid or a person who threatened other people's marriages. In my head the fifties were dying slowly. Like a cargo plane worshiper on a mountaintop in darkest Africa, I was on some runway, waiting for the arrival of unknown, impossible-to-imagine revelations. I was free of a man who himself wanted to be free of me. I was determined to at last make something of myself. I thought I might go to Appalachia and become a public health nurse. I thought I might go to Washington and become a diplomat. I wanted to travel, to take a rucksack and climb a mountain. My child had different needs and other yearnings that did not meld so well with my emerging feminism. I walked along the street with my daughter who was then three years old. I was wearing a miniskirt. I was carrying a sack with her two favorite stuffed animals in it. She refused to leave the house without them. "When," she said, "am I going to see my daddy again?" "Soon," I said, "I hope." I said this whenever she asked that question. The week before he called and said he would take her to his favorite bar, Elaine's, at ten o'clock at night. Patiently

I explained that you don't take a three-year-old child to a bar at night. But I agreed. She waited for him, running to the window, looking for the cab, hiding crayons in the corner of the couch, picking at the scab on her ankle, pulling at the bow of the dress I had chosen, till she fell asleep in the chair at midnight. He didn't call. This was my fault and many other things too.

I could have used an extended family. I could have used a husband who would stay home when I had to leave, with whom I could have taken turns on the night shift. I could have used day care, aunts, uncles, cousins, a community. My child would have benefited from all those, but what she really needed was a father who admired her. Freedom from being fathered was never my child's ambition. My erratic choice of mate was a temporary calamity for me, brushed off in the breeziness of time, but for her its effects rippled on and on. My love for her was never sufficient, not by half. Some women may not need men to open mayonnaise jars, to bring in money, to pump gas or change tires, to carry out the garbage, but many of us need them, father by father, mate by mate, as partners in the home. That is not politics. It is bottom line reality, the kind that hits you at two in the morning when in the darkness the corridors of your own home seem unfamiliar and shadows threaten.

The thin ice that supported my confidence easily cracked. I wasn't yet able to see myself as a product of my culture and my history. I was waiting for the climate to change. I wasn't able yet to understand my marriage to a writer as my own thinly disguised attempt to be a writer. As soon as I had learned to read I had intended to be a writer. I had certain complaints I was eager to register. I hoped that the spirit of Dorothy Parker might live on in me. I kept mean journals. I wrote bad poetry. I also grew up expecting to become a man's refuge. At first I saw myself as a woman who had married badly. Later I understood that, reading through manuscripts offered by eligible young writers in beatnik garb, spending time in bars at the edges of respectable New York, I was more like a vampire, a brain sucker, trying to attach myself to, hide myself behind, ride to vicarious success through the gifts of a male. It wasn't so uncommon in those days. It was culturally logical and a lot of women, with their ambitions in the closet, were borrowing men to fulfill their dreams. It was not nice, not entirely decent.

Today the idea that a woman should achieve through her attachment to a male seems absurd, from another century, or another country, someone babbling about how the Count used to whip his serfs just before the turnips were planted in the sod. But the truth is that at the end of the fifties, if men were abusing women for their own sexual needs, so were women using men to vicariously conquer the world. Half a decade later anyone who could read had figured it out. In America consciousness seemed to be raised in a moment, less time than it takes a culture to sneeze, creating a sharp and sudden dividing line between those women who crossed into the new world and those who stayed behind.

I was ashamed. Nobody I knew was divorced. My mother had been afraid to divorce a man who called her stupid, who called her plain, who said she was too short for him, who lost his temper and lost his clients and borrowed money from her and always had other women, taller women, to amuse him. Sometimes, however, I thought it possible that my life was over, my opportunities gone. I felt like Hester Prynne. A scarlet letter was pinned to my chest. I thought I had used up my one chance at happiness. My mother would have said that no man would want me, with a child, used goods. Nevertheless I wanted a new family, a new husband, more children. I wanted to do it right. I knew by then that right was impossible. I was willing to settle for reasonable, for hopeful, for good. I went to graduate school. I began to write a novel. I went to parties and out on dates. I found out that it was true that a divorced woman is a magnet for other people's marital troubles.

In the suburbs there were orgies and wife-swapping parties. People talked of open marriages and honest sexual behavior when they wanted to play around. To stick to the rules meant you might be missing something. In the sixties nobody wanted to miss anything. A night out in a roomful of writers and artists ended with clothes on strange floors, feelings stretched, mangled, trust gone, exhaustion and boredom rising with the dawn. Being in a roomful of naked people is one of the loneliest experiences imaginable. I was always at home before my child woke so I could pour the cereal, brush her hair, and remind myself that real life was in the daily everyday dull discipline of being there, like the women of the prairie sweeping the dust out the door, milking the cow, sewing the cloth that would cover the windows when winter came.

At the end of the sixties many women were beginning to question authorities, taking control away from institutions as long-established traditions were falling by the wayside. Gynecologists no longer called their patients by their first names. Medical school interviewers could no longer ask female applicants if they planned to get pregnant. Organizations, profit and non-, sprang up to help women enter and reenter the workplace. I had comrades in change. I was nobody's baby, doll, sweetie pie, or dish. But I was still someone's mother and I still wanted to love and be loved. I wanted to get married again so that I could have more children. Other women, many of my close friends, had no desire to "get knocked up."

MOTHERHOOD: GASP! NO, NEVER, NOT ME

In 1954 when I applied to college and was asked on the application what woman I most admired, the answer was easy. It was Eleanor Roosevelt. The majority of my classmates had the same answer. It certainly wasn't Ethel Rosenberg. It wasn't a woman doctor, lawyer, pilot, resistance fighter, author, senator, or CEO. There were some of course but I didn't know any. The woman I admired most was not my mother. However, the woman I longed for most, the person with whom I had the most intense relationship, whom I needed to please, whom I needed to break free from, who had the most ideas about what I should do (Marry well) was my mother. I couldn't write that on my college application. It seemed in those preliberation days as if we lived parallel lives. One was public in which you did math homework as if it mattered and the other private where the tides were carrying you into a place where the body took precedence over the mind and your destiny as a mother waited.

As the sixties turned into the seventies it was very clear that being a mother was an unfortunate surrender to the old social design. In a daring article in *Life* magazine in 1970 Betty Rollin, a reporter and TV journalist, wrote a piece in which she said, Never, never for her, she would not become a mother tied to the will and fortune of her child. She had work to do and she didn't want what she had been told she must want, she wasn't who they, the perpetuators of tradition, the Poloniuses of male chauvinism, the Freudians, the frat boys, the hacks on Madison Avenue, the capitalists who wanted to sell soaps, the purveyors, sellers, and buyers of misogyny thought she was. She was going to be free. She said, "It doesn't make sense anymore to pretend that women need babies when what they really need is themselves. If God were still speaking to us in a voice we could hear, even he would probably say, 'Be fruitful, don't multiply.'" When I read that I winced. She was right and she was wrong. I thought, too late for me, how sad for her.

Simone de Beauvoir had said some years earlier in *The Second Sex,* "The great danger which threatens the infant in our culture lies in the fact that the mother to whom it is confided in all its helplessness is almost always a discontented woman and she will seek to compensate for all these frustrations through her child." When *The Second Sex* first appeared in 1958 it was hard to assimilate, interesting but strange, seeming to have little to do with one's own life. Now in the early seventies with feminism everywhere her meaning was crystal clear. No one wanted to be a discontented mother living through someone else. "My son the doctor" became a nasty joke. Everything about diapers and strollers, school bills and dentist bills, nurturing and picking up pieces of play dough that had strayed under the cushions of the couch was rejected: guilty by association with the life of the trapped female.

All my friends were complaining about their own mothers, how pathetic their lives were, how they hovered, how they wasted their time dusting the furniture, how boring, how they had limited their daughters while encouraging their sons. Everyone had a version of the bitter tale to tell. Sometimes it seemed as if we were engaged in an Olympic competition to decide whose mother was absolutely the worst. Although we were beginning to understand the social realities that had placed our mothers on their respective shelves we were hardly brimming over with sympathy. It was altogether a sad business. What we resented most about our mothers was that they wanted us to be like them when they were so unhappy. We ground them up in our long conversations and spit them out.

Sometimes we even sounded like Philip Wylie, king of the misogynists, who had in 1942 written a sensational best-seller, *Generation of Vipers*. He ranted on and on: "We have turned over most of our fixed wealth to women, — cash has been heaped especially at mom. . . . The infantile unreasonableness of most wives is alone a sufficient cause to wish to escape. . . . After the war the ladies will go back to their clattering cipherdom. The mother of all atrocities we call spoiled children, — is a middle aged hair faced club woman who destroys everything she touches, the murderess, the habitual divorcee, the weeper, the weak sister, the rubbery sex experimenter, the quarreler, the woman forever displeased, the nagger, the female miser — we know as mom and sis. She is Cinderella. She has the prince, the coach, the horses but her soul is a pumpkin, her mind a rat warren, she desperately needs help." Not gentle, this description, and formed out of unabashed hostility. Wylie goes on, "I see her as she is, ridiculous, vain, vicious, a little mad. — Mom is a human calamity." He identifies some original fault in the social structure but doesn't examine it carefully. "The machine has deprived her of her social usefulness, time has stripped away her biological possibilities and man has sealed his own soul by handing her the checkbook and going to work in the service of her caprices — Mom dishes out her sweetness to all fugitives and it turns them not to stone but to slime."

This reads like Rush Limbaugh foaming at the mouth about feminazis and baby murderers, but it portrays the same woman Betty Friedan would bring to our attention with more sympathy twenty years later. This is the bottom line description of the victim of the feminine mystique, the mom whose children are her only expression of purpose: the woman whose depressions, hypochondria, phobias multiply as her days grow emptier with the passing years. The ghost of Philip Wylie haunted our feminist party.

In New York City an organization was formed called People Without Children. They met at the Plaza at regular intervals in order to confirm one another in their desire to be unburdened, not to contribute to population overload, to enjoy the fruits of their labors for themselves, to break with the past and let their DNA die a decent civilized death within their own bodies. Many of them were so young they didn't hear their biological clocks ticking. Many of them were so angry at the way society had demeaned their female minds, bodies, or opportunities that they jumped up and down like children in a tantrum, no, no, no.

"Pregnancy is barbaric," Shulamith Firestone said in her radical book *The Dialectic of Sex*. She believed that women could be freed only by the elimination of motherhood. This she expected to happen through the wonders of technology that could spare women the inconvenience of carrying a child. Gael Greene in *New York Magazine* in 1972 said, "I see many of our friends, some of them with children they hadn't necessarily planned on, bitter, frustrated, vacillating between devotion and despair, screaming at their youngsters, tearing into each other." Greene then asked the question a lot of feminist women were asking themselves: "Whom do I hurt by not having children?" The sugary sweet image of motherhood had been debunked, de-aproned, dethroned.

But I would have been hurt very badly if I had not had children. To care for a child was not an alien duty imposed on me by a hostile culture, it was rather the core, the emotional wellspring, the gravity that held my soul in place. I was having lunch with a feminist writer friend who told me that her oldest son was competing in an interschool spelling bee right then as we munched on our salad. "Why aren't you there?" I asked. She shrugged. "I'm not going to follow little boys around," she said. I thought she was right. I thought she was wrong. I thought of the little boy looking out over the audience of students and parents, searching the seats for his own mother's face. I wished she had gone to the spelling bee. I understood perfectly why she had not.

My friends who had not completed their education were now back in school. Two of them were in management programs and soon would become bankers. An old classmate of mine who had married at eighteen and moved to the suburbs and had three children was divorced by her surgeon husband who had found the head nurse more interesting than his uneducated wife. She enrolled in college on her way to becoming an art historian. My dearest friend who had some years earlier been asked to run for a city council seat and declined because her success would upset her still floundering husband entered a political action public relations firm. By the early seventies the playground was hemorrhaging mothers. Each week there were more and more nannies. I was writing in the mornings. In the afternoons I walked the streets, pushing my stroller, and found myself buying dresses for my daughter, the kind my mother would have bought for her, velvet with lace. It was extravagant of me. She had no place to wear them.

Jessie Bernard, writing in *The Future of Motherhood* in 1974, quoted a nineteenth-century poem by José Echegaray:

There was a young man loved a maid
who taunted him, "are you afraid"
She asked him, "to bring me today
Your mother's heart upon a tray?"

He went and slew his mother dead
Tore from her breast her heart so red
Then towards his lady love he raced
But tripped and fell in all his haste

As the heart rolled on the ground
It gave forth a plaintive sound
And it spoke in accents mild:
"Did you hurt yourself, my child."

So mother love, made absurd by Victorian exaggerations, was now ridiculed again and again by modern feminists. This hilarious poem contains the long and dreadful tale of children's flight and mothers' martyrdom as well as the subsequent infinite guilt that too-loving mothers oozed over their offspring. This long-suffering mom, the American mom who smothered her child with her own repressed ambitions, this mother whom no girl in her right mind could ever have wanted to be and yet so many became, was nobody's true love. The more she sacrificed herself, the less appealing she became. Indeed as this wave of feminism rolled over us it brought with it an openly discussed fear of becoming a mother and a sensible, if fierce, wariness of the whole emotionally sticky, unrewarded process.

Nancy Friday, in *My Mother/My Self,* outlined the growing distance between determined daughters and conventional, traditional mothers. The best way not to be like your mother, it seemed, was not to become a mother at all. However, I stuck to my original plan. I would be unlike my mother by doing my mothering myself with my own two clumsy hands.

My oldest daughter, then repeating kindergarten because of "maturity problems," made a drawing that won the lower school prize. It was of a gnarled bare tree in winter. I framed her drawing and looked at it again and again. I was dazzled. She sat in the chair by the record player and listened to music hour after hour. She learned the lyrics to every song. But she spilled glasses of milk. She lost sweaters and books, ribbons and socks. She interrupted and wouldn't sit in a circle at circle time. She had no interest in learning what was being taught. She daydreamed about a battle between the folk of a distant galaxy. One eye was always crossed as if the signals in her brain were misfiring. She wrote in red Magic Marker on her arms and legs. She would not brush her hair or wash her face or eat calmly. She didn't want to learn to read. She didn't want to learn numbers. She refused to be taught how to tell time or make change. At a prospective new school she told the interviewer that she was playing Heidi in the new Hollywood version of the book and might not have much time for school. She still had bad dreams night after night. I trailed after her picking up things she had dropped. Her teachers were always angry with her. I was angry at her. I loved her to distraction. I loved the smell of her skin, the tangle of her hair. Late at night I read child psychology books: Oral Stage, Anal Stage, Oedipus to follow, merging, separating, Freud, Anna, and Freud, Sigmund, Bettelheim and Spock. I underlined some passages. I memorized others. I tried to figure out the mystery of my child. Would she ever recover from the divorce? I should have asked the tea leaves.

Betty Friedan's *Feminine Mystique* was replaced on the best-seller list by Germaine Greer's *The Female Eunuch*. Susan Brownmiller's *Against Our Will* alerted women to the frequency of sexual attacks by men, and a thousand women wrote down the hard details of their broken marriages in novels that appeared one after another about Mad Housewives, betrayed women (I wrote one myself). We considered — what does the mother owe the child and who must pay and why was the price so high? As if life contained a struggle for one single breath of air: either the child or the mother would survive. The images of mothers that filled our heads, sacrificing, dying in childbirth, saving pennies for their children's education, standing at doorways waving goodbye, putting gold stars on their windows, working as it were for the army, grieving in the shadows behind the curtains, were exposed to the light. We didn't like what we saw. Compared to being a foreign correspondent, compared to being a brain surgeon, compared even to earning a decent wage, compared to traveling to exotic places or working for the social good or for political change, the role of mother, even for the majority of us who had played at house, tended our dolls, bathed and fed them in the first pretends of childhood, mothering appeared neither glamorous, appealing, necessary, nor rewarding. Germaine Greer wrote that if she had a child she would send it away to a commune in Italy. Maybe she would visit once in a while. I was shocked. If someone had tried to take my child from me I would have torn my hair, screamed like a banshee, fought like a tiger, wept till my eyes fell out. I knew it.

I took a significant part of the money my mother had left me and I went to a psychiatrist. "I want to be a good mother," I told him. "I want my child to be all right." "You're not a good mother?" he asked and leaned forward to get a closer look at my face. "I'm not sure," I said. After all, what was therapy without truth? I wanted to tell him how much I wanted for my child, that she play a musical instrument, speak French and Hebrew, use her imagination, want for nothing, that she be triumphant where I was mediocre. I wanted to ask him to save my child from contamination from me, from the inner oil spills, the toxic wastes, the sewers filled with sludge that would surely be revealed by some X ray of my mind and must be dwarfing, stunting my child who deserved a chance. It wasn't so easy to say all that to the psychiatrist. I didn't want him to think I was crazy.

Adrienne Rich wrote, "The patriarchal institution of motherhood is not the 'human condition' any more than rape, prostitution and slavery are." The mother worm had turned and was very angry. But I was left with a puzzle. Yes, cultural expectations and buried hormones may have been tapping secret lemming-like messages inside my skull, but if motherhood was prostitution and slavery, why did I persist in believing that it was my redemption, my core, my holy skywriting?

In a 1974 book called *Pronatalism: The Myth of Mom and Apple Pie,* Ellen Peck and Judith Senderowitz write, "We challenge Pronatalism and the reproductive ethic." Pronatalism, they say, "refers to any attitude or policy that is pro-birth, that encourages reproduction, that exalts the role of parenthood." They go on to promise that "tomorrow's feminists will increasingly include those who desire to devote themselves exclusively to interests outside the domestic sphere and who will not choose to have children." Letty Cottin Pogrebin in *Ms.* magazine in 1973 recognized the growing tension between mothers and nonmothers and quoted a pregnant friend: "I've come full circle to where my grandmother was. Granny had to hide her condition out of modesty. My belly is embarrassing today because it labels me as a population exploder or an exploited baby machine." Of course this mother-to-be was moving on special ground drenched in feminist rain. Pogrebin goes on to say that she "has found herself now and again in fierce arguments with people who can see no merit whatsoever in having children." Word of these arguments naturally sent a chill through the country because everybody, no matter what their religious beliefs or philosophical bent, knows that without children, the human world, the species itself, will end. The Devil will get the last laugh.

The fly in the feminist ointment: somebody has to bear children and somebody has to raise those children.

In 1976 Jane Lazarre wrote *The Mother Knot.* It was the story of her pregnancy with her first son. She describes her image of a mother. "She is quietly strong, selflessly giving, undemanding, unambitious, she is receptive and intelligent in only a moderate concrete way. She is of even temperament, almost always in control of her emotions. She loves her children completely and unambivalently." Of course the author could not live up to this bland ideal of the mother and found herself depressed and frantic as her life seemed to have spun into a dead end, and her capacities for mothering in her ideal terms were found wanting. Lazarre became isolated and half mad with mourning for her former self. She thought, "I am the only mother in the world who had such hateful feelings for the child I loved so intensely, who wished over and over that it had never happened, who finally could understand those women I had met when working for the welfare department who had burnt their babies' arms, beat their faces, killed them." Lazarre was describing a postpartum depression of sorts, but in doing so she captured the pervasive sense of being constantly violated, less than you might be, that motherhood had entailed in prefeminist times. She was describing the plight of the mad housewife, the victim of the feminine mystique, the woman reduced to her motherliness, a sad and forlorn creature she. Lazarre wrote, "Now I'm a mother and that means I'm nothing."

All these wrenching public admissions that maternity was not all it was cracked up to be cleared the air like a summer storm.

The Lazarre book was angry. Women were angry. Postpartum depressions are about anger, hidden rage, turned on the self and sometimes on the baby. They are personal, of course, this one's mother died, this one's father abandoned the family, but postpartum depression also has a social dimension. Women were angry at their collective position in the society. These severe baby blues reflect a woman's grief at losing what she has believed to be a part of herself. The separation that birth entails is painful for some women, who once again face the aloneness of their human state and feel angry at the baby for causing this pain. At its worst the postpartum depression can become the trigger for a madness that reveals itself as rage against the child. But these feelings also arise because a woman who becomes a mother has in reality diminished herself in many ways. In a prefeminist society, becoming a mother is a complicated and burdensome matter. Personal psychology is always political and the political reality contributes to emotional life.

Women were bored. Taking care of a child is boring in many ways. Women today, longing to stay at home with their children, don't know how long the day can be, how stale the air of the nursery can become, how limiting the conversation of a two-year-old really is. Today we have forgotten how dull we became, how our mates wandered off looking for a sparkle, a companion, a challenging female, how little things consumed us and how our minds idled in place, the boredom mingled with anger. Anger released in the culture, anger no longer a taboo female emotion, spread through the playgrounds — it was contagious.

Women were now able to see that a good deal of their previous sorrow was really anger in disguise. Women tend to cry when they want to hit someone. This strange fact was becoming obvious.

There was, among newly liberated, Free To Be Me women a common revulsion against the Freudian dictum anatomy is destiny, and what is the sign, the mark of anatomy but the pregnant belly, the fertile womb, the dripping breasts? Freud had said that women had babies as a compensation for the longed-for penis, a kind of substitute gift from a man substituting for the desired father. The baby in other words was a substitute for the penis itself, a prize in the rivalrous drama between mother and daughter. Women laughed. Keep your penis, keep your baby, we don't want either, they said. The rejection of Freud's penis envy theories by Kate Millett and other early feminists contributed to the growing consensus that the baby was a product of the patriarchy, an unwanted burden, equated still with the unwanted penis but this time rejected, both baby and penis, rather than envied or desired. Women noticed and emphasized that men envied women their wombs, their reproductive capacity. This new glorification of the womb over the penis didn't exactly turn women toward childbearing; rather it settled old scores. It's you who want what I have, not the other way around. The organs of fertility became weapons in the war between the sexes as if the bearing of human children was not after all a joint venture.

Those were heady days, and to speak then of biology was to support the forces of reaction. Tomgirls don't play house, and suddenly all over America there were grown-up tomgirls who didn't want to play house anymore. At least not under the "I promise to obey, I promise to make tuna casseroles, I promise to put you ahead of me ever after" social contract that had bound our own mothers body and soul.

Many of the wives of the artists and writers that I knew already had babies. The babies were sleeping on coats in the bedroom while the party went on. The babies were waking early to sleepy, hung-over mothers. Fathers didn't touch them. Fathers didn't change diapers. Fathers drifted off into other beds after their wives went home. One summer on a Long Island beach my daughter and I were collecting shells when we looked up and saw my ex-husband with someone else's small son on his shoulders. The child's mother, the abandoned wife of a newly famous screenwriter, was by his side. My daughter stared in shock. Her father then promised to come and see her, but the weekend passed and he never came. My daughter rode on the shoulders of the man I was seeing at the time. He was nice about the way she pulled at his hair and kicked her heels into his chest as hard as she could. I can picture his face but I can't remember his name. We didn't know each other that long.

The anti-baby drumbeat continued. Writing in *Feminist Studies* in 1978, Rachel Blau DuPlessis said, "Motherhood under patriarchy means the death of the self." Adrienne Rich said grimly, "Motherhood is the key role, the keystone in the patriarchal arch, for it is also the site of wresting of power from women." We were squeezed between that proverbial rock and hard place. Motherhood by definition requires tending of the other, a sacrifice of self-wishes for the needs of a helpless, hapless human being, and feminism by definition insists on attention being paid to the self, to the full humanity, wishes, desires, capacities of the self. This basic contradiction is not simply the nasty work of a sexist society. It is the lay of the land, the mother of all paradoxes, the irony we cannot bend with mere wishing or might of will. Here are the ingredients of our private and public human tragedy.

Nevertheless I still wanted more children.

HALF-BAKED LUKEWARM POLITICAL SOLUTIONS

There in the early days of this bout of feminism began the division between the women who already had children, those who were staying at home with their children, and those who were planning to storm the boardrooms and faculty lounges of America unencumbered, no sticky fingers clinging to the skirt, no burped orange juice staining a sleeve. Each side looked down on the other. Some of us were card-carrying members of both groups.

In the early nineteen seventies in New York I was walking through the halls of one major network when my guide pointed out a tourist family. Two little girls were holding their mother's hands. They were wearing pink flouncy dresses and black Mary Janes. Each child had a white ribbon in her hair and clutched a small pocketbook printed with strawberries. My blue-jeaned guide sneered. "See," she said, "how those children are being ruined by their parents." Intolerance, a backlash against enforced femininity, became an intolerance of women who led traditional lives. Even little girls from Tulsa in party frocks were subject to our feminist contempt and misplaced pity. Style was political, and motherhood, girlishness, was way out of style. We hadn't shed the conformity. We had just changed its skin. Same snake.

I am not suggesting that early feminists were child-hating witches. We understood full well that women had children and that the adequate care of these children was the rub of the matter, the place where feminism could fall from the sky. The very first NOW conference issued a list of demands. Three of the eight items on this list concerned children. On the manifesto was a call for universal day care, adequate child care for every woman in America. The problem was that the feminist firebrands were not really hell-bent on universal day care, their enthusiasm was weak, their interest in children slim. This was after all an American, individualistic grass-roots movement, and the sexy stuff, the stuff that grabbed the media, was the most personal, the anger, the attacks on chivalry, the championing of female brains, the creation of role models from the past — and present — the opportunity to break down barriers in corporate America, in the army, in the fire department, in politics, how to help abused women, incest victims. Questions of language — Ms., Chairperson, She-kind, God and her dominion — were given more public debate than the issue of child care.

You could say that women were sick of the subject of children. They had heard enough of how to and what ought and who was responsible when what went wrong. Our newly minted feminism seemed to belong with motherhood like maple syrup on sushi.

When I was first divorced I was invited to a party by the wife of an internist I had met in the playground. I needed new friends. At this party after dinner the men went to one side of the room and discussed hospital politics and the women on the other side of the room were discussing toilet training and bribing two-year-olds and where to buy the best asparagus in the neighborhood. I went home early. Some years later I went to a party at the same woman's house. Now she was divorced too and it was an all-female gathering and we discussed orgasms, one kind or two, clitoral or vaginal, real or faked, into the predawn hours. My hostess was becoming a midwife and offered to show her guests how we could examine ourselves vaginally by means of the mirror in our compacts.

In the late sixties and early seventies the most colorful feminists got the best press. Jill Johnston rolled on the floor while Norman Mailer ranted at Carnegie Hall. She wrote angry wild pieces about the piteous state of the male penis. Valerie Solanas founded an organization called SCUM, Society for the Cutting Up of Men. In its manifesto it called for the abolishment of men, the ridiculing and castrating of men: "The few remaining men can exist out their puny days doped out on drugs or strutting around in drag or passively watching the high powered female in action or breeding in the cow pasture with the toadies or they can go off to the nearest friendly neighborhood suicide center where they will be quietly, quickly, and painlessly gassed to death." Some feminists were saying that all married women are prostitutes. These were the media feminists who were never ever caught by the camera taking their kids to the zoo, waiting for hours at the pediatrician's, in parent–teacher conferences, baking cakes for birthday parties. These were the women who talked more about love of other women than about love for kids. As revolutionaries, extremists, tend to do, they altered the climate for everyone, letting out anger, letting in new visions, breaking down the all too rigid images of what a family should be, what a woman must do, but they didn't stop most women from having children, raising children, enduring their children's childhood, bringing drinks to the bedside, saving money for the orthodontist, suffering the slings and arrows of the new and old forms of cultural contempt, their kids' rebellion, their own late-night fears.

Lorena Bobbitt was then just a mote in Valerie Solanas's winking eye. Real-life people no more imitated SCUM than they now imitate Madonna or Michael Jackson. The overwhelming majority of men and women had sex the ordinary way, although perhaps with the sexual revolution they had more of it. There was more confusion and less prejudice, new roles and expectations for women, more same-sex gender choices, but whatever they did in bed and with however many partners of whatever gender orientation, they continued to conceive and bear children, and as the divorce and abandonment rates rose and rose again more and more mothers were taking care of their children alone.

I want to write a book. I have hired a young girl from Switzerland to live as an au pair in our house. My daughter loves her. I have someone to talk to over coffee. My au pair, named Alice, says to me, "You're too picky. You keep breaking up with men. You have to get married again." She wants to buy my daughter a dog. "She needs an animal in her bed then she won't be afraid of the dark," she says. Alice's boyfriend comes over from Zurich. He is a sculptor. He makes alabaster statues in the loft he shares with a friend. He spends the night at my house. He eats a huge amount of food. I come home at one o'clock one morning to find him walking around naked, my daughter curled up in a chair in front of the TV and the au pair in tears in the kitchen. She and her boyfriend have had a loud fight. The au pair moves out although I plead with her to stay. My daughter says she doesn't care. I know she cares. I take a photograph of my daughter on a swing in the park. There are dark circles under her eyes and her face is white as the sand in the sandbox. Her hair is unkempt. Hadn't I combed it? I stay home with my daughter for nights on end. I am restless. I feel like an old lady. I should take up knitting. I wait for something to happen to us. I hire a sweet black lady who comes to us three days a week on the bus from Harlem. I don't want to have some other woman taking care of my child. I don't like it that she needs to do this work. I am opposed to the social injustice implied in her working for me. I don't want my child raised by someone I pay. I don't know what else to do. Should my work on my book be achieved by another woman's work in my home and is that feminist progress or some form of nonsisterly exploitation?

THE LESBIAN FACTOR

With the return of feminism, the release of sexual secrets, the open talk of the frequent horrors of heterosexual marriage, the lesbian option became increasingly more reasonable. It was possible to reject a life of motherhood and legal marriage and still be a respected member of your community. Lesbians organized on campuses, spoke out for one another, against the secrecy that had formerly determined their days. Their voices on all the campuses, in the media, were frequently harshly critical of men. Those women who wanted heterosexual relationships were alarmed. Was feminism trying to drive a wedge between the sexes or was it merely striving for equality of opportunity? Those were confusing times. The fear of being thought a man-hating female drove some women away from feminist activity. The enemies of feminism exploited the new lesbian assertiveness as a way of attempting to frighten women into maintaining the traditional family systems. An atmosphere of suspicion followed. Conservative and traditional America was frightened and angered by the suddenly visible lesbian positions and used them to discredit the feminist movement. My father had always thought that all women who wanted to become lawyers were secret lesbians. Now he thought all feminists were closet lesbians. Many women were afraid of the label. This put a hammer in the hands of the Total Woman which she used to bang on the heads of the rest of us. When Betty Friedan was talking around the country she received nasty letters from lesbian groups and was accused of anti-lesbianism. A speech of hers was canceled because there were bomb threats from outraged lesbians. Your sexual choice became overtly political, no longer just a matter of desire, and sexual issues took center stage, new conformities of language and behavior were imposed, from the left and from the right. Too bad for the rest of us.

There had always been lesbians. There had always been Boston marriages. In every major city in America there were hidden lesbian bars in the fifties where women dressed in tuxedos and danced with each other till dawn, but the taboos against difference, against sexual freedom were very strong. We were a nation that pointed fingers, that took refuge from our own miseries by demanding conformity, by judging the smallest of deviances from the cultural norm. In the dark ages of the fifties, if you wore the wrong color in the wrong month you were looked down upon. If your hair was curly or dark or you were too short or too tall or you left your white gloves at home you were in trouble. If your skin was the wrong color or your accent odd you could be rejected at places as disparate as lunch counters and graduate schools. Hotels turned away vacationing Jews. Hospitals in the South turned away Negroes. We were half a decade away from imprisoning Japanese Americans.

In the nineteen fifties I attended two all-women colleges, Smith and Sarah Lawrence. We were always whispering about someone's lesbian romance. It was the darkest, most titillating idea, something over the threshold of law and order, far beyond normality, a love that made us shiver but one we could all imagine. It was the great forbidden outcome of our crushes. In 1955 flashing a copy of Radclyffe Hall's *Well of Loneliness* was the best way to terrify parents. It was truly rebellious and subversive to dare to be irregular at a time when virginity was still a valuable commodity and every sophomore was pinned to a fellow from Yale or Dartmouth. In those days to have sex with a woman seemed an escape to the moon, a drop into madness, a flight of fancy akin to setting off cross-country with a bank robber or practicing witchcraft in the dormitory kitchen. It was worse than being a communist with its fateful implications of ostracism and exclusion. Nevertheless it happened.

Of course, to have sex at all was to play with fire. Death by abortion was the way the girl across the hall left college. My freshman-year roommate asked me, "Can you lose your virginity if you French kiss standing up?" I was pretty sure that wasn't how you lost your virginity. What was true, what was rumor, what would ruin your life, what would spoil your chances, what would bring shame? Shame in those days was our constant companion. We were a democracy inside of which there were infinite rankings, acceptable and nonacceptable races, ethnicities, sexual choices, length of nose, texture of hair. Lesbians were condemned to social exile. They lived in the dark continent of shame. Feminists understood that homophobia was just another way of driving everyone into the house of conformity, of male dominance and female misery. Sisterhood bound women together no matter their sexual preferences, at least in theory.

In the seventies on campuses the lesbian option became a mark of political wisdom, a kind of badge of courage in the wars against injustice. It was still hard for people to lead their lives with respect and privacy, with dignity in their sexual choices. It was still a circus even if the barker was shouting different slogans and the clowns had changed their costumes. Although now some lesbian couples are having and raising children and creating stable families, in the early days of this new openness the lesbian interest in children was, understandably, not marked. The considerable feminist lesbian constituency could be counted on to support feminist issues across the board, but child care was not in those days one of their priorities.

WHAT TO DO WITH THE KIDS

The question didn't disappear. There was talk of day care centers — Sweden did it right. There was a renewed murmur about the kibbutz, but the response was lukewarm, the women doing the talking were not all that concerned about children and their well-being. The conversation when it turned to how to take care of the next generation was muddled, mystical, and short. It was assumed that in a proper feminist world communal solutions would emerge. Alas, to this day they haven't. Men have not come forward in large numbers to take over the nurturing of children. The state has not stepped in. The women's movement has turned its attention to the apparently more riveting matters of rape and sexual harassment, abortion rights, glass ceilings, and pornography. It has not erupted with creative new solutions for child care. It has not pressured corporations for day care centers. There have been few large marches demanding flextime, longer maternal leaves, time off to care for a sick child. On campuses across the country there have been candlelight vigils against date rape, massive pro-choice rallies, but no organized action on child care.

In 1995 a group of women academics joined with NOW to form a sub-organization called UP from Poverty. This organization lobbies for children and women on welfare. This comes at a time when many parts of the country are ready to abandon all attempts to help the vulnerable. This is a group that should have begun in 1965 with the women's movement itself. Today their voices are mere wisps of smoke on the cultural horizon.

The women's studies departments of various universities are still not talking about motherhood, at least not as most women experience it. Conversations about the need for communal day care are as emotionally dry and politically ignored today as they ever were. We are not a country fond of the communal solution; anything that smacks of socialism sends cold chills down the spine. Early feminism in the sixties and seventies stressed individual rights, grievances for old wrongs, the terror of bad marriages. This unmuzzling of complaint and hope did not create a mood in which children, the endless demands of children, could be heard. Feminism had enough on its agenda attempting to create a revolution between men and women without also seriously attacking the foundations of our traditional family system with loud demands for alien socialist methods of child care.

Feminism was busy attending to its high-priority issues, building up female self-confidence, creating a women's history, doing political analysis of books and movies, and listing male crimes while many women were discovering the drawbacks and advantages to the nursing pump.

Gloria Steinem, the beautiful face of feminism, appeared on the cover of *Time* magazine. "A woman needs a man like a fish needs a bicycle," she said. This is perhaps true, except for the conception of a child and the raising of a child, and the fulfillment of sexual pleasure for the majority of us. But Gloria wasn't thinking about heterosexual sex, conception, or motherhood; she was thinking about independence and money and equal pay for equal work. Although glib enough, Gloria's slogan ignored what other women certainly knew, that a man in your bed can both move and steady the universe at the same time, that a father for a child is not a psychological luxury, like a vacation in the Caribbean. A second breadwinner is not useless and a partner in the care of a child is missed in most profound ways if gone. And so it was that most early feminist writings had little that was good or realistic to say about having a baby, caring for a child. So it was that the universal day care issue drifted off the stage and was replaced by the failed effort to get the Equal Rights Amendment passed and the pro-choice battle began its long fateful rattle across our national stage.

Women began to rediscover the earlier generation of feminists. I read Kate Chopin's *The Awakening*. In this book first published in the 1880s the natural mother who is happy with her many children is portrayed as a kind of cow, insensitive, animal-like, an earth mother with no sexuality, no personality of her own. The heroine of the book, on the other hand, is a woman who responds to color, to light, to art, to music, who has capacities for passion and love that are personal and outside the conventional mode. Her husband is dull and brutish, involved with commerce. Her upper-class New Orleans society binds her mind and crushes her soul. When she finds an illicit love she leaves her home in a desperate attempt to revive her imprisoned spirit, an attempt that drives her ultimately to her death in the sea. Early on her two boys are left to others' care because she has no gift for mothering or any particular interest in it. The novel describes the beautiful heroine as a victim of a world in which her true nature can find no outlet. She is the artist-woman who soars above and falls hard. The division then between mothers and artists, mothers and free spirits, mothers and those who live for themselves is as old as American feminism. Children are the albatrosses that drag us down, our role as mother is our role as slave. Some of us will believe that and some of us won't. *The Awakening,* written before the beginning of the century, still speaks to us: Must creativity clash with motherhood? Are passion and love and beauty irreconcilable with domestic life? Is maternity keeping us from our destiny as creative people? Is the home a shelter or a prison? In the nineteen seventies many women left their husbands in order to find out. Their children were sometimes also left, more often taken along on a voyage they would not appreciate. It seems that in this feminist climate some women stopped sacrificing themselves for their children and instead sacrificed their children for themselves. I read *The Awakening* and knew that I should identify with the heroine who rejects motherhood. Instead I identified with her bovine friend who had baby after baby in a frenzy of maternal oozing. I simply wanted more children, and talk of populations exploding, of mother bondage went right through my bones like a draft from an open window.

When I was remarried we had three children at the wedding. My daughter and my two stepdaughters. The three children wore blue dresses with lace collars. They came with us on our honeymoon. We didn't want them to feel abandoned, left behind.

I had two more daughters. We were a family of sorts. I had my last child when I was thirty-four. I was the oldest mother in her nursery school class. Now I might be among the youngest. I would have had another baby or two, but we were paying high alimony from a settlement created in prefeminist times when women received a lifetime of full support from their ex-husbands if they didn't remarry. We were born too early, but then so is everyone.

We went on peace marches, babies in strollers, the dog with his tongue hanging out from thirst, older children carrying placards they had made with Magic Markers. We stayed at home with the doors double-bolted the day there were riots in Harlem after Martin Luther King was killed, but we too grieved for Dr. King. We went to the Brooklyn Museum to see the Judy Chicago *Dinner Party* with all its ceramic plates dedicated to heroines of the past. We went to Washington to march when Nixon was inaugurated. "Amazing Grace," we sang on the train on the way down. "Be brave," I said to my girls, but I never missed a parent–teacher meeting. Neither did anyone else I knew.

In 1970 I wrote a novel about a woman spending her time in the playground with her two children and imagining herself a foreign correspondent, a revolutionary, a woman engaged in the world, free of entanglements. When the movie was optioned the producers asked me to write the screenplay. They would put me up in a hotel in L.A. for three or four months. I could sip gin and tonics by the pool and have dinner with movie moguls. I was tempted. I was excited. But I had two daughters under the age of four and I had an older child who still waited at the window when I went out and called for me in the predawn hours. I had two stepdaughters who needed to know that there was such a thing as family order, as two parents who could stay together in a nest of their mutual weaving. While my husband could wait, the children could not, for them the time would have seemed an eternity. Even for a few months I could not leave my family enterprise, my fragile patched-up family, my children who needed the day that is to come to be just like the day that was and all the important people in the same place. They needed their ordinary life. I needed them to have what they needed. I turned Hollywood down. Right or wrong decision, good or bad, I felt I had no choice. In fact I wanted the daily drip of want and soothe, clean and feed, the show and tell, the consistent ooze of tears and quarrels, of demand and questions, the tying of shoelaces, the purchase of soap and cereal, the planning of birthday parties, the keeping of appointments with pediatricians, orthodontists, schoolteachers, play dates, the running behind the two-wheel bike, the teaching of time, of the calendar, of how to put in batteries with their pluses and minuses at the right ends. This is not romantic, it is not interesting, it is not material for novels. Mothering is daily, all daily, even if the child is tended by someone else for eight hours, the mother's inner ear is always attuned, attention is paid. The dullness of it, the blandness of it, the work of it is the deal. I agreed with feminists who didn't want to be mothers, mothering is clichéd, wearing, and unglamorous. But if I were not in my home at least now and then, who would tell my children that the dead guinea pig was unlikely to be in heaven whatever the girl next door said? Who would tell them that women could be scientists whatever Wilma Flintstone had reported on the subject? If I were not in my home how could my children become feminists? Perhaps I missed the irony at the time. But the truth remains for me. To be free of one's children is too high a price to pay for freedom.

The irritation between mothers and nonmothers was swept under the rug of sisterhood. The intellectual and emotional misfit between child care and feminism was observed but not solved. Could you really be a feminist and have and care for children? Charlotte Perkins Gilman had scandalized America in the eighteen nineties by leaving her child with her husband and his new wife. Doris Lessing, whose novels presented pioneering left-thinking independent heroines, left her own two children behind in South

Africa claiming the need to follow her star. Ingrid Bergman was censured on the floor of Congress for falling in love with an Italian movie director and leaving her daughter behind when she followed her newest romance. By 1977, when Margaret Trudeau left Prime Minister Pierre Trudeau with three small children, the world was curious but not exactly shocked. Mothers were reconsidering, many women were in flight from domestic responsibility. Although the public sided with the children against the mothers, women who left children behind had escaped and they were slightly envied by those who remained behind.

One of my close friends had four children all delivered at home in her bed with candlelight and a midwife to accompany her. This was a radical defiance of the medical profession. I thought she was brave. She was married to an inventor of toys. She went into psychotherapy because she couldn't stop crying and was having trouble sleeping. Her psychotherapist moved into Manhattan leaving his wife and three children in the suburbs and began an affair with my friend who was blissful for a while and had a baby with him. Her husband moved out of the home. I lost track of her when she left the city for San Francisco and a new life, leaving all the children behind. I admired her courage. I thought she was a coward. I thought she was a selfish person and I wondered if I could do what she had done. I knew the answer. Never, not even in my imagination. I had spent too much time anticipating the return of my own mother to keep a child of my own waiting.

The discipline of child care, the giving up of self-interest required by child love, the sacrifice of opportunity, sex, advancement that are often the unwanted results of having children in both the short and long haul were ignored by some feminists and denounced by others. Charlotte Perkins Gilman in *Herland* written in 1915 describes a utopia in which children are brought up by caring mother substitutes in a communal way, valued, educated, adored equally by each member of the all-female society. According to this hopeful vision personal motherhood with all its attendant impossible griefs and vulnerability to the whims of fate was to be avoided at all costs.

The early feminist turn against children was rejected by most women but it wasn't irrational. The contradiction between the martyr mother and Gloria Steinem was laid out plainly for all to see. Gloria Steinem was beautiful, perfect. Betty Friedan, who had children, was irregular, odd. Gloria Steinem fit our image of Wonder Woman, Amazon warrior. Betty Friedan was a refugee from the suburbs. Gloria Steinem had no stretch marks. Most of her admirers did. Some women were attracted to feminism because of the starkness of the choice, some women were driven away. Most women could not conceive of leaving their children, could not put their own professional or love interests above the needs of their children. They resented women who lived for themselves alone, just as women who left their children resented the ones who stayed behind. One of those women who left said, "I think I've done what many women are scared of doing. I think there's hardly a woman in the country who wouldn't want to leave their kids at some point, quite honestly, only they won't admit it. They've swallowed so much for so long." The tension between mothers who leave and mothers who stay has lasted for nearly half a century.

In 1994 Rosemary Jackson writes a book supportive of mothers who leave their children, saying, "While maternal devotion may be perfectly genuine, this is in fact rarely the case. Maternity is usually a strange mixture of narcissism, altruism, idle daydreaming, sincerity, bad faith, devotion and cynicism." In 1994 nobody is surprised by this statement. It rings true enough. The novelist Fay Weldon writes an introduction to the book, called *Mothers Who Leave*, saying, "The marvel to me is that women have children at all. The marvel is that women so often stay and don't leave. It is wonderfully to their credit when they do, not to their discredit when they don't." This is politics not life as most of us experience it, which includes staying with and supporting, financially and emotionally, our children.

FREE TO BE ME: THE POLITICS OF
REARING FEMINIST CHILDREN

Throughout the seventies women were giving their girls trucks to play with and the boys, not necessarily to their delight, were receiving dolls. Lois Gould wrote a brilliant book for children about Baby X. It told the story of a child whose genitals were kept secret and who grew strong and happy by crossing all the stereotypes, back and forth, and doing just what he/she wanted to. Baby X was a terrific athlete and loved to cook. Baby X also had no mother waiting for him/her at home. This didn't bother Baby X because he/she was a fictional creation. The rest of us worried about our children. I gave my girls trucks but they kept turning them into dolls' beds. One of my daughters wanted a gun. The Vietnam War was on. I hated seeing her on the stairs, pointing her cowboy pistol at my guests in the living room. I didn't say anything, or at least not much of anything. I didn't want my girls as clean and polite as I had been. I didn't want them to curtsey as I had whenever I was introduced to an adult. I didn't want them fearful, gentle, and focused on their appearance. In principle I wanted them to be openly aggressive. In reality I couldn't stand it. I hushed them, calmed them, made constant liberal noises about other people's feelings. And yet, when a relative purchased a Barbie doll beauty parlor for one of their birthdays I removed it from their room the next day using the lame but not incredible excuse that the dog had chewed it up. My messages were probably as confused as I was. Was playing with a truck the reason why boys had power and girls had none, or did boys play with trucks because they had power and girls had none? By the mid-seventies it was clear to those of us in the trenches of child rearing that gender distinctions were coming at our children from all over and the children were imitating their peers as well as their mothers, and I could be only a mixed role model, wanting them to be free of stereotypes of all sorts even as I carried so many of those same stereotypes around just under the conscious skin.

Researchers told us that we handled our children differently according to gender from the first seconds that we held them in our arms. Boys were treated rougher, girls were rocked gently. Girls were more talked to, boys were pushed to stand and walk. The layers of gender-learned behavior were so thick that my palliatives, my trucks, my baseballs, even my reluctant toy pistols weren't going to change my children into true Baby X's. One of the little girls loved horses and one summer at camp learned to jump over high hurdles, but lots of little girls, way before feminism spread across the land, took up horses just before they took up boys. Another daughter was cautious, avoided sudden movements, unexpected drops. As a baby she had been afraid of the smallest breeze, screaming in the swing because the air was brushing past her face. What kind of Wonder Woman is afraid of the wind?

I wanted my daughters to become scientists and mathematicians. I purchased chemistry sets, toy microscopes. I spent hours with them putting together the Visible Woman, a see-through plastic model with all the internal organs carefully labeled. They weren't interested. Did I do something wrong or was I defeated by the real world which seems still to produce few women scientists? Every now and then I would buy one of them a doll of the sort my mother would have bought them, a baby doll wearing a dress with pleats and pearl buttons. This was bad from the point of view of liberation, mine and theirs, but it felt good. It is clear that the mix of home and genetics, of culture and hormones, of sexual communal clues and childhood experience cause stereotypical masculine and feminine behaviors to appear and disappear throughout childhood and after.

Eventually I gave up trying to shape my girls into Madame Curies. They were hell-bent to avoid that fate. I finally had to assume that the Baby X model was a metaphor, an ideal, a kind of Ur-baby that we couldn't create in the real world. I followed the children's lead and let them play with what they wanted. Not because I was so wise or because I approved of all their games but because the culture rolled over me as a mother, bringing with it both conventional rules of older traditional times and the new feminist truths. The girls would have to sort it out, make sense of the mixed messages themselves. If a *Ms.* magazine poster child existed, she wasn't in my house. My children were still playing house. Perhaps this is because I was not a good model. Wistfully I bought myself a brown briefcase. I carried it around all the time. I had always wanted to be the sort of person who needed a briefcase.

Once in the summer we were at the beach and the two littlest girls were running along the water's edge, the older one cautious, hanging back from the oncoming surf, the younger one splashing, letting the spray fall over her small body. All along the shore the outgoing tide had left starfish. Every few inches another lay encrusted in sand, most still alive, arms moving helplessly, fatally drying in the sun. The older one told the younger one to pick up a starfish and put it back in the water. "We'll save them," she said, "we'll save them all." "You can't," I said. "It's nature. Death is a part of nature." They looked at me and grabbed their orange plastic pails. "We'll save them," they said, and all afternoon they ran up and down the edge of the shore, gathering starfish and tossing them back into the sea. "It's futile," I said. "They'll be good mothers," my husband said. "They'll be nutty liberals," I answered. I was not ashamed of them, not at all.

The talk is still there at the end of the century about girls learning differently, girls losing confidence in adolescence, about bolstering girls academically, about leading them into the sciences, but most mothers seem, a generation after feminism became a household icon, less concerned than we were at the beginning with bringing up girls free of stereotypical gender limitations. Barbie still sells, little girls play with baby dolls, fewer of them are given trucks for birthday presents. Madonna is a heroine because she combines female beauty, female sexuality, masochism and sadism with success, aggression, action, wealth. This is a combination most of us could not have dreamed of in the early seventies. Now it seems as if the entire culture has backed off the Platonic ideal of pure unisex behavior. That no longer appears to be the route to freedom from prejudice, escape from imposed social boundaries. All that unisex talk was just another one of those ideologies that didn't stick to real people.

Whenever ideology and reality clashed, reality won.

THE POPULATION EXPLOSION

Despite the fact that nobody believed in happily ever after anymore, despite the growing lack of trust between the genders, right in the middle of the sexual revolution women who wrote and spoke against having babies had babies themselves, ten years later, just in the nick of time. Motherhood seemed to have an appeal, a staying power, that made it bend with the winds of feminism but not break. By the late seventies friends of mine who had delayed pregnancy until their late thirties became pregnant if they still could, remarried friends had children with new spouses, some women had children with no spouse or with a female partner, and while the men around them offered new and appreciated help, it was still the woman who woke for the early feedings, still the woman who felt most humiliated when her child was not accepted at a school of her choice, still the woman whose mothering was considered decisive for the mental health of her offspring. It seems that in turning a collective back on biology the feminist movement had made a mistake.

This desire of women for children is not just some social construct, not some male misogynist plot, not some patriarchal desire to control the inheritance of the next generation. It is some unstoppable species urge, some delicate strand of our genes that makes so many of us smile back at a baby smiling at us, makes us reach out with open arms to a child who reaches up to us, makes us think — lawyers, professors, architects all, secretaries, factory workers, insurance salespersons all — that we must have a child to make our lives move forward, to mold ourselves into our time, to make family, and we always want to make family better than it was made for us. Our optimism despite all we know of human experience is one of our strangest but sweetest follies.

Gender might not require a woman to stay home and raise the kids but it was clear that biology could not be erased just like that. Women, while delaying perhaps the first birth till after the graduate school degree had been conferred, the job promotion won, still had children if they could. The fact was that American women were simply not willing to give up the experience of childbirth, child raising, even if motherhood mixed badly with their other newer aspirations. There was birth control, after 1974 there was legal abortion: still there were children. Motherhood myths, "baby traps," as Ellen Peck called them, were exposed, but most women went right on conceiving and bringing infants to term. It seems that most of us did not after all want to be liberated from that basic biological experience, from that life course. The pull to reproduce was not a political decision but deeply primordial, a response to rhythms and tides not always accessible to reason.

THE ABORTION ISSUE TURNS INTO A POLITICAL-RELIGIOUS WAR

That's not to say that family life, tending babies, raising children is for every woman at every time of her life. Pregnancy at certain times, under certain circumstances, can be a real tragedy. This is an ancient truth and was not created by modern feminism. In the days before the society became more open and the double standard ruled, women were stigmatized by pregnancy out of wedlock. The child was a bastard and life of mother and child could truly be ruined. Sexual rules were always being broken, someone was always being shamed. Even for a married woman with other children the conception of another child is not necessarily welcome. This is true for women with financial problems with or without mates, it is true for women who are in the midst of their education or training, it is true for women who simply don't feel ready or able to take on the immense burden of a baby or a child. It is also true for women whose pregnancies have occurred through rape or incest, or with men who have left them alone. The fierceness of the desire to have a child is equally balanced by the necessity of not having a child sometimes, under some circumstances. Abortion is as old as history and existed way before feminism made the woman's ownership of her own body a major issue. Abortion is the face of harsh reality and always has been. Before technology, before sterilization, before contraception, the birth of a child was not always the cause for rejoicing. It still isn't. These days abortion intersects so clearly with feminist goals that it appears to be a feminist wish, to abort the fetus, or so the enemies of abortion and feminism would have us think.

Abortion has become a symbolic public issue. The desire to keep women dependent and at home, to hold on to something sacred in a world that tends to strip everything down to its commercial use, to prevent the casual sexual encounter out of puritan sensibility, fear of sexual disorder (which is usually a fear of one's own sexual impulses raging out of control), fear of a world in which life and death are not just God's domain — these are matters that inform the abortion battles.

Abortion has become the issue that divides the fundamentally religious from the anti-traditional, those who seek personal freedom from those who seek obedience to the decreed ways. Shame, since the upheaval of the nineteen seventies, is no longer a player in the discussion, although certain conservatives would like to control sexual behavior with that old splintered billy club. Now the fight in America is between clashing worldviews, oppositions that can barely coexist. The abortion issue signals an ongoing if unrecognized civil war that may yet lead to our undoing as a civil nation. What presents itself here as a feminist issue of control over one's own body is in fact entangled in questions of ambiguity, contrasting visions of freedom that belong to the religious wars of history. It's amazing that so little blood has been shed so far.

The right to an abortion is so central to a woman's dignity, hope, education, prospects for independence that it must be a feminist issue. When motherhood is an imposition not a choice, a tragedy not a desire, then women are reduced to their biology, and life with its accumulated disappointments becomes a prison: depression where joy should be. On the other hand, when feminists fight for legal abortion they appear to be fighting against the child that will come. They do in fact appear to be more interested in preventing motherhood than in making life better for the new mothers and children that continually spill across the country, uncountable like the stars in the Milky Way. This matter of image has serious political consequences. To be pro-child is in fact to be pro-choice, to be pro-choice is to be pro-child, but it is easy to make that appear untrue. Every child a wanted child is a less dramatic slogan, less visual, heart-tugging, morally unambiguous, than Save the baby, Life, a beautiful choice, or Child murderer. The feminist movement has allowed itself to be out-maneuvered, out-sloganed, by the rigid right who claim to love children more than the rest of us. It's a false claim, it's a sleight of hand, but it hurts. We have not made the case that every child must be a wanted child strongly enough because that would involve an open public expression of women's love for children which to some feminists seems like stoking the reactionary fires. We don't want to make such a fuss over the wonder of babies that someone might suggest we should go back into the nursery and stay there. Calling for legal abortion is a more attractive position for women so newly liberated from exclusive child care than carrying on about the beautiful choice of a wanted child.

The pro-life movement takes out TV ads in which adorable children emerge from behind a school door, they share a sandwich, they sit on the swings, they jump rope, they smile shyly at the camera, and the voice-over says, "Life, what a beautiful choice." The ad speaks in terms so blatantly sentimental that it's hard to resist. We can despise their cleaned-up view of the unwanted child, the way they leave out the bruises of abuse, the effects of poverty, but we can't help but be touched by the living blush of real children at the beginning of their lives. They got us. They got us because our position appears like a negative, a reverse of their image, our position is a graveyard, a collection of fetuses in a jar, stillness in place of movement.

When we debated abortion back in the prelegal days, we discussed the beginning of life, when was it exactly, and we held hard to the line that life was about breathing air, working lungs, fetal viability. Life could only be extrauterine we said. That was our story. This was philosophically interesting but actually meaningless. The real line between the life that would be if left alone and the life that wasn't because it wasn't left alone is clearly more ambiguous than we would have liked. The advent of sonograms, the earlier age of fetal survival, the knowledge that every pregnant woman has, even in the first days after she discovers that she is pregnant, certainly when the baby kicks within her, that life is really there, means that our position was intellectually weak, more wish than reality. However, their position was no better, simple but not necessarily moral. We drew our line on the absolute question: Is or isn't the embryo alive? We should have drawn the line on whether the fetus was or was not wanted and shaped the debate on that issue instead of getting mired in metaphysics or theology about the beginning of life.

In some circumstances life is not sacred. To say this is to end the old debate and begin a new one on which we are on firmer ground. To say this is not to instigate massacres or social mayhem. We have always had those, and not because a nation or a tribe allowed legal abortion. To be able to take a shading on the moral chart, to declare that you can't kill a fifteen-month-old child but you can a six-week-old fetus is to accept ambiguity, complications, things that are not black and white but private, morally sticky, sometimes necessary. Every woman who has been pregnant knows that the life within her is life whether she chooses to end it or not. Just as the two-year-old will likely become twenty, so the undisturbed fetus will likely become one. To kill a fetus, however, is not the same as to kill a baby and everyone knows that. To kill a baby without a brain is not the same as to kill a baby with a club foot and everyone knows that too. Life is sacred but sometimes the sacred thing to do is to end life. It is true we stand on a slippery slope but reality and morality are formed and lived on slippery slopes. To be able to make difficult decisions that are not based on immutable rules is a sign of human complexity and indicates a capacity for moral thought as opposed to sheer obedience.

The morality of abortion lies in our capacity to make distinctions of quality, to balance one good against another, one evil against another. The moral outrage of the pro-lifers would be blunted if we made the argument that civilized people can hold the line against murder while acknowledging that sometimes life is not a necessary outcome of its earliest beginning.

The women's movement would be better able to fight off the pro-life forces if we had expressed a deeper concern for children, for family, for the sacrifices that children require of a parent, of a society. If the issue is women's freedom alone it becomes suspect. If the desire for the legalization of abortion is prompted by concern for the welfare of children, of mothers, of families, then we can go on the moral offensive, not just when they try to shoot our doctors but the rest of the time as well.

My oldest daughter is seventeen. She is in her senior year of high school. She hangs out in the park and smokes in her room and once a friend of hers dropped a lighted cigarette into a chair and later smoke filled the house and the fire trucks came. She wakes up at night and sleeps during the day, like a nocturnal animal. Her eyes are often red. I have sent her to my gynecologist. She knows about birth control. She forgets her books, her bus money, her scarf. She has been tested by a psychologist. The report comes back. There is no good news. She thinks about death. She has a new psychiatrist. She misses appointments. There are bottles under her bed. "Be careful, be careful," I say. "You don't trust me," she says. "Be careful," I say. "You hate me," she says. I follow her around the city with phone calls. She's just been there. She's expected soon. I watch. I wait for her at the window and often she comes home hours late. In the house she seems like an exhausted child, asleep in odd places, writing poetry on the back of matchbooks.

Then she tells me she is pregnant. We make an appointment at a clinic. I go with her. I wait in the waiting room. There are boyfriends pacing up and down. There are girlfriends running back and forth to the bank of telephones in the outer hall. There is another mother. We avoid each other's eyes. I try to read. I can't. The walls are a peaceful blue. There is a painting of a ship sailing around a cliff. I am sitting in a waiting room while my first grandchild loses life. There is no ceremony for this. The moment just slips by slowly. I am not a romantic. There is no point in thinking about it. I cannot stop. I am grateful that she can have a legal abortion. I am sad at her loss, my loss. I don't think it was nothing. I do think it was necessary and morally right. The ethical scales are balanced correctly but that doesn't mean that ambivalence, doubt, and sorrow aren't weighed in.

THE LITTLE FAMILIES THAT COULDN'T

In 1974 abortion was made legal. The pill was everywhere and so was divorce. It seemed as if our social structure was breaking down. The late sixties had brought us orgies and swapping and open marriages. In the seventies we were divorcing. Is it some sort of linguistic irony that love, liberation, and loneliness all start with the same letter of the alphabet? In the two decades since then the divorce rate has continued to climb. Men who talk a lot about becoming new fathers may share custody or have custody of their children in rising numbers and the stigma of the broken home is gone, but the bleakness of it all hasn't changed. It was hard then just as it is hard now to be a single parent, and the many young women who don't opt for abortion but bear their children because they want them are now an army of single mothers, straggling, scattered, unprepared, wounded. It seems an incredible irony that during the same time that abortion was made legal, many women were deciding to bear their children, to raise them in poverty, to forgo their education, to burden the society with their needs. This is not just the result of anti-abortion fieldwork but some clear expression of our social failure, our cruel divisions between men and women, children and parents, that has further fragmented families, left men unconnected to their children and children so desperate for affection that they have children themselves to fill needs as deep as the ocean, as wide as the sky.

Feminists find themselves astounded by the numbers of out-of-wedlock births and astounded by the numbers of men deserting children. This was certainly not part of the original design. It is a feather in no feminist cap that in the years since the first NOW conference, since abortion first became legal, the instances of child abuse, the numbers of teenage mothers, the numbers of divorced mothers bringing up children alone living under the poverty line have so drastically multiplied. To own one's body, to bring a child to term only if wanted, was a reasonable goal for those who did not fetishize the fetus. Unfortunately it was clearly not enough, not sufficient to create the kind of social well-being for women and children that was once imagined. Legal abortion is a fine thing as far as it goes but it doesn't go far enough. To whatever extent feminism contributed to the idea that women could do without men, that families were not necessary for human protection, growth, happiness, that women could stand alone, that we were not bound together in marriage, in community, it is complicit in the ills we see everywhere.

That said, let no one forget that the seemingly well glued society of the fifties stood on a foundation riddled with rot. It was built on a swamp of conformity, repression, and bigotry against anyone who differed. There was nothing peaceful, lovely, fine about the way it was. Nostalgia can easily make fools of us all. Homes like my parents' where divorce did not occur were not necessarily homes in which love, respect, honor, and honesty flourished. We complain these days about the talk shows in which dirty secrets are flashed before millions of people, but remember the silence of the fifties, the secrecy of sex, the fear of public exposure of homosexuals, the ridicule of spinsters, the fear of being a freak, the increased anxiety because no one knew what went on in anybody else's house. The talk shows, commercial bazaar or not, are a cultural corrective to the conformities and private shames that dominated America in the past. They may not be so bad after all if the alternative is to put the lid back on: hush, hush, shame, shame.

ANGER RISES AND RISES SOME MORE

We talked about men endlessly. We began to talk about male doctors. We saw our obstetricians as domineering, condescending, calling each of us by our first names while we referred to them as Doctor So-and-So. Women in increasing numbers became angry at a medical establishment that allowed so few women into its top ranks, controlled the way women experienced the birth of their children. There was much that needed correcting, and the list of wrongs done to women by the male obstetrical hierarchy is long indeed. In the holy but masculine name of science the midwife, who probably knew what she was doing, was replaced with the male doctor who overused forceps, who made the mother-to-be lie down flat, who brought deathly sepsis into the birth canal with his unclean hands and removed the mother from her birthing place in the family to the alien cold world of the hospital where infections spread and so many women in the nineteenth century died. But before you work up a head of steam about male control, patriarchal medicine, etc., remember that's only half the picture. Male doctors also discovered ways of saving babies and mothers and as twentieth-century medicine progressed they increasingly were able to protect the mother from the ravages of toxemia and to restore babies born in frail and precarious states. Dr. Lamaze was a male and so were the inventors of the sonogram and amniocentesis, which offer a much-improved opportunity for a healthy birth. This combination of good and bad has also been true of the psychologists' and psychoanalysts' influence on motherhood and child care, although many more of them were women from the start. The humane and wonderful Women's Health Book Collective in Boston published *Our Bodies, Ourselves* and reminded us that childbirth was *ours*, not *theirs*. However, the anti–male doctor ethos that was running through the women's movement put some women at risk by encouraging them to use home remedies and avoid modern science and its lifesaving technology. It also fed the anger against males that spread through the culture like a particularly contagious if oddly satisfying virus.

Published in 1981, Betty Friedan's book *The Second Stage* was accused of sliding backwards because she called for attention to family issues, to children's issues, to the home. Betty Friedan wrote this book to remind feminists that the time had come to collaborate with men, to work together to build a better way to live in equal partnership. Betty Friedan was not honored in some feminist circles because she was bucking the now strong current of the women's movement. Some women were feeling and expressing a previously inexpressible fury at the male animal. Their anger at their fathers, brothers, or grandfathers metamorphosed into a blanket rage against the patriarchy. The rage against the patriarchy began to turn into a deep suspicion of men in general. This anger could be seen on the grim faces of the women attending the Lorena Bobbitt trial (at Columbia University a sign read "What about the ones that got away?"), in the anti-pornography movement in its extremes, in the sudden sharp focus on abused women, incest victims. The recovered memory phenomenon which swept the nation in the early nineties was about the evil doings of fathers. On a Toronto talk show a woman, tight-lipped, ashen, wearing army fatigues, says she is doing a book on a single family in which twenty-four members were sexually attacked as children by their fathers and uncles.

Incest and sexual abuse of children by neighbors or relatives or strangers is a hideous matter. When my husband ran a therapeutic nursery for children under the age of three from the inner city he would on occasion see venereal sores on children's mouths, a sure sign of sexual abuse. What kind of animal attacks its young? The idea of so harming a baby is sickening. The idea of any adult sexually using any child of any age is shocking and distressing and we know it happens again and again. Too many men are indeed morally dwarfed and truly demonic. One case of incest alone would be enough to indict the entire species in a heavenly court, but the question arises, and it is an important question, are all men tainted by the moral lacunae of some, and what is that some, and what happened to them that they are so maimed, and how many are there actually?

It is not a denial of the multigenerational horror of real incest to say that in past years the inflated numbers, the hysteria, the memories elicited by dedicated therapists with preconceived ideas had more to do with a climate of female rage against men than about actual incest rates. In the eighties and early nineties it seemed as if almost every new novel contained at its center a revelation of incest: i.e., Jane Smiley's *A Thousand Acres,* Mary Gaitskill's *Two Girls, Fat and Thin,* Kathryn Harrison's *Exposure,* E. Annie Proulx's *Shipping News,* Alice Walker's *The Color Purple,* Margaret Atwood's *Robber Bride.* In fact it is almost impossible to name a novel written by a woman published in the last several years that doesn't include an incest scene. (Male novelists picked up the plot — Russell Banks, Geoffrey Wolff, for example.) I am writing here of incest's sudden commonplaceness, its role as a plot device in contemporary fiction, its cultural reasons for coming to prominence. The incest theme fueled and reflected some feminists' belief that the male animal is by nature an abuser, a rapist, and an oppressor. This view of father and brother, lover and male friend spread across certain parts of female America.

I was at a meeting at the *New York Times* in the late seventies. A group of women writers was attempting to put pressure on the magazine and book review sections to hire more women editors. The magazine had run an article about the Los Angeles freeways several weeks earlier. In the article the reporter, male, had described a scene in which panties and a bra were found on the highway. The reporter had interpreted this as pleasure occurring in a car. One of my colleagues at this meeting insisted that every woman knew that a rape had taken place. I wasn't sure, after all, many of us had made out, made love, in the back seat of a car. Another writer insisted that no female editor would have approved the article on male heart attacks that suggested that women should cook low-fat foods for their husbands. "Who cares about what men eat or what they die of?" she said. "I do," I mumbled, but very quietly. I didn't want to be counterproductive. I really did want more women editors at the paper. But after the meeting I decided that my activist political career would have to end. There was no way around it. I wanted my husband to eat well even though he was the cook in the family. I didn't fit in.

WHAT FEMINISM DID TO FREUD

The incest, incest everywhere cry was abetted by Jeffrey Moussaieff Masson's attack on Freud and the Freud archives. He claimed that Freud had sold out in creating his Oedipus theory by attributing sexual wishes to children and denying the cases he had seen of actual incest. Masson accused Freud of an opportunist collusion with Victorian daddies in their nasty practices. In fact Freud always acknowledged real incest as a part of the social reality. His theories concerned a child's normal sexuality, which, he observed, existed independent of any real paternal action. He never ruled out real sexual abuse, and in fact his theories on Oedipal sexuality explain why incest is such a psychologically disastrous event, crippling and haunting its victims for the rest of their lives. Most psychiatrists today listen carefully to their patients and believe that most of the time they can discriminate between the buried childhood Oedipal trace and actual physical harm suffered by some at the hands of their male relatives.

Freud ran into tremendous opposition in Vienna in the early nineteen hundreds and was in fact denounced by the University of

Vienna because at the time the idea of children, innocence incarnate, bearing sexual desire was itself revolutionary and unsettling. So much for Freud's opportunism. However, Masson's attack on Freud added fuel to the popular feminist attack against his theories on women. The image of the male as his daughter's worst enemy fell on fertile soil, and anything that debunked Freud and illustrated the evil carnality of men was welcome news. Incest, however, is hardly the common experience of daughters, and its prominence in our art, in our psychotherapy today has more to do with political streams running together and overflowing their banks than with actual male monsters loose in every other family.

The attack on Freud by feminists was justified insofar as it exposed the weak place in his theory — female sexual development — and it caused more than a few psychoanalysts to alter their expectations for their female patients. There was a time in the forties and fifties when many women were routinely pushed by their therapists toward mothering and domestic existence. But even in those days many therapists listened carefully to their patients and if their needs included work and self-expression they encouraged those patients regardless of sex to move forward. Anne Sexton's therapist, Dr. Orne, despite betraying her after her death by giving tapes of her sessions to her biographer, did at least support her poetry.

Sometime in the late sixties I am sitting in the soft deep chair in my therapist's office. The noisy fan clinks and purrs. The light is a half light, coming through closed blinds, striping the carpet. I am in love with my therapist. I know it's only an illusion, a by-product of the artificial intimacy. If he asked me to clean his closets or swim the English Channel, I would. "I had a dream," I say. "Not today," he says. "My mother once said," I begin. He sits back in his chair. I hear him breathing. I am silent. "You want to hear about what my daughter did at dinner last night?" "No," he says. "I'm thinking," I say, "about writing a story." He sits up straight, leans forward. "You," he said. "What nerve." Irony. I heard him.

Some in the women's movement appeared ready in their anger to throw out all the Freudian insights, the proverbial baby with the bath water so to speak. Their anger at ideas like penis envy, female impaired conscience, and inherently female passivity and masochism was certainly justified. The problem with anger is that it overwhelms cool reason and becomes at full intensity incompatible with intellectual activity.

The feminist anger at Freud was at bottom an anger against men talking about women, about male control of the culture, male control of science, males positing the male model as the norm and the female as deviant. The anger was at Freud for saying that childbirth was female fulfillment and home the woman's proper domain. This anger was justified but its proper target was the entire Victorian culture, not so much the eminent scientist who was trying to make sense out of it all while living within it. Feminist anger went too far dismissing interesting avenues of intellectual exploration, it became too blanket, undiscriminating, silly. Freud could be seen as a great genius who was wrong about female sexuality or as a demonic cultural force keeping women in their secondary place. The latter view fed the anti-male sentiments of many feminists but drove others away.

Freud said a good many foolish and insulting things about women. Man of his time, scientist and genius that he was, he couldn't see past his culture when it came to women's development. This has been made clear not only by popular feminists such as Kate Millett, Germaine Greer, and Phyllis Chesler but also by his followers and supporters, many of them women psychoanalysts (Karen Horney, Melanie Klein, Nancy Chodorow, the psychologist Dorothy Dinnerstein). But he also made remarkable discoveries into the nature of the human mind, female as well as male. He told us that we have an unconscious that is made up of nasty thoughts, wishes, primitive desires. He told us that childhood is a time when sexual fantasies seem real and attainable. He explained our chronic guilt, our fear of retaliation for sexual transgressions that exist only in our unconscious wishes. He explained ambivalence, how love and hate are intertwined in most human relationships. He opened childhood to the idea of cause and effect, the impact of the child's experiences on the adult to be. He showed us how we tame our animal selves and what price we pay for that taming, how hard it is to dose ourselves with the right amount of guilt, neither too little nor too much. He showed us how we harm ourselves in our internal psychic struggles. And perhaps most important of all he showed us that self-knowledge is the way to freedom, that patterns of the past can be broken when we understand them, when we recognize ourselves in our fate.

When Gloria Steinem attacks Freud, ridiculing his concepts of penis envy and female passivity, she ignores all the great advances of knowledge that he did give us and focuses only on those of his theories that do not stand the test of culture's change. She simplifies and attacks at will, even calling Anna Freud a disaster, this woman who ran Hampstead clinic for years, was a distinguished theoretician, a respected colleague, and lived a life of good work and deep friendships that would make anyone proud. Gloria Steinem forgets that so much of what we understand about ourselves we understand through Freud's explorations of previously uncharted territory. She doesn't grasp that the questions Freud asked, the how and why of human unconscious experience, the how and why of the mind-body dance, opened the door for new understandings of our civilization, our symbols, ourselves.

THE CONSPIRACY: "THEY 'AGAINST' US"

When we speak of the patriarchy we speak of a social organization, a means of distributing power and kinship relations within society. We can look at how the patriarchy works, at kings, fathers, heads of departments, CEOs, etc. But the women's movement transformed the patriarchy into something harder to observe and pin down, a "they." This "they," like the one supposedly described by the *Protocols of the Elders of Zion,* is an almost mystical entity, exerting its influence as a mysterious atmosphere, as a conspiracy of a part of society, as a plan against the others, as an intentional activity. A friend of mine told me that "they" were trying to get women to buy lipstick because "they" were connected to petroleum interests worldwide. Another "they" exists in Marilyn French's work, in Phyllis Chesler's attack on fathers and child custody issues. This invisible conspiratorial "they" became a trope to which stuck all kinds of female anger. Actually the most rotten things in the world come about because of the cocktail of human passions, the weird turns of historical forces, the effects of the economy, religion, the whims of individuals, etc. There just isn't any "they" planning to make life uncomfortable for you and me, and when we start to think like that our anger gets in our way and trouble lies ahead.

Susan Brownmiller's best-selling book on rape, *Against Our Will,* presented the origins of human society as the impressing of male sexuality on women they had corralled into groups for their own sexual use. In that view the great cathedrals of Europe, the achievements of Mozart, the wonders of modern medicine, the paintings of Picasso, the invention of the wheel and the airplane are all built on the corrupt foundation of male penises forcing their way into unwilling vaginas. Yes, said many women who smarted and burned from the exclusion from power that was the patriarchal norm, yes, said women who had been unloved or couldn't love. The river of rage that was released was too strong for Betty Friedan's more humanistic voice.

The anger at the domination of women was of course natural. So was the fury of the crowds that cheered on the wagons carrying the sorry nobility to the guillotine in 1789. The anger of the oppressed is always dangerous and global, missing the right target, blanketing whole populations, seeking the satisfaction of revenge and never quite finding it. The problem is that this anger, stronger in one woman than another because of her personal experience, is aimed at the one who should be her love object, her partner, her shelter as she should be his. It makes it difficult to love and be loved and support a child in a family if rage is blazing in the hearth.

In 1979 Jean Bethke Elshtain, an associate professor of political science at the University of Massachusetts, wrote: "To have a war one needs enemies, and radical feminism has no difficulty finding him. The portrait of man which emerges from radical feminist texts is that of an implacable enemy, an incorrigible and dangerous beast who has as his chief aim in life the oppression and domination of women. Ti-Grace Atkinson attributes this male compulsion to man's a priori need to oppress others, an imperative termed 'metaphysical cannibalism,' from which women are exempt. . . . Susan Brownmiller's male is tainted with animus dominandi which makes him a 'natural predator.' Mary Daly's male is less bestial more ghoulish, a vampire who 'feeds on the bodies and minds of women.'" Elshtain points out that in radical feminist rantings the fetus is labeled a tenant, a parasite, and an uninvited guest.

Sara Ruddick, teacher of philosophy and women's studies at the New School for Social Research, wrote in 1990 of her ideal for women: "Secure in near exclusively female enclaves that are governed by ideals of gender justice, women could undertake a politico-spiritual journey in which they (almost all) relinquished heterosexuality though not necessarily mothering, overcame their dependence on fathers and fears of fatherlessness and claimed for themselves personal autonomy and collective political and cultural power." She goes on to point out that "if an absent father is depressingly disappointing, a present father can be dangerous to mothers and children." While this is literally sometimes true, this fear of the male is out of proportion and most of us know it in our bones. Some men are monsters, so are some women. Most men and women are not dangerous to each other and a worldview that sees men as alligators and women as babes wading in the shallow water does not convince us.

Rape, domestic violence, sexual crimes became increasingly a subject of discussion in the culture. The abuse of the female body by the disturbed male had long been a terrible secret, a shame we needed to expose. However, the byproduct of all the talk, films, TV shows, campus pamphlets was a further split between the sexes, a good-and-evil divide that ran along gender lines, spawning and intensifying female rage, a rage that was very righteous indeed. In a cultural sense the propaganda war was won by the feminists. The Anita Hill–Clarence Thomas hearings were the high point of cultural confusion about correct sexual behavior. At the end many women were convinced that men just didn't get it and that women were offended by sexual innuendo, propositions, harassment in frightening numbers. The added publicity given the issue of sexual harassment by the Navy Tailhook convention, and the Paula Jones harassment suit against President Clinton, as well as the Bob Packwood scandal, led to a cultural environment thick with sexual accusations, assuming a kind of female purity and absence of expressed lust, a desire not to have desire, a denial of female desire. This contradiction in feminist terms, a sort of Victorian revival, was a natural outgrowth of the anti-male railings that had become the hallmark of contemporary feminism.

Despite the fact that the media in the last ten years have presented program after program about male rapists, wife beaters, sexual harassers, incest perpetrators, we didn't all become Thelmas and Louises running off a cliff. Despite the attitude toward men that seems to come out of many feminist centers most of us continue to seek out men, to enjoy their admiration, to encourage them to respond to us as sexual beings some of the time.

My youngest daughter has just become a teenager. With a pack of friends she has begun hanging out in a local department store, testing all the cosmetics. "What about your homework, what about your mind," I mutter on and on. She looks at me from beneath heavily mascaraed lashes, as if I have lost my wits. When we walk down the street together men stare at her, turn around and continue looking after she has passed. Stop that, I want to call out. On the other hand, I know she's releasing a barely decent scent. It precedes us, it follows us as we walk around. I feel old, dowdy, slightly envious of the way the sun shines on her skin, the way the muscles in her legs flex, the way she walks trying out a discreet hip swing from side to side, the way her hand flips through her hair. Then she has a boyfriend and she stops going to the department store. She spends her time in her room with him. When she goes away for a few weeks over the summer I see him every day sitting all afternoon on the steps of the brownstone across the street staring at our building. Then she comes back and his sidewalk vigil is over. One night we come home from dinner with friends and find him, shaggy haired, big hands, big feet, weeping in our living room. My daughter has developed a migraine headache and has been in pain for hours. She has vomited over his shirt. He is crying because he doesn't know what to do to help her. He is fourteen years old and able to love even when the glamour has gone. Young romance may not last but it opens a path. It begins one of the truest stories we will ever know. Hormones make their own political parameters.

Despite the flight from hearth by some women most of us would never under any circumstances leave our children. We have a hard enough time leaving them to go to work, leaving them with a cold in the head or a baby sitter they don't know. It's not a matter of social shame. Our mothering is daily, constant, urgent, necessary. Are we crazy to hold our families so? I am reading *Babar* to my youngest daughter. I feel her hand on my leg press down hard. I look in her face and see the look of terror that the elephant mother's death has caused. I see how pale she is, how her foot shakes in a nervous spasm. "It's all right," I say, "I'm not going to be shot by an elephant hunter. I promise." She moves away from me. "I don't want to read anymore," she says. "But the story is good," I say. "You'll see," I say, "everything will be fine." "No," she says, "it will never be fine again." Later I find myself shivering. That is a terrible story. I stay heartbroken for hours.

Most women in America preferred to dismiss feminists than to dismiss the interests of their hearts and bodies, their needs for vital human connections. Most women in America hearing this loud anti-male beat in the feminist movement distanced themselves from political feminism while absorbing the more practical feminist lessons of self-worth, economic independence, and aspiration. They continued to have children not because a conspiracy of male patriarchal forces was pulling the wool over their eyes but because they wanted to.

THE PROBLEM THAT WON'T GO AWAY

At an academically excellent all-girls private school on the Upper East Side of Manhattan a few years back the principal held a special assembly so the girls could meet a woman who was a partner in a major law firm and had just been asked to serve on an important city commission. This was to be a significant role model experience, so the principal intended. The lawyer spoke to the girls about her work, her training, and her interest in First Amendment issues. When she finished, the first question asked was what hour did she get home. The second question asked was who took care of her children during the day. The third question was about what happened if one of her children was sick. The students, most of them daughters of working women, professional women who had left their children in the care of au pairs, nannies from Jamaica or Trinidad, did not take kindly to this lawyer and her accomplishments. They hissed her answers to those questions. These private school girls, with their plaid skirts, braces, acne, socks falling down over their sneakers, were not brainwashed by Phyllis Schlafly or

Marabel Morgan. They must have felt truly deprived of their mothers. How much they need us, how crucial we are, how important is the word *mother*. How sad is the loss of a mother. How deep is the yearning for mother. This need will not go away. It is not a cultural artifact, like the male need for a wife to keep his supper warm, it is a deep implant, a hook that snares us, a connection both treacherous and wondrous. A child without a mother is so horribly sad that we can't tolerate the thought. A child with a nose pressed to the window waiting for mother is an image like water torture that drip-drips through our days. Feminism used to say that the personal is political. If so the personal grief of the children who need better mothering, who need better family, who need voices speaking for them is our new politics.

If, as it appears, children have paid the price for our feminist gains, we can expand our vision, recognizing the ancient rub between mother and child. Without capitulating to the religious right, without setting back the clock on female progress, without turning ourselves into brownie bakers, we have to address this hard uneasy tension between motherhood and feminism, otherwise it will return to haunt us in our children's fates, in our politics. If our children are unhappy we cannot be happy. And most of us cannot be happy without children.

We are on vacation in St. Croix. We have rented a house for a month on the far side of the mountains. The water is turquoise, the clouds come like periods in a sonnet. Each morning we work a few hours and then go down to the beach with the children. We carry a picnic lunch, sand toys, suntan oil, and a first aid kit. My second stepdaughter's hair turns golden. She sits on the blanket making tiny houses out of tissues. So fragile is her home. The baby walks and adds words, firefly, lizard, coconut. The children sleep on a screened porch at night, the stars seem within reaching distance. My older daughter refuses to wear a bathing suit top. She runs into the surf and throws herself backwards and forwards. She glides, she sinks. Her dark hair hangs down to her waist. Her knees are skinned from the rocks she has climbed. She moves up and down the beach chasing after bugs. She stays in the warm clear water for hours. Her limbs are strong and her body is lithe. She sings to herself as she dives. She does not swim a conventional stroke. She wouldn't do it the way she was told. She never did anything the way she was told. She calls out to us, "Come in, come in." No one can stay in the water as long as she can. Her hands are wrinkled. She tells us she is a fish, a purple fish. I watch her.

What I know is that she should never have to wear clothes. She should never have appointments to keep, lists to make, assignments to complete. She should never have to do math problems or calculate distances. She should always be free to run, a creature without restraint. Glory, glory, her happiness in the silver shining surf brings me terror. If I moved to Tahiti, if I became a madwoman on an island with a child, eating fruit from the trees and telling the seasons by the tilt of the stars in the sky, she might be all right. Her hair is caked with sand. There is peach juice running down her chest. Civilization will kill her I think. At night my eyes scan the horizon for the mythical green flash that some say marks the sunset at the equator. If I see it I think it will be a sign that she will be all right. I don't see it. My husband laughs. He doesn't believe that I'm praying to a green flash. At night in our beds we hear drums. There is a Black Power group organizing on the island. There are some unpleasant incidents. Our dog is kidnapped and never returned. I am trying to become pregnant again. Like the crabs that had come down from the mountains in the thousands, knocking their shells against one another, a massive carpet of moving creatures making their way to the shore to mate, reversing themselves the next day, returning up to the mountains, a massive army of moving shells, I am driven by instinct. I must have more children.

PART II

GUILT:
WHAT IT DOES TO US

ATONAL MUSIC: WHEN MOTHER AND
CHILD SING DIFFERENT SONGS

I am divorced. My first child is two and a half. My mother has died. I have to find a way to make a living. I'm running out of money. I am sitting in the playground watching my daughter climb up and down the jungle gym. She is reckless, bold, careless, and flushed with pleasure. I am tense, frightened, hold myself back from stopping her. I want her to explore. I want her to have dirt on her knees, to dare. I also want her to be careful. I bite my lip till it bleeds. I bring her home and fix supper. She doesn't want what I have prepared. I sit with her and beg. I make faces, I read a story. I put on a record. I give her crayons. I prepare something else. She is pale now and tired. I give her a bath. She moves away from the washcloth. I chase her. I notice a mole on her shoulder. Is it growing? I should ask the doctor about that. I think about melanoma. The doorbell rings. The baby sitter has arrived. I have a graduate school class. My daughter knows this baby sitter. She sees her and climbs out of the tub and grabs my knees. I need to get my books. I need to comb my hair and change my clothes. I carry my daughter in my arms as I do these things. Her fingers are pressed into my neck. I set her down. I am going. I am going out the door. My daughter begins to scream. She screams not like a child in pain but as if a nightmare were progressing, as if deep within her everything was falling apart. These are shrieks and sobs combined. She loses her breath, her face is red. She gasps for air. "I will be back. I always come back. I will be back by eleven o'clock. I promise I will be back," I say. She screams harder, she tries to grab my hair. I know she is screaming because she has only me, I am the sole parent. That is my fault. I pry her loose. I know what I have to do. I open the door. The baby sitter holds my daughter in a firm grip. I run out the door. I ring the elevator bell. I hear her screaming. I hear her as I ride down the elevator, all the way to the first floor I hear her cries. I am soaking wet. I have perspired through my shirt. I feel faint. Should I go back upstairs? I wait a moment or two. My heart stops pounding. I head off toward the subway. The churning in my stomach is not all sympathy and love. Something else, a desire to leave has entered. This only makes me more guilty, guilty as charged, leaving a child. I have never been more miserable.

I understand perfectly what Adrienne Rich meant by "the invisible violence of the institution of motherhood . . . the guilt, the powerless responsibility for human lives, the judgments and condemnations, the fear of her own power, the guilt, the guilt, the guilt."

In 1924 A. A. Milne wrote what I suppose he thought of as an amusing poem. It is called "Disobedience" and it refers to the mother's sin, not the child's.

> James James
> Morrison Morrison
> Weatherby George Dupree
> Took great
> Care of his Mother
> Though he was only three.
> James James,
> Said to his Mother,
> "Mother," he said, said he:

"You must never go down to the end of the town
   if you don't go down with me."

James James
Morrison's Mother
Put on a golden gown,
James James
Morrison's Mother
Drove to the end of the town.
James James
Morrison's Mother
Said to herself said she:
"I can get right down to the end of the town
   and be back in time for tea."

Of course she wasn't, and the rest of the poem chronicles how her son goes to look for her but she is never found again. This little poem is the author's accurate perception of a child's wish to control his mother's whereabouts, to keep her close by his side, and it speaks of his deepest fear that he will lose his mother to the attractive, beckoning, but frightening outside world which is down there at the end of town where she goes all dressed up, leaving him behind. This common childhood experience hardly ever ends in permanent loss, but the drama is high, the threat is real, and women these days who go off to town on a daily basis must know that the child they leave behind fears the worst, time and again, over and over.

And it isn't as if mothers don't want to go down to the end of town, at least sometimes. The child may always wish to be with the mother but the mother often has other desires, friends, work, family. She is attracted, distracted, needful of the outside world just when the child requires her to be focused, steady, home, near. What mother hasn't had secret dreams of escape? What mother hasn't had moments when the strain overwhelms, when the child whines once too often, when the exhaustion of soothing a colicky baby grows too intense, when the struggle between siblings sets off a desire to flee? What mother hasn't wondered sometimes if she really loves her children, enough, too much, at all? What if she really has to go to work?

Adrienne Rich writes most pointedly about this mother guilt: "For years I believed that I should never have been anyone's mother, that because I felt my own needs acutely and often expressed them violently, I was Kali, Medea, the sow that devours her farrow, the unwomanly woman in flight from womanhood, a Nietzschean monster." This is expressed in somewhat hysterical language but the truth in it is recognizable even to those of us with less volatile or literary temperaments. There is inherent in motherhood a continual giving up of self, and few of us take to that without resentment, which itself creates a river of guilt. Adrienne Rich is able to call on the figures of Kali and Medea because culture has provided images of the all-purpose destructive woman, the cruel and consuming mother who like an animal gone wild will eat her young. These are male-created images but women recognize them too. We fear the destructiveness inside ourselves. Most of us are afraid that if we caught our true face in the mirror we might see not the most beautiful queen in the land but the wicked stepmother, the Medusa who turns her enemies to stone. This makes us feel guilty.

One of the reasons it's hard to express satisfaction with your life when you have children is that everywhere, every day there is anger. Not the life-threatening kind that caused Susan Smith to kill her boys, not the dark rage of depression that caused Sylvia Plath to put her head in the oven with her two babies in the house, but the quick summer storm kind of anger, the slow burn anger, the underground anger that sometimes affects what you do or say without your even knowing that it was there. There are the terrible twos when a child asserting independence refuses to wear mittens on a freezing cold day and for a moment your frustration turns you into a wild thing. There's the other kind of anger that comes when you need sleep and the child wakes or you need to soak in the bath and the child wants you to see his block tower. There's the anger that rises out of frustration when a child gives up the violin after you hocked the family jewels to buy him the instrument and pay for the lessons. There's the bleakness that follows a bad report card when you know a child can do better. There's the hard-to-express kind of anger you feel when you know the child can't do better. Anger is everywhere in the rough-and-tumble of child rearing as you find out what you can't tolerate, what kind of a demon witch you really are, what causes you to flare, to stifle fury or to stuff it back down the throat, to let it out all of a sudden: the room is a mess, the dinner not eaten, the fight with a sibling, the toy broken, the rule broken, the thing undone, the thing done. Added to the complication are old angers that belong in scenes long gone, angers against a father who never took you to the circus, the way you took your child who is right now jumping over the seats, or angers against a mother who wouldn't let you have or told you that or died too soon. These old angers get a second chance to do damage when children evoke, provoke, provide opportunity. Mastering anger, not letting it trample the child, not letting it turn inward and strangle the spirit, this is a task that many of us cannot do or do not do as well as we would have liked. None of this is simple. Domestic squalor is dark and serious. It leaves behind guilt or sadness. Anger bestows on you a portrait of your soul. It is often followed by guilt. The portrait is more detailed if you have children.

I was driving the car in city traffic. In the back seat my two youngest daughters were whispering. I had picked them up at school for reasons I forget. The older one had been asked to baby-sit for a neighbor. It was her first job. It was her first time baby-sitting. She was eleven and her younger sister was nine. She was going across the street to a neighbor's house. I was to be on call in case there was any problem. She was excited and began to talk about how she would spend the fifty cents an hour she was going to be making. Suddenly the younger sister shrieked, "I want a baby-sitting job too. I am as responsible. I can do it. I should go with her." The older one said no, this was her job. I could hear the tremble in her voice. The younger one said yes, she was entitled. She should be baby-sitting too. She was shouting. She was not going to let the older one grow up faster, have a privilege ahead of her, take authority, make money. She was not going to be the baby in our family left behind as the others went out into the world. She sounded ferocious. The older one held firm. "This is my job. I am old enough, not you." I felt squeezed. The older one had a right to be older. She had a right to grow up first. The younger one had a right to object, to be hurt, to scramble to keep up. The older one was white as ash when I glanced in the mirror. The younger one was red and there were tears in her eyes. I made a decision. "No," I said, "baby-sitting is a one-person job and they asked your sister so she is going alone. She is the older sister," I said, announcing a fact that was always in dispute. The younger one collapsed in deep sobs. The older one was quiet in victory. The younger one said, "I want to die. I need to see a psychiatrist right away."

Then I was angry. This was manipulation, this was threat. This was playing on my nerves. "No," I said, "you don't need a psychiatrist. You aren't old enough to go baby-sitting and that's all."

"I can't stand my life," she said. "I don't care," I said. "Send me to a psychiatrist," she said between sobs. "Send yourself," I said. "I have no money," she wailed, "because you won't let me baby-sit," she added. "Too bad," I said. Later I worried. In preserving the right of the elder had I wounded the younger beyond repair? Did she need a psychiatrist? Why did ordinary rivalry and entitlement cause her such pain? Was that normal? Had I been cruel? Should I have forced the older one to share her grown-up moment with the younger? The scene plays over and over in my mind, half funny, half tragic, and each time it brings with it a feeling of futility, of helplessness. I know it sounds like nothing now, but then . . .

There is always the fear of death. When my children were young it came over me all the time. I could not bear to think of them grieving for me. I could not bear to think of them missing me. I was afraid to fly. From liftoff to touchdown I thought of them needing and not having a mother and I would imagine their loss in specific detail. The pain of it was quite extraordinary, especially since I was alive and all that loss was purely anticipated, conjured. In those days I would worry about car accidents, mutating cells, sudden strokes, slowly debilitating nerve diseases, all because I could not tolerate the idea of my children hurt the way my death would hurt them. As soon as they all became old enough so that my desire to survive had to be for reasons other than their urgent need I became a fearless flier, a person stoical about illness and ready if need be to let my life go. Relief is what I felt. My death had become my own again. The terror departed, or almost departed.

It returned whenever I thought something might happen to one of them.

This musing on death, my death, their death, was in part a product of anger, a way of punishing myself, a way of playing with a wound, a way of expressing the hard-to-express guilt.

Anna Freud said, "No child is wholly loved." She knew that in each sacred mother-and-child circle there is in addition to all the necessary well-touted tenderness a mutual anger, a mutual distaste that bides its time, holds its place, but bursts through now and then like a summer squall, hard and brief, startling, turning the leaves around on the branches and drenching the ground. The hostility a mother may feel for her children is natural enough, harmless enough, except in the cases of postpartum depression when the hormonal stew brews a malicious kind of toxin and mothers can actually harm their children, do fear harming their children, can themselves die under the effort to keep their rage contained. But the anger is there in diluted form in most mothers and in most babies. There is the baby's primordial fear and rage at the engulfing mother. We've all known babies to bite, scream, hit, pinch, grit their teeth and kick. The baby needs to be a separate self and pushes against the mother who holds him. The baby can't help but hate the mother who holds back the hand, who says no, who does not supply what is needed fast enough. The mother returns the sentiment. She may be enraged with loss of sleep. She may be mourning for her clipped wings, wanting her body back again for herself alone.

Maternal guilt. If there is too much anger there can be too much guilt. If there is too much guilt we can have trouble letting our children go off to explore the room, the school, the world. If we are too guilty we become frantic with the need to prove to ourselves and others what good mothers we really are. Most of us, feminist or traditional woman, at home or at work, manage to contain the small showers of maternal anger and guilt that are simply a part of normal weather conditions. Some of us do not.

Being able to let go of the child, be he toddler or teenager, is one of the requirements of motherhood, but the delicate balancing between holding on and fostering growth is not so easy to maintain. At the time of birth the old issues arise: How alone am I? Some mothers are overwhelmed with helpless anger both at the inner emptiness they suddenly feel after nine months of carrying and at the constant demands of the child. This reaction when more than a passing mood becomes pathology, but it tells us something about how all women experience the birth of their children, about the seeds of hostility that are built in to the most loving of bonds. James James Morrison Morrison's mother may have fled because she couldn't tolerate being a mother any longer. At the end of town her anger at James couldn't hurt him. Perhaps in her flight she was protecting him from herself. She wouldn't be the first mother to do so.

My two younger girls are fighting. It's nothing special. The older one has ordered the younger one around beyond endurance. The younger one rebels. The older won't play anymore. The younger in frustration screams. I have an old intolerance for the sounds of fighting. My parents turned dinner tables, car rides, vacations into scenes of mayhem and grief. The sound of open anger, which is after all the harmless fuel of family living, brings an unreasonable but uncontrollable fury to my heart. I get up from the table where I am working and go into the children's room and I demand order, restraint, niceness, the appearance if not the fact of sisterly love. I do so between clenched teeth. I feel ten feet tall. I am implacable. I hate them for the hatred they have evoked with their harmless squabble. I look in their eyes and see that I have frightened them. Good. They are quiet. I go back to work but my fingers tremble when I place them on the typewriter keys. I have frightened myself. What have I done to them? If they can't express themselves in a normal battle, what will become of the rivalry they feel? What have I begun? What well do I poison with this haunting from my childhood? I am guilty of confusing past and present. I will not be able to stop. I know I will not be able to stop. They will have to bend to my storms. I am drenched in guilt.

A partial list of things my children have done that have made me angry:

> Be cruel to one another.
> My oldest daughter lost books, shoes, money, clothes.
> Be rude to me.
> Be rude to one another.
> Keep their music too loud.
> Keep their secrets to themselves.
> Smoke, drink, or worse.

Accuse me of reading private journals left on the dining table
  (I didn't).

Lie — some of my children never, some of my children
  always.

Not take good care of themselves.

Not let me know where they were at night.

Express disdain for something or someone I love.

Go through a room as if I wasn't in it.

One of my stepdaughters told my brother something I said
  that hurt him badly.

One of my stepdaughters stole something valuable from me.

One of my stepdaughters invited me to lunch as a birthday
  present which made me happy but then she didn't call to
  arrange a date.

Whether my anger at them was justified or not by some objective
standard, each burst of anger was followed by guilt. Had I done
something wrong to cause them to do whatever it was they did?
Was the unhappiness that floated through our home sometimes my
fault? Had I not been firm enough? Had I confused the past with
the present? Was I contaminated by my past so that I could not
create loving children?

Firing a good baby sitter because she seems too attached to your
child is another effect of guilt and anger. Staying in a bad marriage,
getting into a bad marriage, making your life more miserable than it
need be — these are sometimes the mark of a too guilty mother.
However, this dark fear and rage between mother and child is quite
simply to some degree or another always one of the foundations on
which our homes are built. So much the worse for us.

The baby's needs are endless, consuming, and often boring. The
ideal mother may always be smiling through the sleepless nights,
through the curtailed days, through the milk that comes and the

diapers that need changing but most of us, far short of the ideal, survive with a mixture of pleasure and exhaustion. Tedium is hardly rare and the metamorphosing of the selfish self into the caregiver is a slow and painful process varying in difficulty from woman to woman but never a pure delight, never a Hallmark greeting card, always a recall of long-buried feelings, always a hostile thought or two directed at the child, directed at one's own parents, drifting just behind the lullabies. Rock-a-bye baby on the treetop, down will come baby, cradle and all — branches come tumbling down in this song (there, if you doubted it, lies revealed the universal hostility to the child) because mothers are not so lovely, despite the gentle melody, not all the time, not without reservations. Remember the childhood game, *Step on a crack and break your mother's back*. Discussing the birth of the child Adrienne Rich says it clearly: "The depths of this conflict, between self-preservation and maternal feelings, can be experienced — I have experienced it — as a primal agony."

I look at a picture in our album, I am holding another newborn. She rests on my shoulder, her wide eyes are looking fiercely out at the room. My neck is bent down to her face, my body presses against hers. Summer light pours through the window, everything is still as if the scene were from a Vermeer painting. There is some truth in the vertical black and white of the photo, mother and child caught in such calm, but photographs also conceal.

To be a mother who wants to be a mother is not necessarily to be blind to the difficulty, unworn by the work, unmindful of the high stakes of the game you are playing. You don't have to turn against mothering because you know how hard it is, how it has its ugly abrasive side. You don't have to be gullible, naive, or ignorant to want to be a mother despite its complications. Most of us know the score or learn it well before our second child is born. Most of us still find motherhood essential, riveting. We know that being a mother is not the happiest state in the world and we know that we are not capable of endless giving, unlimited love, still we have no desire to escape — at least not permanently.

When Susan Smith admitted pushing her two sons into the lake strapped down in the back seat of her car, her South Carolina neighbors turned on her with fury. How could she have changed into the witch mother, the destroying mother, the vengeful mother even as they were praying for the safe return of her babies? Our television sets showed us wreaths of flowers, pictures, notes left at the launching site at the lake. The oft-repeated sympathy for the boys shown in the tear-stained faces of many of the women who gathered at this almost gravesite was intensified by the common denial of their own much better contained maternal rage. Every mother knows, even if she cannot consciously admit it, that she doesn't always love her child and that the desire to be free of the baby rises, hardly acknowledged, there at the edge of the mind, in the bad dream, the excessive anxiety, the overprotectiveness that disguises angry wishes. Each of us knows that part of being a good mother is disciplining, repressing, banishing the evil mother that lives within. It all makes for free-floating guilt: such is the human drama that even the most natural of acts, the care of a child, becomes tinged with our complications, our always pushing and punishing souls. When God said Eve would give birth in pain He meant more than the expulsion of the infant down the birth canal. He was talking about the whole experience of creating the next generation.

There has always been a bad mommy around. In other times fairy tales and myths split the bad mother off from the good mother, giving us wicked stepmothers, witches, evil queens who might harm a child, turn him into a stone statue, as in C. S. Lewis's *The Lion, the Witch, and the Wardrobe,* or more familiarly push him into an oven, turning him into a cookie as in Hansel and Gretel. Our best-beloved stories include stepmothers dealing in poisonous apples, fairies making sure that princesses are stabbed with spinning wheel needles and put to sleep for a hundred years. These are the common shared myths of our mother-fearing imaginations.

I am sitting on the floor holding my oldest daughter. Her body is pressed into mine. She has had a nightmare. She woke screaming. She thought she saw the door to her room move off its hinges and come to crush her. I have turned on the lights. I am rocking her gently, slowly, back and forth on my heels. Her legs are tight about my waist. Her hands are digging into my shoulders. I watch the traffic lights on the avenue change, smears of red and green. The buildings across the street are dark, the doormen are drowsing at their posts. The sliver of the moon I can see over the rooftops is dim, covered in clouds. What if something happens to me, a cancer cell divides, a car strikes, a brick falls, a blood vessel bursts, what if I am not there, what if she calls for me and I cannot come? I am cold in the dark. If she is left without me — the pain shoots through my arms — some things are too hard to think about. It is exactly those things that one does think about in the first hours of a new day when everyone else sleeps. What if she is having a nightmare about me? What if I am the door moving toward her? What if I am the spider, tiger, witch of other dreams on other nights? I try to put her down in her bed promising to stay in her room. She cries again. I smell the wet damp sweat off her neck. I lie down in her bed with her. What else is there to do? I remember how I used to play field hockey running down to the goal, the biting air of fall pressing into my chest, my knees stained from scrapes and grass, calling to my teammates, our red pinnies stuck to our backs. I always wanted to win, to score, to dash on. I was never tired, or I never admitted it. Now I was tired. It wasn't the child's fault. But whose fault was it? I felt anger. I felt guilt.

This is and is not a feminist political problem. The feminist movement as it functions in public is very much concerned with the bad deeds of men, the abusing father, the harassing boss, the violent husband, the squelching patriarch, the army general, the male priest, the rapist, the condescending male doctor, the glazier of the corporate ceiling. The feminist movement has made all this quite clear. We have pointed a lot of fingers at others. What has been less clear is how we feel about our own children. What we are to do with our own confusions as mothers? It's easy enough to be angry at the frat boys on your campus who look on girls as sexual prey but what about the politicians who cut funds for day care, what about the boss who won't give you enough maternity leave, what about the fathers who promise to share the burdens and then don't or can't? What to do about our own feeling that we are not doing right by our children, that we are squeezed between what we know they need and what we feel we need? What about being angry at a child who exhausts you, defies you, disappoints you? You can't chase away guilt with a political slogan.

HOW THE FINGER GOT POINTED AT MOM

In the nineteen thirties and forties children were punished with the rod, children were made to stand in closets, shamed in school, boys were told that if they touched themselves their penises would fall off. In order to stop my constant thumb sucking metal mitts were placed on my hands at bedtime. Children were not told the facts of menstruation, of birth. If I asked a sex question my mouth was washed out with soap. As an infant I was fed every four hours on schedule, picked up only if it was feeding time. I was toilet trained before I was one, God knows how. I was told that if I wasn't kind to my baby brother the kidnappers would get me. Afraid of the water I was pushed in, afraid of the dark I was blindfolded. Children were often thought of like horses, they needed to be broken. The information on child development that began with psychoanalysis in Vienna was for the most part both astonishing and helpful. It was a vast improvement on the way people had viewed and understood children before. Prior to Freud children were considered born with an evil inclination, in need of strict discipline. Some thought of children as tabula rasas, blank slates on which society could write its commands. Some thought children were better seen than heard. Many thought that children reeked of original sin. They were laborers or delinquents, strangers to be controlled by behavioral designs that included frightening them, beating them, and lying to them. My governess used to read to me from a German book called *Struepel Pater*. It was about a little boy named Peter. When he misbehaved his fingers were cut off, one by one. This was socialization by terror. As the Freudian psychoanalysts came over to America from Europe they brought word of the importance of childhood, of infancy. They taught us that the child was not a cipher, that children did not have empty minds but were seething with passions and needs. We learned from Freud that the child had misperceptions about the body's products, confusions about what belongs to the body and what doesn't, real sexual desires, sexual curiosities, gender identity issues, longings and illusions of power. We learned to go gently with our children, to listen to their fears, to interpret reality to them, to understand that all the great passions of life — jealousy, fear of death, lust, love and its opposite — flow through childhood. We learned that in earliest childhood the character is shaped, sexuality emerges, the path is determined, the mind stimulated or dulled. We learned the importance, the short- and long-run significance of mothering. That was good. What was not so good was that all this consciousness about the maternal power over the well-being of the tiny infant also produced guilt. What if I do something wrong?

In the nineteen fifties *Parents'* magazine published a cautionary article which is today both quaint and not so quaint: "A mother must ask herself whether her working will result in a happy child, a satisfied husband, a companionable home life, a better community or will her working cause her youngster to feel deprived of a normal happy childhood, her husband to feel he is an inadequate provider? Will her home become a schedule ridden household? Because of her decision to work will the community eventually have to deal with a broken home or a potentially delinquent child?"

Into this cultural atmosphere where women seemed to hold the fate of the family in their delicate hands Bruno Bettelheim came to America teaching about the schizophrenogenic mother, God help us, remember her? She was the ice lady who couldn't respond with her melting molding arms, with her smile, with her instant empathy to the infant, and her child literally went mad, withdrawing from human voices, faces, language. It was her fault. It turned out that Dr. Bettelheim and a generation of psychiatrists had it wrong. Many mothers of autistic children had other normal children. Many mothers of autistic children appeared to be withdrawn from their damaged children because the baby offered them no response from the earliest moments of life. On the other hand some rotten, cold, undependable mothers had responsive, exuberant, sane children. It has now been firmly established that autism is the result of a catastrophe in the genes. One in ten thousand births produces it regularly everywhere. The psychiatrists who made mother-blaming pronouncements about autism were like so many Wizards of Oz manipulating magic from behind a curtain, humbugs all. But imagine the guilt these mothers felt, their children's illness marking them to themselves and the public as bad mothers, imagine how marriages strained and shredded under the accusing psychiatric eye. There were thousands of mothers so judged and so injured. And for everyone else the autistic child and his ice mother became a cautionary tale, symbolic of dreadful maternal power. How you behave as a mother will determine the mental health of your child.

Male homosexuality was then also considered a byproduct of maternal error. The emasculating mother, the smothering mother, the mother who really wanted a girl, perhaps only unconsciously, was considered the prime suspect in her son's homosexuality. God knows what Hemingway's mother did to him by dressing him up in ribbons and bows for the first five years of his life. This example of assumed maternal power was intimidating. Women whose sons grew up to prefer men were culturally accused of some kind of defilement, castration of their sons, unbounded penis envy, etc. Female homosexuality was almost beyond discussion but was tarred with the same brush: maternal misdeed. In 1987 homosexuality as an illness was removed from the *Diagnostic and Statistical Manual.* This is the psychiatrists' official list of symptoms and diseases. Today no one assumes that homosexuality derives from a mother who was either overly possessive, smothering, or jealous of her son's masculinity. The politically correct cause is assumed to be the genes themselves. Some psychiatrists who dare to defy the current politics of diagnostic judgment would say that complicated interactions of environment as well as the prompting of genes affect erotic choice and gender issues. We at least know what we don't know. The Bible thumpers who feel that homosexuality is sin assume that sexual behavior is chosen. They speak of natural and unnatural, of disgusting and not so disgusting. They walk through the valley of sexuality like Mr. Magoo, knocking at things with their canes.

Most of us no longer believe that homosexuality is a moral evil or a human tragedy but almost all parents would nevertheless like to create in their sons and daughters the desire for heterosexual relationships. We have done away with the ugly word "normal," but nevertheless it hangs around us. Deep in their secret heart most mothers, even the most politically correct mothers, worry, will my children be normal? Who else is to blame if they are not? Even mothers who understand that the proclivities of genes and the chemistry of proteins affect sexual choice wonder if it was their own genes that led their sons away from women or if they might have done something wrong, loved too much, loved too little. The questions may be politically incorrect but they haunt nevertheless.

The one thing that has emerged from the smoke of battle is that the mother probably didn't do it, not singlehandedly, not because she loved her son too little or too much or wished for a girl or wished herself to be a male. Sexual identity and gender role are now seen as such complex matters, embedded as they are in biology and early development, that simple causalities are ruled out. We are not yet able completely to understand, predict, or alter the varieties of human sexual choice that hide themselves under the psychiatrist's couch and most often we cover our ears at his words. If sexuality as we now perceive it is born in the earliest years of childhood, if fetishes and perversions such as sado-masochism are rooted in early sexual fright, misunderstanding, fears for the intact survival of the body, then mothers, who are most responsible for the infancy period, are implicated even if no one wants to come right out and point a finger anymore. Guilt is always around and, like our shadow, follows at our heels.

Although officially let off the hook on homosexuality and autism, mothers are still considered responsible for many aspects of their children's emotional well-being. School phobias, fear of the dark or of dogs or of vacuum cleaners, temper tantrums, inability to make friends, acute shyness, kleptomania, adolescent rebellion, addictions, obsessions, ritual hand washing, constant counting, hair pulling, food disorders, the full range of emotional afflictions are still attributed to maternal handling, to the misfortune of having been born to a mother who lacks the capacity for good, nontoxic mother love.

The psychoanalysts working in England and America on child development came up with a phrase, originally Dr. D. W. Winnicott's, "the good-enough mother." The phrase has lasted because it sums up what a child needs. It doesn't imply perfection, it's meant to allow for the range of human maternal ambivalence, self-interest, the desire for a little peace now and then. It too, however, has terrifying resonances. Am I a good-enough mother? Are you?

One of my younger girls was shy. She talked up a storm at home but seemed almost mute with strangers. "Don't worry," said my spouse. I worried. I worried when she wouldn't talk to the pediatrician. I worried when she wouldn't look at neighbors who complimented her new dress. I worried when she wouldn't speak to other children in the playground. "Give her time," said my husband. Why, I wondered, was she so shy? What had I done to make her believe that the outside world was filled with threat? She stared at everything with wide eyes. She looked sometimes like a fawn who had paused, frozen in place, after hearing a rustle in a distant tree. On a summer vacation she talked for three solid hours in the car till we were hoping for silence. But on picnics with our friends and their children she stayed by my side, silent as a reproachful ghost. At school she was quiet, spoke only if spoken to, and held herself aloof from other children. Slowly she made friends. By the time she lost her first tooth I could hear her talking to other children all the time. At last she was invited to birthday parties and play dates. Later she spoke to teachers freely, and finally to strangers on the bus. My relief was enormous. I could tell by how great my relief was how deep had been my fear. For years afterward she would become silent in strange situations, in new places. I grew to understand that was her way. Her silence was not a defect. It was a strategy.

How many children sucked their thumbs too long or wet their beds or didn't do well in school or were too timid or too aggressive? Truth is most children are far from perfect and their flaws, their development lags, their irregularities were in the postwar flush of psychiatry seen by everyone as the result of something the mother did or did not do. Something in her personality, in her way of handling the child was not up to snuff. Fear of creating neurosis, fear of harming your child, fear of being a bad parent sent waves of guilt across the country. In the forties and fifties guilt was always at high tide. When mothers had no other work in life, no other purpose, financial or social, than their mothering, they were especially vulnerable to guilt over any trouble in their children's lives. We are still, however, even the most modern of nineties mothers, hostage to our children's fortune. Now our egos may seem bolstered by jobs, professions, promotions, successes large and small in the big world outside the home, but who doesn't know what it feels like to receive a note from a teacher complaining about a child's behavior or to notice something disturbing, maybe it's nothing, of course it's nothing, but what if the four-year-old is dressing in your shoes, what if the eight-year-old bit his four-year-old sister, what if reading skills lag or your child won't play with the others, the sinking feeling in the stomach, the heart beating, the mind searching out reasons, excuses: the acute stench of failure that follows — I wonder how much it's really changed?

Most mothers have an additional mission, one that is barely conscious but is very important to us. We want to undo the melancholy of our own childhood in the childhoods we are creating. We can't. Our failures to spare our children pain also create guilt. When my oldest daughter was three my closest friend's daughter, who was just a little older, said to her, "I have a father and you don't." My child replied, "I don't want one." Her words haunted me. I still remember them a quarter of a century later. I had intended to give my child the very thing I didn't have, a storybook home, loving and caring parents. I grieved. I felt guilt. Despair followed: What was the point if generation after generation repeated the mistakes of the past? I had failed at what I considered a sacred matter. I had desecrated her childhood. Guilt was my companion.

Of course, children from a very early age on understand the high-stakes game of guilt. They play it very well. My mother was afraid of dogs. She would press her body against the wall if one passed her on the street, even small ones with rhinestones on their collars. I wanted a dog more than anything else in the world. I wished on stars. I wished on my birthday cake. I waited. When I was twelve I began to pretend I had an imaginary dog. I would talk to it aloud as I walked through the room where my mother was playing cards with her friends. I heard them say, "Blanche, you have to get that child a dog. She needs a dog." "She's unhappy," said one. I strolled back through the room. "Sit," I commanded my imaginary dog. I knew what I was doing. I was giving my mother guilt. She couldn't bear being publicly exposed as a bad mother and at last she bought me a dog. The dog gave my brother asthma and so it was sent away, but that's another story. For years one of my daughters could get me to agree to most anything by mentioning how ashamed and upset she was when she was three years old and I sent her off to a birthday party, forgetting to put on her underpants. She spent the entire party hiding in the bathroom. My guilt was clear. Now, many years later, when I think of her embarrassment and my responsibility for it I grow hot and shame floods all my inner systems. Guilt in families piles up like so many I.O.U.s and most of us are drowning in debt.

Dr. Benjamin Spock was the bridge between the psychoanalysts working in their offices, meeting in small institutes in major cities, and the American public. The women's magazines did the rest. The word was out. No one can measure how many children's lives were improved, but we can assume that children who were not traumatized by toilet training, who were more carefully listened to, whose fears were more likely understood and taken seriously, whose curiosity about sex was not met with hostility or evasiveness stood a better chance of enjoying their full humanity. Too bad all this new information also made mothers feel guilty when things did not, as they hardly ever do, go altogether smoothly.

Here is a partial list of things I know I did wrong:

Let my baby see me wander dazed after the divorce.

Find it hard to say no.

Let my child see me with too many different men between marriages.

Bribe.

Not make firm enough rules.

Be too fearful of some things and not fearful enough of others.

Change some of our family traditions midstream as my religious interests altered.

Have too specific ambitions for my children, to want them to do the exact thing I had not been able to do.

Other items that I either cannot write or do not know. Those of course are the important ones.

The problem for us is that the basic information about childhood, the Freudian revolution in how we think of children, is not humbug and will not be so easily disproved or dismissed. Selma Fraiberg, who wrote *The Magic Years,* appears to be the number one enemy of feminist thinking because she so insistently calls to the American public to pay attention to children's needs for reliable steady attachment. She says, "A baby cannot switch partners and bestow his love on a stranger." John Bowlby, the British psychoanalyst who led the field in observing infants and theorizing about their development, contended that a warm, intimate connection with the mother, continuous, unbroken, is essential in the early years. Erik Erikson wrote, "At this early time of life the actions of the mother and her libidinal cathexis" — that means loving connection — "and involvement with the child exert a selective growth of some and hold back or fail to stimulate and libidinize the growth of other potentialities. This determines basic trends in the child concerning his motility, the earliness or lateness of his verbalization, confidence, basic trust." This language is a bit wooly but the message is clear, a skillion books on child care have pounded home the point, how well your child walks, talks, feels by the age of two is a direct reflection of your continuous love and care.

Psychiatrists have announced the importance of early bonding, of mutual gazing, of early stimulation. Infancy, which was once thought of as a kind of sweet long sleep, is now understood as a crucial building block of human personality. It's almost hard to imagine that generations of aristocrats in France sent their newborns off to the country to live with wet nurses. Almost every American woman has heard the news either through Penelope Leach, T. Berry Brazelton, *Parents'* magazine, *Family Circle,* or her sister down the street — the baby needs more than physical care, its tiny soul is resting in your small decisions, in your mothering style, in your care.

And as if that weren't enough to make a feminist squirm Anna Freud discovered in her work with war orphans and those sent out of Europe or away from their homes for their protection during World War II that the life-threatening dangers of war were not as destructive to the minds and emotions of the children whom she housed at her clinic in Hampstead as the separation from their parents.

Every how-to baby book, every psychiatrist's paper on the subject, all the available evidence tells us what by now is our common truth, believed by talk show hosts and Harvard professors alike: if you don't listen to your children, they will grow up emotionally deaf, sexually weird, socially incompetent. Here it is expressed by Dr. Louise Kaplan, author of a book on childhood called *Oneness and Separateness:* "A mother's presence in a baby's life absorbs, contains, and tolerates the baby's unruly lusts and thereby tames and humanizes them. Her presence illuminates the contours of the infant's world, making the unknown feel familiar, recognizable, and safe." Of course this could just be fashion, the latest style in child care, but I doubt it, the evidence is too real, as real as the germ, as real as DNA. Attachment is not a hem length and it will not go out of style.

Psychiatrists were loudly confirming that to be born to a good mother is more of a stroke of luck than having a silver spoon stuffed down your throat just as women were finding more and more pressing reasons not to be in the home all the time, not to make mothering the central focus of their lives. This was an unexpected and unwelcome irony. Our newer insights into child development and our oldest human aspirations were pulling us in one direction and our feminist politics and our shrinking economy in another.

In 1964 my oldest daughter is going to nursery school. At least she is trying to go to nursery school. I am sitting in the classroom. I am the last mother left. All the other children have begun to get used to the doll corner, to the blocks, to the teachers, to sitting in a circle at juice time. My daughter will not let me leave. When I stand up, eyes at the back of her head see me and she collapses on the floor in tears. I explain to the teacher, "I am divorced, my mother has died, she is afraid of losing me." The teacher is sympathetic. She offers me cookies and juice. I want to go to work. I want to be off. I sit there and read the newspaper cover to cover and then over again. "Your daughter seems a little tense," another mother says to me as we arrive one morning. "Are you having trouble letting her get on with her life, grow up?" asks the head of the school, calling me into her office one day. I blush, of course it's my fault. It's a small thing isn't it, whether or not a child takes to nursery school, uses the potty, acts like all the other children? Or is it perhaps everything? I am still in my twenties. I feel older. It's a wonder I still have my teeth.

Finally, sometime around Thanksgiving, my daughter decided I could leave her classroom.

GUILT WILL FOLLOW US INTO THE GALAXIES

Everywhere technology alters our most private and intimate moments but it doesn't free us from guilt. The technology for refrigerating milk frees us from the need to breast-feed for so many years. The technology of fertility gives us the opportunity to conceive and carry a child when we are older. We can now tell more about the fetus's health. We can avoid crippling illnesses like spina bifida, Down syndrome, and fatal ones like Tay-Sachs. Throughout all my pregnancies, which took place before sonograms and amniocentesis, I had bad dreams about giving birth to monsters. My mother had told me that sexual sins produce cleft palates. I was afraid of Down syndrome. I thought about children with no legs and no arms. We weren't told to stop drinking, to stop smoking. Instead we waited, each pregnant woman chasing her own worst fear alone, not wanting to say the magic words aloud, fingers, toes, brains, gullet, esophagus, liver, spine.

We no longer risk our own lives with each birth. The technology of abortion and birth control gives us some measure of choice whether to bear a child at all. The endless pieces of plastic equipment each baby seems to require make life easier if not more portable. The inventiveness that made all this possible is uniquely human and therefore perfectly natural. It is as much a part of our story as the basic facts of reproduction. We are bound by our bodies but not exactly. Our female biology is more under our control and yet it still isn't. It certainly hasn't gone away. Our uniquely human imagination can take us almost anywhere, yet the most modern of technologies does not free us from guilt which will follow us right into the starships of the future. The tie to the infant, built in to his or her survival, is also built in to us and cannot be so easily waved aside. We struggle with the consequences of our similarity to apes and our remarkable differences. We have to keep our children from feeling abandoned by us or else they won't grow. We have to attach ourselves to them so that they will be able to free themselves from us at the right time. Psychiatrists say that this is about death, separation fear is our fear of dying, and our fear of dying is the fear of separation. James James Morrison Morrison Weatherby George Dupree will die without his mother, or part of him will, or so he fears. Guiltless she cannot run to the end of town. If this attaching and separating (the work of childhood, the essence of mothering) is all about avoiding death, what a bad Halloween joke it is.

We consulted a child psychiatrist about my oldest daughter. Her homework was never done, her shoes were often lost, she bounced and jumped, ran up and down the stairs. She was insistent, clinging, needing constant calming, she was still unwilling to sit in a circle, to play by the rules, to wait her turn. She was wild and beautiful, running up and down the hill, tumbling in the woods in the fall leaves. She drew pictures, dropping her crayons everywhere, she was excessive, a wind that restlessly moaned through the night. Teachers were puzzled. Other children were impatient with her. She lied like an experienced con artist. Sometimes we knew she was lying. Sometimes we didn't. "I don't know who ate all the chocolates in the box. I would have been home in time but the bus bumped into a truck. I met Ringo Starr in the playground and he invited me to tour with him." Her long brown hair was hardly ever combed. We tried discipline, restrictions, reminders, extra time spent reading or playing together. We tried tutors. She remembered the lyrics to every song she had ever heard. She didn't know where her toothbrush had gone, where her math pages could be, where the time had flown. One day she ate all the Flintstone vitamins in the bottle at once and the pediatrician was called. He never had seen anything like that before. We worried about liver damage.

If asked to set the table, to carry a plate to the kitchen, to pick up a pair of socks, she stalled, she forgot, she ran off. Once my husband wondered aloud if she had been nursed by a wolf. I was the wolf. I was guilty as charged. My heart broke. When I was unbearably angry at her she would write me a poem. I pressed her poems into a scrapbook I kept by my bedside and when at night I couldn't sleep I would read her words over and over. I thought about Anne Sexton and Sylvia Plath, were they difficult children too? Why was poetry so close to madness? Why did the child who made metaphors without effort struggle so to keep anxiety at bay, to hold herself together, to run fast enough to escape the demons that seemed always to be chasing her? I knew that the poems were a smoke signal. They were not happy poems. But might they be enough to save her? Save her from what? From the way we lived, the way of numbers and rules, assignments and levels of achievement, of finances and bank balances, of schools and offices, of jobs and pension plans.

When I had married her biological father I had believed that art was the last refuge in a world without order or reason. When I had married a writer I was a kind of beatnik moll who talked dirty to God. When I realized that my daughter was not just a child with a strong will but a child whose nights might never be peaceful I grieved for her. I grieved for the vision I had of myself. I was a mother who had fallen far short of her grandest, most personal, most dearly held ambitions. I loved her like I loved the crooked part of myself, the reflection of my mistakes, the product of my own romance with social defiance. She was my firstborn, the one on whom my own pride, my handprint rested, like the mark of Cain. Can anyone heal my child? I heard myself think these words like a mantra fifty times a day. Of course they can, of course they will, I reassured myself with another mantra. When I knew, and the knowledge was gradual, an accumulation of teachers' reports, of public response, of other children's comments, that my special child was special in ways that were euphemistic and not so welcome, I could hardly look at myself in the mirror, as if a finger was pointing, because a massive failure had occurred, a trust had been broken, as if all the king's horses and all the king's men could never put my body and soul back together again. Like a car that's survived a bad accident, the worth of my mother-self will never be the same, just under the hood the cracks run deep. Someone will understand, someone will make her better, that was my last hope. The child psychiatrist mumbled things about frustration tolerance and impulse control. Whose fault was that? Of course I considered my divorce responsible. I also considered the fact that she had lost her biological father, lived in fact through most of her early childhood without any father. I knew fathers were important. I passed the buck and took it back again. I saw, I denied, I saw again.

Things I have read in psychiatrists' waiting rooms:

> *National Geographic*
> *Birds of Eastern Connecticut*
> *Catalogue of Jewish Athletes*
> *Field and Stream*
> Metropolitan Museum bulletins
> All of *War and Peace*

CHILD CARE: YOU'RE DAMNED IF YOU DO AND DAMNED IF YOU DON'T

In today's world we are also guilty over our child care arrangements. If we are at home sacrificing either money or ambition for our child we can't help some anger floating up at our condition, no matter how deliberately we have chosen it. If we go to work, as most of us do, we are guilty about leaving our children, and angry at being made to feel guilty, and the anger makes us more guilty, and the guilt makes us feel more angry, and so it goes, serpent biting its tail. Despite the feminist call to leave the home, despite the economic necessities that shape our decisions, a mother feels guilty when she leaves her children. Her child may cry. Her baby may turn his face away from her when she returns many hours later. Her toddler may wake in terror at night calling her name. Her child may get sick at school and no one is able to bring her home for hours. Most mothers are beset with problems like changing baby sitters, day care arrangements that are expensive and don't always supply either the stimulation or the affection that the mother wishes. We know how carefully a mother listens to her child, her ear and eye in constant alert to the sigh, the rub of the eye, the extra fidget, the shiver, the pallor, the pinch of the sibling, the whine, the opportunity to teach a new word, a new concept, respond to a question. We know about the constant flow of empathy, at least in the ideal we have of ourselves, the care that is automatic, steady, fueled by the intensity of the connection, our overwhelmingly powerful investment in the child. We have our doubts that anyone else will be able to get our children through the day. Guilt is the handmaiden of this awful state of affairs.

We know our children need to feel secure in their homes, safe in their world. We know they need familiar, stable surroundings. We aren't always able to provide them. And even if we are we carry the guilt of not being on call for the twenty-four hours of each day ourselves. In our heads lurk ghastly images of the stranger rebuffing, ignoring, harming our children. We think of our children faltering and falling as icy hands button their coats, indifferent fingers cut the crusts of their sandwiches and do the laundry. It's hard to believe that if you weren't at home when your child came down with a fever and a stomach pain someone else could comfort him, that his hold on reality hasn't been shaken, his trust in his mother broken. Guilt follows us wherever we go, whatever we do. It weighs us down. Quality time is a wonderful idea but it's hard to find and hard to believe that it suffices. We feel what our children feel. To deprive them of the simplest thing, a second dessert, a toy in the store, hurts us. How much more it hurts us to deprive them of our presence if we believe that's what they need.

Then we are met by irony. If the substitute caretaker is loving to the child and the child responds with a firm attachment to the person who spends the larger part of the day with him, the mother feels left out, a dark jealousy can grab her, a sinister, unreasonable displeasure that things are working out so well. The mother-child twosome has been continued, just with someone else, and the biological mother who has gone to work, either because she has to or because she wants to, finds herself outside the magic circle. This too provokes maternal pain. Part of us wants, reasonably or not, to be our child's sole love, primary protector, essential center. When our child does not appear to miss us as much as we think he should, there follows a piercing sense of loss, injustice, envy of the other woman's place. We cannot win, the child care is either too good or not good enough, discomfort follows us to work and back home again because somehow we, even the most modern, liberated among us, are not sure that it is all right not to be with our children all the time. We are afraid of what we might be missing: the day the first tooth falls out, the important questions we wanted to answer, the trip to the firehouse. The need to work, the going off to work, is accompanied by a sense of deprivation. Home is where the real action appears to be, especially if you're not there. Things always seem slightly out of joint.

If we stay home with our children day after day we have other kinds of guilt. Why didn't you use your education? What are you doing, you who used to be able to do the crossword puzzles in three minutes flat? What is becoming of your gifts? How come you haven't heard of the latest novel, play, art show? Where have you been? We know also that the homemaker is leaving the full economic burden for the family on the shoulders of her mate. Is that fair? Is that feminist? We know that the self-sacrificing mother is not necessarily a saint and won't be rewarded by her children's love, at least not necessarily. We've heard all the jokes. The home-maker also feels guilty. She is out of step, aware of her difference from most American women, slightly ashamed of her role. The homemaker is angry at those who would make her feel guilty for being at home. She knows she has closed an open door. Her stay in the doll's house is voluntary. Scratch the anger and you find guilt and shame. It's true of all of us, nobody is sure of herself whatever her chosen path. You can't escape maternal guilt by staying home. At least not today, not ever.

I am working on a magazine article. I have left my two youngest daughters with my trusted housekeeper. The rain has been falling since noon. The buses moved slowly. I am late getting home. There is a silent heavy quiet on our block. The sound of water running down the drains, of cars suddenly braking, of the wind blowing mixes with the splashing of my feet in the puddles that gather in the slopes and heaves of our sidewalk. The older sister is playing with a friend. I see them in their room, a horse show, stuffed animals sitting in rows, sheets for curtains, pillows on the floor. I look for my youngest daughter. I can't find her. I call her name. I run up the stairs. I run down the stairs. I go into my bedroom. I see her small red sneaker. I open the door to my closet and there she is, curled up on the hard floor. Her face is stained with dirt. Her hair is tangled. She is as pale as an Edward Gorey character walking through a graveyard. Her older sister hadn't allowed her in the game. She was alone. She wanted to play too. She had nobody to play with. The sad story was told with full emotion, with bitten lip, with tears caught in her eyelashes.

I should have been home to read her a story. I should have been home to take her out in the rain to buy ice cream at the store. I should have been there to take her away when her sister closed the door. She felt like a waif, like an orphan, like a sisterless, motherless child. She was waiting in the closet for me to come home. I knew this was not the end of the world, that dramas like this are the stuff of childhood. Without knowing loneliness how can we be human? I knew that she would be all right, I knew that her older sister's friend would leave at the end of the afternoon and the younger one would be restored to her position as playmate of the hour. Still the stark, empty, dark look in the younger one's eyes made my stomach turn. I should have been there for her.

Later we played an endless game of Candyland. But I couldn't forget so easily. It was my responsibility to keep at bay the nightmares of childhood and I had failed: what is worse than being left out, hearing the whispers of sister and friend? I had made an unspoken, unthought-out promise, no fingers crossed, at the moment I conceived this wanted child that I would always be there, but of course I didn't mean all the time, I didn't mean day and night, and I had no way of knowing that it would rain and the buses would take so long and that her sister wouldn't let her play. So what harm was done? Yet the feeling stayed: What kind of mother is out pursuing her own fortune when her child is lying there on the closet floor?

This story, of my daughter on the closet floor, has remained in my mind for twenty years despite the fact that nothing extraordinary happened. Think, then, of the power to frighten a trusting parent that lies inside the nursery school. Think of the already guilt-ridden mother who drops her child off at her local day care center while through her mind run terrible pictures. What exactly is being done to her child in her absence? The imagination can run riot. Starting with the first reports about sexual indecencies in preschools in California and lasting at least until the overturn in 1994 of the conviction of a nursery school teacher imprisoned in New Jersey, America watched, glued to the TV, as an alarming new form of witch trial spread across the country. The persecuted were accused child abusers, alleged sexual perverts who seemed to have permeated the day care center and used little children for all kinds of polymorphous perverse acts, sometimes in the guise of quite amazing Satanic rituals. Teachers were convicted on the testimony of small children who were coached and encouraged by therapists. The stories these three- and four-year-olds told grew wilder and wilder the more the therapists pressed on. America was both entertained and upset by this horrendous tale of children being threatened, sodomized, covered in the blood of animals who had been sacrificed in the dress-up corner, blood smeared on the juice and cookies table. Eventually psychologists were able to demonstrate how easy it is to evoke a story about almost anything from a child. Eventually communities shot through with fears of Satan's blood dripping on toddlers' heads or of rape in the corridors calmed down, but the phenomenon of the abusing nursery school teacher was a socially significant one, calibrated exactly to coincide with the rising tide of maternal guilt.

It rose in reaction to the many women going off to work, needing their day care, nursery schools, as never before. The dark imaginings of sexual nightmares in the place where children were being tended by others can be understood as a response to our collective guilt about leaving our children in the first place. The nursery school sexual abuse hysteria reflects our fear about what will happen to our children if we go out to work. It also reflects our anger at the children. After all, we allowed our lurid imaginations to invent the most dreadful punishments for our babies whose suffering then was less at the hands of their caretakers and more in the minds of their parents. The culture had changed from the nineteen fifties, when magazines could openly scold the working mother for potentially endangering her child, but the attitudes that lay behind that scolding have not altogether disappeared. Those reproaches to the working mother came back dressed as a Satan worshiper who puts things into toddlers' anuses and threatens to rip out their tongues if they tell.

My youngest daughter has her twentieth birthday dinner at a Chinese restaurant. We are all there. Her sisters, one husband, two boyfriends remember that when she was little she had taken to biting when furious. When she was accused of the deed, she explained that the porcupine had quills and the skunk had a smell and the elephant had big feet but all she had were her teeth. "Still," I had said, "you must never bite again." She had cried. But she stopped biting. As we struggle with the menu, each sister hating most what the others love best, my youngest daughter says, "You remember the day you went to the hospital and left me alone." "We never left you alone," I say. "You did," she says. It seems that I had carried out her older sister and gone to the hospital. The younger one, ten at the time, was frightened but decided to fix dinner for her father when he finished work. She set the table for the two of them. She had made a spaghetti sauce and was boiling the water for the spaghetti. She had decided they would have chocolate ice cream for dessert. When my husband came out of his office and went upstairs he put on his coat and left immediately for the hospital where I was waiting for him in the pediatric intensive care unit. On his way out he brusquely told our youngest daughter that he couldn't eat dinner. He had to go right away. She sat at the table alone. It was, she said, the worst night of her life. We had all forgotten her. "It was an emergency," I say. "I know," she says. I think of her at ten, with her bangs growing over her eyes, her love of animals, her fierce loyalties, her sharp logic, and her fearless roaming over the backyard fence. All through her birthday dinner ten years after the event I feel an aching, a blueness of mood that I can't shake.

The Macaulay Culkin hit *Home Alone* — in which, most improbably, the parents discover they have forgotten their son while on a plane to Paris for a family vacation — was an extremely popular movie not only because it was funny but also because it told the story of a child with active parents not quite there. Every parent watching that film heard the question, are my children home alone? Of course they aren't literally, but psychologically? That is very much a contemporary question, guilt-provoking, anxiety-making, a part of the constant perceived tension between feminism and family. The joke in *Home Alone* is that the child is quite able to take care of himself. Poor thing, he has to be.

On the other hand, remember that mothers bore the guilt for the errata in the souls of their children when they stayed home all the time. Remember Mrs. Portnoy trying to get her rebellious son to eat a few peas at dinner. Remember how he claims she threatened him with a knife. When we were home all the time we were accused of smothering, living through, pushing for achievement, passing on phobias, sexually inhibiting, seducing our children, turning them into satyrs, rendering them frigid. While atavistically we think we should be there, we know better. Being there all the time did not prevent children from wetting their beds, stammering, sleepwalking, fighting, refusing to go to school, getting stomachaches, etc. When we were home all the time nobody loved us, our spouses got bored with us, our children were angry at us. We were angry with them and felt guilty all the time. Now that we are not home we are blamed for not being there and we feel guilty about our absences and angry at our children for making us feel guilty. Progress moves in mysterious ways.

Now in urban centers everywhere as women rush to pick up their children from day care, to fill in for a sick baby sitter, to find time to take a child to the dentist, as women bring up children without partners, without their own mothers to help, without enough money or job security, they are haunted, liberated or not, by guilt and reproached by the faces of their children preparing themselves again and again for partings and arrivals.

When a Swiss au pair, in a suburb outside New York City, was accused of having burned an infant to death in an act of arson, every mother was riveted to the story. The person who is taking care of my child is perhaps a killer, a traitor to me, a psychopath. The baby caretakers, including au pairs from clean European countries, have to be resentful of their employers. They after all are doing all the hard work while the mother reaps the pride and joy. New mothers can't help resenting the baby sitter who spends the day rocking the child. This resentment makes a mother feel guilty. She may imagine that it's the baby sitter who resents the mother not the other way around. Sometimes she may be right. Could these bad feelings turn to murder or maltreatment? The new mothers, returning to work after their maternity leaves, do not feel safe.

Mothers who would never ever harm their children do sometimes have preconscious, unconscious, fleetingly conscious thoughts about their children that are not so nice. We have them in anxiety dreams when we picture our children falling, drowning, or lost. We have them when we become overly anxious about trips they may be taking or accidents that might befall them. When we are overly anxious about our children the anxiety does not stem from love. Anxiety rises when anger erupts from the place in the soul where we usually store it and makes fearful pictures in our heads. We suffer from these bad thoughts because each one is followed by a heavy dose of guilt. The only way to avoid this guilt is to be a saint and for the most part saints don't have children. This cycle of bad thoughts and guilt adds to our worry when we leave our children in the care of others.

We know after thirty years of feminist consciousness that going to work is good for a woman's self-esteem, good for her pocketbook, good for her marriage and its myriad balancing acts. We know in these less than lush economic times that most families need two working partners. We know that marriage is not necessarily permanent and that widowhood or divorce can throw a woman into poverty faster than lightning can strike. So she had better be prepared to stand on her own, balance her checkbook, pay her taxes, have some marketable skills. We know that careers and the fulfillment and satisfaction they can bring are as important for women as for men. We know that child rearing hardly consumes the entire life span of a woman. Its intense phase is for most mothers under ten years of their eighty-year life expectancy. We know that women can perform well in every area, as pilots and firefighters, as corporate lawyers and neurosurgeons. What we don't know exactly (at least not so we can quantify it) is how this affects their children. This open question makes us most uneasy.

That the question remains open is not from want of trying on the part of sociologists in academe. So many of them have done studies and written up their results that one can't resist the image of all those clowns pouring out of the circus Volkswagen, tripping on one another, pushing, elbowing, tumbling through the trap that must lie under the sawdust floor. These clowns, however, unlike Molière's Bourgeois Gentilhomme, don't speak prose. They mumble, shout, cajole, wonder, pray, often in statistics, as if they were rural Rotarians or Elks or Moose or Masons playing around with a secret language at their annual convention banquet.

Here are some of their conclusions. If you're expecting clarity, don't hold your breath. From a book called *Maternal Employment and Children's Development Longitudinal Research,* edited by Adele Eskeles Gottfried and Allen W. Gottfried, published in 1988, I gathered this information. "The fewer types of child care arrangements, the more satisfied mothers were with their work ($N = 36$, $r = -.70$ p 1.001). If the number of child care arrangements is conceptualized as a potential 'hassle' — the less this hassle is experienced, the greater the satisfaction with the roles and patterns of daily living."

In other words it's tough to go back to work right after the birth of your baby. Ah ha!

Other sociologists report that "whereas the main effect of maternal employment was not significant for children's ego resilience, neither ego resiliency nor language ability as measured by the PPVT was predicted by toddlerhood maternal employment." In other words kids with mothers who worked spoke as well and were pains in the neck just as often as kids whose mothers stayed home with them.

Further studies tell us that many changes in alternative care during infancy were associated with a greater likelihood of toddlers having at least one insecure attachment. So you're skating on thin ice if your child is moved from place to place, if one baby sitter runs off with the delivery boy and the next decides to go back to school. If this is an argument for staying home, listen to this conclusion I found in a sociology text: "Women who were in their preferred status [working or at home] felt more satisfied with their lives and were able to respond more positively to all of their roles, including motherhood." So if you are happier at work and have chosen to work, you will be a better mother than if you stay at home resenting your domestic condition. If you have to work and hate it, your child is in trouble too. Your happiness also depends on the behavior of your spouse. One sociologist counted the hours husbands worked and concluded (to whose surprise?) that the more hours the husband spent at work the more likely the wife was to feel depressed, worthless, guilty, and isolated. Also she smoked more. This study, however, didn't examine the happiness quotient of the working woman whose husband stays at home because he keeps losing his job, drinks too much, and/or is writing the great American novel.

The sociologists contradict one another. Another pair found that children whose mothers were employed were "temperamentally easier" although Gottfried and Gottfried found no significant difference in temperament from infancy through childhood owing to the mother's employment status. (Is easier a good thing? Do artists and creative types have easy temperaments?) Can the intensity of a child's spirit really be determined by the number of hours the mother spends at work?

I have a friend whose teen years were spent in Auschwitz, where her parents and siblings died. She went on to become a prominent doctor, a wife and a mother of three, and she glows with happiness, warmth for others. I am at a meeting with her in Portugal and after the dinner speeches I see her dancing in a bright red dress. She spins and spins, catching my eye, she smiles and waves. Either children are sturdier than we think or there are more routes to a good life than the professionals can imagine. A child in my daughter's second grade class is left at home alone by parents who have gone to a cocktail party and have not come back. It is nine o'clock at night. The child in a panic calls our house. We go over to get her and leave a note pinned to the door. The parents call us the next morning. They had gone out to dinner and had a few drinks too many. This child soon has trouble in school. Years later she ends up following the Grateful Dead around the country. Maybe it's better to come back to a child when you say you will. How could the sociologists chart that one?

One study found that mothers' employment status at three months was unrelated to infants' security of attachment at twelve months, though infants whose mothers were employed at three months showed more resistance to being left in a strange place. In other words the mothers who went back to work when or before their infants were three months old were putting some kind of strain on their children, what kind of strain, what exactly is the effect, we don't know. Gottfried and Gottfried found that maternal employment status during toddlerhood was not related to separation anxiety, ego resiliency, or language ability. A different study found no cognitive, intellectual, social, or behavioral difference between the children of working mothers and those of nonworking mothers.

Some of these conclusions may be wishful thinking or seeing what someone hoped to see. Some of these conclusions are so obvious that our common sense and life experience tells us that they're true enough, in most instances, except for the family down the street, probably. This sociology cannot give us the answer to questions of how we should live with our small children, how guilty we should feel about working and when. The categories are broad, the statistical samples can point in a direction we might follow, but they are clearly cartoons of real life, fortune cookies compared to novels. It seems impossible for social scientists to measure the thousands of variables that make each of our homes fraught, feverish, each with its own drama. The truth appears to be like God, in the details, in the individualities. The social scientists tell us that it's all right to go back to work but the psychiatrists remind us how important attachment is, how the young child builds a separate self, how insecurity threatens the first steps toward independence, how sexual identity, future sexual pleasure are embedded in the toddler years. How could we not be guilty, how could we not feel guilty, no matter what we do. Someone is getting short shrift: most often that someone is ourselves. T. Berry Brazelton, the child psychiatrist from Harvard, has come to the view that a loved child can manage day care if given good time with caring parents. Most psychiatrists today, many of whom are working women themselves, see leaving their child with a nanny or in some form of day care as a necessary option and in no way harmful to the child. Despite professional reassurances, however, most mothers still have qualms. In part our image of the perfect mom of the fifties has outlasted her actual existence and hangs around reproaching us with our continued active lives. Also, our children frequently make clear their preference for us as caretakers. Their desire not to be left, however it is expressed, is painful for us.

One thing that is absolutely clear is that from a very early age children know that their own parents are the center of their lives. Nannies, baby sitters, day care providers may become familiar and beloved, may be welcomed with a smile and let go with a clinging cry, but the children know which person is Mommy and they know that Mommy is the force that holds their universe together. They know this because the power over the child's life lies with the mother and father. This comes across even to the very young child. Babies of mothers who work have attachments to their own mothers exactly like those of a child whose mother is in constant attendance. The mother is the center of the child's universe no matter how much authority she delegates or how much real time she spends in the daily care of her child. This means that her personality, her kind of humor, her love of music, the way she bites her lip, the way she counts the pennies in her purse, these are what the child, with all the antennas at his or her disposal, catches, absorbs, stores away. That is the way we absorb our culture, the way we focus on anyone we desperately need and so assume we love.

That even the very young child is not confused about its real parent is an assertion, not a piece of scientific data. However, this is the belief of child psychiatrists. It is the belief of people who work with children in day care centers, in schools. It is not so easy to prove — how do you measure the way the heart beats quicker when someone enters the room, the way the eyes focus sharply, the way the needs that have been held back all day burst forth? — but each mother knows (aside from early moments of anxiety and unnecessary nanny competitiveness) that she is not replaceable by her nanny no matter how good that nanny may be.

I remember the way my last baby would follow me with her

eyes as I worked in the kitchen. It was different from the way she looked at any of the other people in the room. I remember the way she pinched me hard and turned red in the face when I returned even though she had spent the afternoon with a familiar and loved housekeeper. I remember the way she looked through me like I wasn't there the time I left her for a few days to go off with the older girls. On our return she smiled happily at her father but for hours seemed not to know me at all. This was fury not indifference. Although just over a year she was capable of feeling betrayed and expressing it. Some babies turn their heads away from the departing mother, some from the returning mother but the tension of separation is always there and the child knows and the mother knows that each parting is a drama and the main characters, mother and child, are never confused about the plot.

THE POLITICS OF MOTHERHOOD: HOW WE MISSED THE BOAT

In the early days of the current feminist movement we taught ourselves to respect nonconventional lives. Old maids, spinsters, lesbians were no longer shameful, no longer outside the normal social order. We learned not to whisper about the nonconventional, nonstereotyped gender decisions of both sexes. We certainly talked about sisterhood, and when we marched together in pro-choice marches, 200,000, 300,000, 500,000 of us, we felt it, a kind of woman power that throbbed in the streets, made us giddy with pleasure. We never thought of bonding together as mothers, as parents, as needing one another through the lifelong journey of motherhood. We thought of motherhood as a thing one did on the side, a kind of private hobby, like playing the flute. We each made our own arrangements and struggled with the consequences. If we thought about motherhood politically at all it was in connection with surrogacy or custody issues, where we had a chance to stake our claim against that of the despised male. We missed the boat. We should have talked about mother love, what does it mean, what price does it exact, what do we share in common, what can we do to make our mothering better, our children's lives better? When we thought of ourselves as Wonder Women with magic bracelets, a flat midriff, and a bow and arrow pointed at the heart of a male enemy we were magnificent. When we thought of ourselves pushing strollers, dropping pieces of Lego across the living room floor, rushing home to give a sick child Tylenol, we just let it go, let the mothering side of ourselves become silent, almost as if we were ashamed of ourselves as nurturers, as protectors of the young. We suffered our maternal guilt house by house, woman by woman, the old-fashioned way.

Alice Rossi writing in *Daedalus* in the spring of 1977 reminds us of the "central biological fact that the core function of any family system is human continuity through reproduction and child rearing," a statement that comes from the belly of the Social Science Beast who eats statistics for breakfast and poets for lunch. However, this drive for human continuity translates into the intensity of feeling we have for our own kids. It explains the fierce pull to have children and raise them which puts prospective parents through the kinds of fertility nightmares we hear so much about — the timing of ovulation, the expensive and anguishing in vitro fertilizations, surrogacy, etc. Alice Rossi points out that we have inherited our biological equipment from our 65 million-year-long mammalian past. Only 40,000 years ago Homo sapiens, you and me, evolved from primitive hominids. Ninety percent of human history has been spent in hunting-and-gathering societies where the muscular man went out and killed a big fearsome horned beast while the woman stayed close to home with her needy, totally dependent offspring, probably whining at her, "I only want the big red berries." The skinny raw helpless soft-headed mewly baby we produce is certainly a half-baked creature. In the words of the anthropologists we are a rearing society not a catching one. Rossi reminds us that Westernized human beings now living in a technological world are still genetically equipped only with an ancient primate heritage that evolved largely through adaptations appropriate to much earlier times. No wonder we women get a crazy feeling in our heads when we are asked to leave behind our small children and go out to work. No wonder we women get a crazy feeling in our heads when we are asked to stay home with our small children and live as if we were still in the caves and plains of our ancestors. No wonder we still have children. Whether we like it or not Darwin gets under our bedclothes and drives us on.

PART III

WOMEN AGAINST MEN:
THE FATHERING ISSUE

THE NEW MALE MONSTER AND HOW
THE ACADEMICS FED HIM

The last quarter of a century has been a time of turning things upside down. In the Court of Good Opinion the white male who once ruled everything is at last suffering from bad p.r., a taste of his own medicine.

As women met in consciousness-raising groups, as we wrote down our stories and added our own particular voices to the mounting cry, we discovered that we had been insulted, our brains and bodies demeaned. I remembered the Hebrew teacher arriving at our house, not for me but for my brother. "Just for boys," said my mother. "Not you," said my aunt. I can still see my brother's face as he held his first Hebrew workbook in his hands. His great pleasure was increased by my real grief. I remember a boy in my second grade class named Louis Adler who said that girls couldn't do math. I punched him, but then I stopped listening in math. I remember that my father said that Golda Meir became prime minister because she was too ugly to keep a man. I remember that my father announced that a woman whose play was being produced on Broadway was a stupid bitch who wished she was a man. When her play was a huge success I felt great joy, but nevertheless a few years later I married a playwright instead of trying to write a play myself. My mother slapped me on the face when I began to menstruate. It was what her mother had done to her. Female bleeding was a stigma to be kept hidden. It was a sign of disfavor. It was the curse. Double standards pricked at my pride. What was sauce for the gander was not sauce for the gander's sister. My mother refused to pay for graduate school for me. She was afraid I would educate myself out of the marriage market. My brother became a doctor. Everywhere my virginity was being protected even as it was being stormed. Was I a cow to be worshiped or was I hamburger? Women were indeed victims of male violence and were ashamed to admit it. Women were abused by stronger arms and stronger chests. The only status most girls could attain was through beauty and beauty was only the surface of the soul. The real self was always in hiding until we came out of hiding and began to complain. If my mother had lived longer she would have heard that women were not the sum of their mates, the helpless leashed pets of the house. She would have, maybe she would have, become a theater producer, a stockbroker, a business-woman. Maybe it was too late.

In the beginning this telling of stories was liberation. But as the anger from under the ground spewed up into the atmosphere it began to darken the sky and flood the terrain with irrational waters. The anger was not without just cause but it dominated some women, it blocked human sympathy, it prompted sloppy thinking and silly thoughts. Some women were saying that men were responsible for war, misery, and pollution. Women once again were everything nice, environmentally clean, and good. Instead of establishing equality between the sexes, all the banging of the con-sciousness-raising drum had somehow managed to reverse the po-larity. Good was now female and bad was male. This was an im-provement if you were a woman but not quite the social solution most of us had hoped for.

The academic feminists stockpiled stories for the gender wars. The Ph.D.'s and their students were doing good work toiling in the libraries, rescuing from obscurity female writers and historical fig-ures. In the process they developed a counterlanguage of their own to discuss women's tropes, discourses, etc. These activities, a mingling of scholarship, revenge disguised as scholarship, and politics disguised as scholarship, are located in women's studies programs in almost every prominent university. These departments spawn their own kind who go forth and teach the same point of view. They offer a necessary and important corrective to a culture all too prone to forget that women always played a part, that nothing happened in history without them, that the view from the distaff quarters is as interesting and significant as any other. But some of these academic sisters tend to grow tight-lipped, white-faced, mad with the constant fanning of their past oppression. Some of them are partisan scholars, academics with an ax that they hide under their jargon. The nonacademics among us don't read their journals or attend their meetings but we hear little waftings, whisperings, we gather and surmise. The air we breathe mingles with theirs. Personal history isn't scholarship. Sometimes your heart can lead your mind astray, causing you to see the shadow of a monster against the wall when it is only the base of your lamp caught in the moonlight.

Here is feminist Rachel Blau DuPlessis: "All the social, sexual, economic, psychological, and legal constraints on women contribute to the oppressive system of patriarchal motherhood." Something about this ungraceful language, something about this self-righteous tone, something about the use of the word "patriarchy" makes most of us uneasy, not to mention cross-eyed. Patriarchy describes power relations, inheritance patterns. While it can be identified in economics, religion, politics, it doesn't completely explain the factor of lust, greed, fear, jealousy, or the myriad gremlins that seem to make the world go round. It is not the totality of those experiences. Like class and mass and proletariat and other ideas from our late not so lamented past, the view of the world as a giant evil patriarchal system seems headed for eventual ridicule and oblivion. Patriarchy describes a system in which men are in control but the adjectives now attached to it may not be specifically or exclusively male. Feminists have long since agreed that the adjectives describing femininity — passive, pure, sweet, irrational, emotional, fearful — are the result of both prejudices and social expectations rather than inherent qualities. Logic tells us that the same must be true of so-called male qualities: aggressive, active, angry, etc.

Sometimes women's studies departments have served as an academic arm of the women's movement, the separatist part, the furious part, the military branch. Scholars such as Mary Daly say heavy things like "Mothers in our culture are cajoled into killing off the self-actualization of their daughters who learn to hate them" or "Men envy the womb and woman's creative energy in all its forms — their attraction is to all that is dead, dying, and purely mechanical." Over and over these professors say that nuclear reactors and the poisons they produce, stockpiles of atomic bombs, ozone-destroying aerosol spray propellants, oil tankers designed to self-destruct in the ocean: these are male. Some years back when giving a lecture at Harvard Mary Daly refused to take questions from male students. This is the politics of revenge. Daly has suggested some kind of retreat to a coven in which female power will protect the world from ecological disaster. This is a brilliant tactic: it turns formerly despised crones and witches into leading figures of the resistance, reversing bad into good and putting a thumb in the male eye along the way. Most women wouldn't mind a coven of their own that could work black magic from time to time but most women would not want every night to be Halloween. Some of us would miss Valentine's Day. It's hard to believe that men want the world to blow up in a nuclear storm or that they want the oceans to drift in a stew of oil while birds and fish, weighted down with slime, die on the blackened shore. It's equally hard to believe, as the zero population growth feminists were saying in the seventies, that human reproduction, the coming of the next generation, will actually be fatal to the planet. It would certainly be fatal to humankind if there were no reproduction, no fetuses brought to term. This kind of mudslinging gets the juices flowing but leaves most of us as puzzled as ever as to the root cause of evil in the world. If, as feminists have insisted, God may be a she, isn't it also probable that the Devil has her feminine wiles?

What gets left behind on the battlefields of these sexual wars is prejudices that were more appropriate for the Cleavers than for the families of today. Heather Jon Maroney in an essay that appeared in *Feminism Now: Theory and Practice* says that matriarchal society is thought to have been "cooperative, natural, sex positive and permissive, peaceful, able to integrate males on a basis of equal exchange. In contrast patriarchy is hierarchical, technologically rational, sexually repressive and violent for women, associated with militarism and the state and the oppressive exploitation of female productive and reproductive powers." This language makes me sleepy. It makes my ankles swell. At bottom this is the school of "we're so nice and they're so nasty." This is the stuff of nursery rhymes, sugar and spice vs. puppy dogs' tails, snails, etc.: never mind that the actual existence of once upon a time ideal matriarchal societies is in doubt, never mind that splitting the virtues and vices along gender lines repeats the bad habits of the past. If we label everything in the male as bad, as causing the obvious pains of the human condition, then we mirror image, we imitate the way of thinking which has demeaned females all these years. If, for example, we have working superegos, good consciousness, and they do not, then all we are is the upside-down version of them. We repeat the error (Freud's error in particular), we do not correct it. Mirror, mirror, on the wall, who is the fairest of them all? is perhaps not the best question to jump-start a social justice inquiry.

This theory of male the root of all evil can be found in the charming but pointed vision of an all-female world in Charlotte Perkins Gilman's 1915 *Herland,* now commonly taught in feminist studies programs. Gilman imagined a utopia in a distant South American landscape far down the Amazon River from which men were excluded and where women developed the capacity for bearing babies without them. In this book most males are described as the embodiment of worldly corruption, deaf ears, and personal greed. Females are just, kind, loving, the essence of light opposing the dark. In *Herland* everything is shared, orderly, in harmony, equality and balance are everywhere. When some inquisitive exploring men discover this distant utopia they bring into it their own possessiveness, domination, desires, patriarchal prejudices. They threaten the equilibrium of paradise. *Herland* is one of these visions that assumes an inherent difference in male and female character and capacity and makes everything of it. Read as a corrective to male arrogance it's a wonderful fable. Read as a map of our predetermined nature it becomes a fairy tale. It's not completely untrue, it's just not all there is. Everyone who has ever been in a girls' school, on a girls' basketball team, within a female organization knows that women are not without aggression, competition, cruelty, or hierarchies.

Woman's cruelty in prefeminist times was largely writ around issues of inclusion or exclusion from the in-group. I remember the day I lost my best friend in the second grade. I had black thick curly hair, frizzy and unruly. I had been absent for two days. When I returned I found a note on my desk. "Brillo head," it said in red crayon. I turned around and saw my friend and another girl, both with silky blond braids, whispering together. They saw me watching. They whispered more and laughed. My heart has been broken since then but never again has the world seemed so bleak, never again have I felt so alone among others. That was in the nineteen forties, when little girls still curtseyed when greeting adults and wore pinafores to school. Margaret Atwood's book *Cat's Eye* describes with sickening familiarity the way little girls bully, gang up on the most vulnerable among them, threaten with excommunication, and come to the edge of emotional violence in their play. The anger women felt at the restrictions of a prefeminist world was certainly communicated to their daughters, taken out on those daughters, even as they taught those same little girls to fold napkins, to hem curtains, to scrub the toilet bowls. Little girls might be mean to one another because they reflect the unfortunate lives their mothers have lived, but that seems more like ideology than real life. The simpler explanation is that little girls are mean because human beings are mean. It appears unlikely that if women ruled, anger would disappear.

SEXUAL WARS: AN OLD BATTLEFIELD WITH A NEW LOOK

The female anger against the patriarchy gained intensity and focus around highly charged sexual issues. Women objected to being seen as sexual objects. We began to complain about double standards of sexual behavior. We began to resist men opening doors for us, and men looking at us with open desire. We began to notice exactly how bestial the male animal was, and where was he revealed at his absolute worst but in his pornography where lust is stripped of pretense and civilization is reduced to mere props for raw fantasy. The anti-pornography issue caught fire and has continued to smolder on because it expresses so succinctly some women's view of the dangerous and insensitive male about to turn into a rapist, harboring humiliating thoughts about females in his head. Such men exist of course in shockingly large numbers, but the movement to quash pornography grew because it so conveniently fed and nourished the anti-male fevers that were raging across the land.

To be a sexual object has never seemed to me so terrible, not when I was younger, not now. If someone looked at me with lust I did not feel bad or exploited or visually attacked. I thought, Would I like that? the way I do when I pass through strange neighborhoods on a train. If I walked past a construction site and the guys whistled I thought I must be looking good. I didn't assume I had turned into an object to be used by someone else. So the anti-pornography movement has me puzzled. If someone looks at a dirty picture and his sexual response is stimulated I'm not sure I think that's such a sin. Of course, if the woman is roped and tied and if she has been sold to white slavers that's a sorrowful thing, and if looking at such a picture is the only way that guy gets pleasure, why poor him. But if she was willing to pose and if he is willing to let his imagination light up his sexual wires, I'm not so sure I see the oppression in the act. Perhaps it is my fifties eyes, perhaps it is my desire not to make desire once again a taboo for women as well as men, but I don't hate men for liking dirty pictures. I don't quite get it myself but that seems to have something to do with female psychology, or it may be the result of my repressive upbringing. It is not a moral statement. Most women, including me, are also not so fond of W. C. Fields. I don't understand why boys like baseball statistics or how they know the make of every car that rolls past their window. We don't have to make a federal case out of it. The anti-pornography and other sexual issues that began to take up the attention of the women's movement in the mid-seventies certainly made men feel guilty but many women became confused. Was it unfeminist to want to be desired? They went right on wanting it. Fashion magazines went right on showing the latest styles. Women went right on doing their own desiring. Did all the noise about pornography make the world a more loving place? Hardly.

The question of sado-masochism and its role in our erotic lives is complicated. The idea that some men are turned on by pain inflicted on women is ghastly. On the other hand, we know that some women too are turned on by pain inflicted on themselves or on men. What this tells us about our souls, about our sexuality is certainly bad news. The why of it must lie in the sexual wiring and the way our most infantile angers and fears get tangled up with erotic urges and responses. Psychoanalysts know something about this but not everything and much remains to be understood. The recesses of the mind are breeding spots for horrid expressions of the inseparability of hatred and love. Do men act on their sadistic or masochistic fantasies? Rarely. Do women? Hardly ever. Can we banish the fantasies by banishing the public pictures? Probably not. Are we better people if we only acknowledge the squeaky clean parts of our souls? I can't see why.

The First Amendment lawyers are there to protect our freedom to read and look at what we will. I am not so concerned with censorship winning the day. We are a long way from the time when Catharine MacKinnon gets to take her delete button to the corner bookstore. But I am concerned about the blurring of lines between action and thought, between the ugly sexuality that we haven't banished from the minds of either sex and the peculiar idea that men will turn into wild beasts, rapists, and murderers if they are exposed to one another's fantasies in X-rated comic books. I am more interested in understanding our sexual fantasies than in banishing them. They won't be banished for long anyhow.

The emphasis on pornography, which is after all not a major issue for most women who are trying to hold down a job, take care of the kids, and find a little love on the side, is an emphasis that contributes to the male-as-monster theme, the tiger that we have caught by the tail. If enough men can see dirty pictures and then rush out in the night to rape or kill or maim, then we have to beware of them all. Who knows what cruel fantasies are percolating in the mind of the man next to you on the subway, at the neighboring desk, walking the dog down the street, waiting in line at the post office?

All this talk about the evil patriarchy creates a drumbeat of sourness throughout the culture. In 1989 a survey showed that eighty-nine percent of women thought that rape was the predominant problem facing women today. There is no question that rape is a serious and calamitous event far too prevalent in our culture and everything possible must be done to prevent it, to change cultural attitudes that have encouraged it, to punish it, and to understand its causes and effects. Nevertheless, issues of child care, economics, education, family, love, divorce have too often been dwarfed by the more sensational and black and white issues of rape and male violence.

Most of us do not accept a vision of the world in which men should be scorned and women idealized. Nevertheless, today there are real women all over who believe that men are dangerous and bad. All too many women have suffered emotional damage around sexual issues, and they are not going to be overly calm or rational about male behaviors. These are the women who have been harmed, frozen out, terrorized by fathers and brothers and husbands in our society. Their versions of the story may be one-sided, heroines and villains, male vs. female, but we can't doubt that there is genuinely felt hatred between the sexes, that many homes are not what they should be, that love between male and female is not as easy as we would hope, and that fathers and husbands disappoint, disappear, and worse. But that's not the whole story.

Terrible things happened to males also. Poverty, drunkenness, abuse, neglect, and all the human ills are poured on the heads of little boys as well as little girls. While women are surely less openly violent than men, they too commit acts of emotional terror, engage in cruel acts of dominance and submission, abandon children, pour scalding water on them, harass them, withhold from them their rightful share of human joy. That human life is often a cruel brutish thing is true enough, but the rage of one gender against the other is likely to be the result, not the single cause, of the tragedy.

WHEN PSYCHOLOGISTS BECAME FEMINISTS: OR THE POLITICS OF SELF-ESTEEM

Contributing to the general cultural complaint against males is the public debate between victim feminists and anti-victim feminists, between male blamers and their defenders, between cultural observers of difference like Deborah Tannen, author of *You Just Don't Understand,* and her opponents who deny the importance of style. There's Wendy Kaminer, author of *I'm Dysfunctional, You're Dysfunctional,* and the anti–Wendy Kaminer, difference feminists and those who think that all acknowledgment of difference will boomerang onto the heads of women. All points of view are backed up with studies, everybody else's study is accused of fixing the data, forgetting a crucial factor, studying only college students or auto executives. There's all this talk about girls' self-esteem and all that counting of hands raised in the classroom, two boys to every girl, etc. It is not clear to me who is absolutely right in these culture wars. I imagine most people are like me, holding their spinning heads, knowing what they know whatever anybody says: male and female are so bound together in the biological purpose of life that one can never be thought of without the other. As the DNA wraps around its double helix, so male and female entwine each with the other.

The self-esteem issue hinges on the idea that men feel better about themselves than do women and this self-confidence translates into worldly triumph. Men not only have hogged the best jobs but also have taken the lion's share of confidence away from women. The self-esteem issue is very significant. If girls are really still made to feel less capable in our society and still expect less of their minds, then the society must be changed even more drastically. If, however, something is off in the testing, if in fact self-esteem is such a chimera that we can hardly measure it, then we are chasing social justice up the wrong tree. How you feel about yourself, how you regard your place in the world may be a more individual matter, more psychological, affected by geography and class and parental love than political dogma would have us believe.

As every mother of sons knows, self-esteem, a word that reminds us of twelve steps and warm milk, is as hard for boys to achieve as for girls, whatever the tests may show. Boys are afraid of being too short, acned, refused, rebuffed, rejected by colleges, coaches, girls, whether they say so when asked by testers or not. Their lot is not easy and their images of themselves, like their voices, change. Holden Caulfield did not become a hero to generations of adolescents because sanity is so easy for the male.

My own adolescence in the nineteen fifties was one blighted by sexual terror. I was not afraid of being raped; I was afraid of being talked about. Those days the boys were playing games about scoring and getting to second base and the girls were trying to do two contradictory things at once, satisfy the boys and be good girls or else. Hands that went too far, responses that seemed too eager could get you on a list, but responses that did not go far enough could leave you out in the cold. I was never sure where the lines were, which game I should be playing. Abortion was unavailable and could kill you. I knew that pregnancy would ruin my life — not because I would have a child that I would have to raise but because the disgrace would be unbearable. I knew that boys were interested in sex and girls were supposed to be pure. My own purity was always in question. The result was confusion, early marriage. So when feminism began to talk back about boys' sexual behavior and girls' right to their own desires I applauded as loudly as I could.

Biology plays a role in matters of self-esteem also. Girls' menstrual cycle, their earlier physical maturity must require psychic energy, must create a temporary imbalance of self-image and alter their sense of being in control. Boys may appear to be more confident at fourteen (but are they really, and is the edge permanent or temporary?), they think too well of themselves while we think too little, so the researchers are saying. The entire debate leads us to see men as cocky while women shiver in the background. Men are increasingly perceived as insensitive brutes who inhabit our homes, while we are timid rabbits with no sexual wishes of our own.

ON THE OTHER HAND, MAYBE MEN
AREN'T SO BAD AFTER ALL

Despite the fact that I had a father who was heart dead his entire life and a first husband who was, throughout the seven years of our marriage, either drunk because he was crazy or crazy because he was drunk, there are many things that I have liked about men. I like the way they smell after exercise. I like the way they try to hide their tears. I like to put my hand in a male hand and feel the difference in size, in hardness, between my hand and his hand. I have looked at a sleeping man and wanted to cover him with a blanket. I have lain down next to a sleeping man and felt him holding on to me as if I might drift away. I have felt protected by men. I have also protected men. I like the wideness of the male chest and its hairiness. I like the grizzle on the face and how easily a man can lift and carry heavy objects. I've known men who couldn't tell you what they felt and men who never stop telling you what they feel. I have met men who can repeat all the baseball statistics and others who know only classical music. I have had dinner with men who respect my work and some who don't. I know why their bodies are made differently from mine and what good can come from that difference.

Despite Charlotte Perkins Gilman's opinion the person I now have breakfast with is not an environment-trashing monster: like me, he works to make a living, is always coping with forces beyond his control, loving sometimes, sometimes not. He was in a war while still in his teens but has spent his life in a profession that commits him to do no harm. The realities of our lives occur out of sight of these antipatriarchal theorists. We pick up the napkin that fell to the floor. We market for milk that the house needs. We listen to the news and shiver in our ethnic boots. Some nights we fall exhausted into bed and in our sleep we have bad dreams, if we can sleep at all. Other nights we lie close whispering, telling stories, making plans. We also pay our taxes, watch movies on our VCR, call our siblings on the phone, attend to crabgrass, tooth decay, mildew on the bathroom tiles.

We know that many males, if not most males, themselves feel powerless, frightened, threatened by real enough specters — loss of job, loss of love, inability to perform sexually, to stay young forever, to be strong enough forever. The men of the militia, the little boys in their dangerous gangs, the drunks and the paranoids who cruise our streets do not feel powerful. They feel weak. Their antisocial behaviors stem from their weakness, not from their strength. Even the abusing husband, the incestuous father are examples not of male power but of male terror, male weakness, male fear of ridicule, betrayal, rage at the weakness they sense within themselves.

The Red Badge of Courage by Stephen Crane tells a Civil War story about a young boy whose greatest fear and whose deepest thoughts are about the possibility that he will behave like a coward, or seem like a coward to others. The postfeminist world has changed men to the degree that Air Force pilot Scott O'Grady, trapped behind enemy lines in Bosnia, said when rescued that he wasn't brave, he was more like a "scared bunny." But so was the hero of *The Red Badge of Courage* and the hero of Tim O'Brien's Vietnam War stories, so also the heroes of *All Quiet on the Western Front, Grand Illusion, Farewell to Arms, The Thin Red Line*. This fear of weakness does not excuse male brutality nor fully explain it. Feminist rhetoric, however, often blurs the picture. In our culture the male is not uncommonly powerless to gain what he needs for himself, shivering behind his own walls, like Adam in the Garden hiding from God, sometimes striking out in terror, sometimes monstrous, shut off from his own feelings, often alone, afraid of the dark. The male may be a patriarch in the anthropological categorical sense. But we know there is more to the story than that. The patriarchal label is pasted over male fragility and diverts us from the rains of fearfulness and sorrow that fall equally on both sexes: bad weather since our exile from Eden. The division of the world along sexual lines leaves out so many other factors that affect our lives — physical beauty or physical defect, place of birth, rich or poor, urban or rural, healthy or sick, smart or dumb, black or white, with or without God.

Things that I have hated my second husband for:

> Not letting me close to him: sometimes.
> Not understanding how I felt: sometimes.
> Not wanting to talk when I wanted to talk: sometimes.
> Not telling me the important parts of a story.
> Not admitting he was sick until he had to go to the emergency room.
> Not ever telling me he was afraid.
> Not telling me that his family had been evicted from their home during the depression until we had been married for twelve years.
> Not wanting to have a sixth child when I did.
> Wanting to save our money for the third millennium.

Some of these sins arise from male-female differences. We were brought up each of us in times of severe gender separations. But we have managed to find bridges, mutual respect, to give up on what can't be changed. He sits at the head of the table. He drives the car when we go places. He tells the waiter what I want to order. He puts an umbrella over my head. Nevertheless, in the things that matter we have passed into a place where dominance and submission are not the point. We journey together. He is the father of my children and I am the mother of most of his and the stepmother of the rest. That he adopted my child from my first marriage makes him be-loved by me and my daughter. However, I am not grateful for his simple humanity, nor is he for mine. It is just assumed, presumed, like the sky overhead: the weather changes, but the atmosphere remains, enough oxygen to get through.

Yes, I was lucky not to have been raped or physically abused by spouse or father. I was also fortunate enough to escape polio and leukemia, earthquake and landslide, terrorist bombers, Nazi soldiers, locusts and flood so far. The same can be said for a substantial number of women. Despite being underfoot, occasionally stinging, creating allergic reactions, men are not like insects, life forms that most women could easily live without.

It's true that up until very recently men controlled everything interesting in the world and kept women in the house and that the divisions of labor in a prefeminist world were unjust to everyone, and of course we must make sure our consciousness stays at least at sea level if not above. Misogyny and the cruelty of a system that deprives women of worldly opportunity are real and worthy adversaries. The system of male control of all the major social arenas with the exception of child care has been a disaster for both sexes. It may have begun in the caves of primitive man but in its extension into our modern world it brings with it all kinds of social inequities and potential for abuse. By now that's old news. Some men beat their wives, some men think of women as sex kittens, some men lust after their daughters or attack strange women in elevators, but most men do not. The language of the feminist theorists, such as Catharine MacKinnon's "To be about to be raped is to be gender female in the process of going about life as usual," posits a split between the sexes that seems for many average-citizen women unreal, unlike their lives, creating bogeymen that are unlike their fathers, boyfriends, mates. This feminist language often factors out the waves of love and sexual attraction that accompany so many of us through our days. This kind of feminist language washes away our real tenderness toward the male, both man and boy. This language which keeps insisting on THEIR venality and OUR virtue forgets the sweetness of the bed and the things that happen there, most of which are not violent and would be sorely missed in a world without males. All this scowling at the patriarchy, while it may correctly identify some systemic injustices, overlooks the pleasure of a walk with a man, the exchange of perspectives, the mutuality of touch, the excitement in differences writ large and small. The young college women who become converts to this brand of male-fearing feminism are finding solutions to inner problems that are ready-made and offer community and identity. Like the ideologies of other eras, this kind of feminism contains more than a hint of stiff-backed humorless religion and reeks of that most dangerous human emotion: certainty.

DADDY: NOW AND THEN

One of my daughters now twelve years old has been sick with a high fever for days. She has been breathing in gasps. I follow the doctor's instructions. I keep her cool with alcohol. I sit by her bed. I keep taking her temperature. The doctor comes in the early morning. "Keep in touch with me," he says. She has a solo part in her seventh grade production of Gilbert and Sullivan's *Gondoliers*. "I'm missing rehearsal," she whispers in a barely audible voice, again and again. In midafternoon as the winter light drains away I see that she has become still, her skin is a pale blue. The doctor says, "Go to the hospital, right now." I pick her up. I can hardly carry her. She is too weak to walk. I stand by the door in our house behind which my husband's office lies. I know he is with a patient. Shall I tell him, shall I knock, shall I shout? A psychoanalyst should not be interrupted when he is seeing patients. I decide. Alone, I drag my daughter to the corner to a cab. In the taxi she faints and she lies there, her lips blue, her eyes closed, in her flannel pajamas, heavy like a marble statue on a grave. At the emergency room the driver helps me carry her through the doors. She has pneumonia. She is in the pediatric intensive care unit. Her fever is 106. They place an oxygen mask on her face. "Daddy," she pleads. "Daddy," she repeats.

Later he says I should have knocked on his door. I should have let him help me carry her to the hospital. I should have. I hadn't known that was what he would have wanted. I thought in the final analysis, in emergencies, I should take over. I thought of myself like the heroine in the novel about an Appalachian family in the forties. That mother performed a tracheotomy on her child by the road as they were walking miles to the nearest hospital. I thought that fathers were after all not quite mothers. My husband was sad that I had not turned to him. "These things are not so clear," I said.

What does the mother do? What does the father do? Why are both parents so frequently not quite there? These are not new questions. But the twist that contemporary feminism has given the problem is that women too are barely at home. Women have their own doors that are often closed. Fathers who are expected to fill in either can't or won't most of the time. Every story that tells us about a good father seems to be pointing a finger at female absence. The guilt and responsibility have been spread more equally between the sexes, which is an improvement but not one to shout about, not yet.

It wasn't that feminists didn't think of it. If fathers took fifty percent of the care of children, then we would be free to go out and have the same lives they did. The women's movement was talking softly, of course, about men filling in the holes, doing their share, becoming more intimate with their children, less authoritarian. Then we could have family and work, income and love, and why not? Women attached to progressive and sympathetic males pushed the idea and everywhere you saw more men carrying diaper bags, pushing strollers, showing up at school meetings. It was no longer all right for men in certain circles to leave the dishes in the sink and the toddler in the playground with his mom. Paternity leave became a possibility if not a widespread reality. This was certainly an improvement for those families that saw the light, for those men who were willing and able to participate, who discovered what women already knew, that taking care of a child, day to day, is hard work but good for the soul. YES!

Unfortunately, however, the work of transforming the macho male into the nurturing father began just as many marriages were breaking up, and many women found themselves alone with their children. At the same time as the talk began about Daddy taking the midnight feeding there was a release into the culture of long pent-up animus against the male. A major male editor at the *New York Times* took a well-known feminist writer to lunch at Sardi's. At the end of the meal he held her coat for her. Instead of slipping her arms into the proper openings, she turned around and kneed him in the groin. He told everyone. She told everyone. Men were held in contempt for previously ordinary acts of chivalry like opening the door and carrying packages. The theory was that you didn't get any real respect from someone who put you on a pedestal. Problem was an awful lot of women had no one to respect them on or off a pedestal. Kneeing men in the groin got them to back off quickly, but it didn't do much for bringing them into the nursery. In the preliberation days men were expected to take care of their wives and children economically. Alimony was a lifetime bitter obligation. With the new emphasis on woman's ability to take care of herself, with men being told to keep their seats in the bus, cut out the condescending patriarchal view, many men stopped thinking of themselves as economically and emotionally responsible for their families. For every man who carried a pacifier in his breast pocket another two just went off. (This is not a statistic. It is a heartfelt guess based on having been there.)

The feminist attempt to get men into the home, involved in child care, was only half-baked, only halfheartedly entered into, and affected primarily a small segment of the society. It helped, of course, and the new approach to fatherhood contributed to the breakdown of the old stereotypes of what male and female must be. But the rising anti-male sentiment (the male as abuser–rapist–incestuous monster) collided with the male as good father putting Pampers into the shopping cart. These two contrasting visions of men squared off against each other. Contradictions included, both these images are still with us.

My own father was an athlete who stayed hours at his club playing squash. My father was a man with a love of good clothes. Conservative clothes, silk ties, well-fitting suits, and tennis whites. He was a lawyer who often lost his temper; he had punched out a client on more than one occasion. He despised anyone who expressed an opinion that he deemed pink. Pink in the nineteen fifties was the color of political shame. It remains the color for girls. He ground his teeth in his sleep. He had migraines. He spent long hours at his athletic club, playing squash with the boys. His eyes were Tartar eyes, dark-sealed, narrow. When you looked into his eyes you could see the Mongolian steppe where the snow drifted across the empty plains. When I was a child I thought he had snake eyes. He did. My mother would beg him to take my brother and me for a walk in the park. When he did he strode far ahead of us. He stopped to make phone calls from every corner. He had his own schemes: rendezvous with ladies, get-rich-quick plans that died on the vine. He was disappointed in his son who was not an athlete, given to asthma and classical music. He was disappointed in me because I was an athlete and could never learn to be quiet. He did not enjoy our company. He did not fix our broken toys or read us his favorite books. He did not teach us to ride bikes or throw balls. He was not typical because the moat that surrounded his castle was particularly deep and the walls could not be breached, but his style of fathering was common enough. In those days sugar daddies were not offering sweets to their children.

Years after my childhood ended I called my father to tell him that a book of mine had been optioned for a movie. There was silence on the phone. He said, "Well one day your brother will get a Nobel Prize." I have remembered that. He was a creature of his culture and I was lucky to come of age at the time of the transition. I was told the old things but was given the new in the nick of time.

Even today, every time I see a commercial with a father holding a baby, with a child running into a man's arms, with a reunion at a rail station or an airport, unbidden tears come, ridiculous tears. These are not tears for toothpaste, jeeps, or dog food. If you don't have a good father you mourn for him always.

MOVIE DADS AND REAL DADS: THE STORIES WE TOLD OURSELVES

So you can imagine that I wept till my nose turned red throughout the many movies stuffed with good fathers, men discovering the wonders of fathering. Some feminists saw *Kramer vs. Kramer* as a backlash movie because it portrays the mother, seeking to find her place, as selfish and the father as good. But that wasn't all the movie was about. The nurturing father was an image that should have pleased most women, who were also someone's daughters, and who welcomed the male into the household. In *Kramer vs. Kramer* the problem is put in some extreme way, the mother leaves to find herself, forcing the father and son to discover each other. The sympathy the movie evokes for fathers in the ever appealing person of Dustin Hoffman trying to make French toast is one that most women found agreeable, but the bottom line in this modern urban myth is the discovery of fatherhood. The same theme appeared in *Three Men and a Baby*, in which three studs become attached to an infant left in their hilariously unprepared but ultimately well meaning care. They come to love the child and are forever changed. The movie *Parenthood* shows Steve Martin defending his family, particularly his awkward son, at the expense of his job, and the audience applauds his discovery of his real strength as a dad. The movie is funny but it works because it plays on our most central and rarely fulfilled wish, a good father. Again the story is told in Robin Williams's *Mrs. Doubtfire.* Here the feminism is taken for granted. The thing that gets twisted around is the gender roles. The father is the one who is good with the kids. The mother is out at work. How can he get back in the house after he is thrown out? He pretends to be a woman. The movie plays with our confusions about what is male and what is female in a changing world. It plays on female guilt about being out of the house and it makes fun of the father who is at home while still extolling his virtues. The movie was a successful nod in all directions at once.

What were all these daddy movies about? We have disguised, under the apparent focus on all this good fathering, a long riff on maternal guilt. Mothers are at work — architects, lawyers, executives — their absence leaves a void and father must fill in. Perhaps we were busy thinking about the good father so as to avoid our real worry: Where are the mothers and what are they doing? Implicit in these movies is some reproach to women who have indeed abandoned their traditional role. But these movies also reflect a genuine social concern. Who is bringing up baby now? Only if you believe in conspiracies could you see these movies as trying to herd females back into the kitchen or the nursery, but they do express an anxious rumble, an end-of-the-century tremble, explorations of the father solution. Also through these movies we were indulging in a communal wish-fulfillment dream. Everyone's eyes were filling up with tears at the sight of fathers cooing over their infants. Certainly the success of *Sleepless in Seattle,* in which Tom Hanks is a widower who is taking care of his son and therefore becomes the most desired male in the country, tells us that women are yearning for good fathers for themselves, for their children. In a later movie, *Forrest Gump,* which is a kind of family values, religious right propaganda film in which the adventurousness of women, the protest against the Vietnam War, the sixties itself, are seen as the evil eye cast upon us all, the hero ends up taking care of a child. He may be a damaged intellect but he is a good father. Dream on, America. Our movies reveal what we wish to believe about ourselves, what worries us at night because we know it isn't so.

IF FATHERS WERE MOTHERS

Some of the extremes of misogyny can be seen in the images of castrating, consuming females that seem to rattle around in the male brain revealing themselves in art, sculpture, fairy tale, myth, literature, and Alfred Hitchcock movies. This current anti-male talk on the part of some feminists is just the other shoe dropping. Some psychoanalytically oriented feminists have begun to investigate the why of this, the where it all began of sexual antagonism.

In academic circles Dorothy Dinnerstein's *The Mermaid and the Minotaur,* Nancy Chodorow's *Femininity and Psychoanalysis,* and Jessica Benjamin's *The Bonds of Love* are read often enough, and quoted all the time, but the major import of their work seems to be swept aside by the general public. Because their work is academic and grew in psychoanalytic soil it's not a surprise that Chodorow, Dinnerstein, and Benjamin have not been translated into slogans to march by, shouts to be shouted at your congressperson, quotes to be cherished and acted upon. That, however, is a pity because their ideas about motherhood are startling and far more apt to take us somewhere than fish without bicycles or bicycles without fish.

The work that stems from this pioneering psychoanalytic thinking leads to a practical political conclusion that men, far from being the evil other, must be brought into the nursery. This psychoanalytic view proposes that radical change in our child care assumptions will produce a very different world, one in which patriarchy, misogyny, and all their attendant injustices to both male and female will fade away. This may seem like an old idea, and it is one that was put out in the late sixties as women struggled with changing roles, but it was never, except in a small elite population, put into wide and complete practice and it was not given the careful intellectual examination by the general public that it deserved. Full participation in the work of raising children was regarded as something men should do as reparations, for the sake of justice, because their service in the home would contribute to women's liberation. The Chodorow–Dinnerstein perspective points us in another direction, illustrating the effect on our male and female experience, on our best stories, of mother-dominated childhoods. Their careful analysis of how we become adults, afraid of dependence on mothers, angry at mothers, building on the experiences of babyhood, points the way toward real change, as deep as our characters, as pervasive as our humanity. They intend to alter the most intimate of inner spaces: our minds.

When I am a married women with two young daughters my father comes on a rare visit. The little girls are in the bathtub. They are six and four. I go downstairs to greet my father. The children come running after. They have no clothes on. My father stares at them. "Well," he says, "they don't have bad bodies for girls." I send them off to get dressed. It is true, some men never get used to the idea that some bodies do not have penises. This childhood sexual mystery continues to affect us long after we should know better. We hear its echoes in the ravings of Philip Wylie, in the curtain that separates Orthodox Jewish women from Jewish men, in the back rooms of porno shops, in sado-masochistic practices, in some of the perversions.

A major Hollywood portrait of mothers appeared in the *Alien* series with Sigourney Weaver. Feminist critics have pointed out that the mother in these horror films is represented as a monster with monster babies that will enter your guts and eat you up from the inside. Slimy, disgusting, with jaws of steel, popeyes, and maternal tentacles, the alien is mother stripped of her human form. Her tentacles enter her human victims. She consumes them from the inside, providing food for her babies, who slither and crawl, the nonhuman other, the precise embodiment of our fear of babies, that their dependency will eat up our lives. What is metaphor becomes in the horror film reality. That was the pleasure of it, the success of it. The alien mother monster expresses the male fear of his mother and simultaneously carries the male fear of the pregnant fertile woman. This is Hollywood's Kali, Hollywood's Philip Wylie Mom. The *Alien* monster also embodies the female fear of her own mother and her own babies. There is nothing simple about it.

Philip Wylie had said in 1942, "I give you the destroying mother. I give you the angel and point to the sword in her hand. I give you the harpies, and the witches and the fates. I give you Pandora — I give you Prosephine, Queen of Hell, Lilith the Black widow who is poisonous and eats her mate." This imagery reappears in a film made in the nineteen eighties postfeminist world. This time out it carries also the female fear of becoming a mother, the feminist version of the same hate. As Sigourney Weaver makes her way through the destroyed space vehicle, through pipes and pieces of wondrous internal technology, the alien jumps, spits, vomits, and consumes. This is motherhood in the modern version, stripped of idealization. We are down to the ferocity alone, and as we jump and squeal in our movie seats we are reminded that the threat to female independence comes from mothering, our own mothers, the mothers we might become. As Sigourney Weaver battles the mother monster, she represents for us the warrior woman who will not be consumed by her own babies.

The father of my oldest child was not with me in the delivery room. That was not allowed in 1960. When I came home from the hospital he did not want to hold his baby. "I have a hangover," he said. "You wanted the baby, you take care of her," he said. Soon he was gone. The home with a child was repugnant to a man whose mind was on art and immortality. It contained body odors, diapers in cans, stained sheets, juice on the counter. There was a discipline in getting up in the middle of the night, in tending the baby in the early hours of the morning, in catching naps between things, in not having time to read the paper or a book or go drinking with friends. I was not surprised that he left us. Then I believed that mother discipline was too much for men. I thought of men as crippled, limited in some way, feebleminded when it came to love. Men after all are not mothers, and mothers I thought in those feminist dark ages are drawn as if by a magnet to their young, and the same magnet repels men, sends them off in the other direction just as forcefully. I thought it was in the nature of the magnet that this was so. Just as women were excused from combat in wartime, I thought men like tomcats had to be excused from home, the window kept open for easy escape. Poor things, I thought, what they are missing.

Times changed quickly. The father of my youngest children could put them to sleep faster than I could. He knew about holding babies close into the body and if they spit up on his jacket he wiped it off — of course, he trained as a pediatrician. He knew about letting them eat by themselves no matter what the mess. He knew what to do if they had a fever or fell down or lost a friend at school or had a tantrum. He made them scrambled eggs at our stove. He was pleased if they liked his French toast, his biscuits, his chicken. He told them stories. He read *The Wind in the Willows* aloud, and there were tears in his eyes when Toad is taken to jail. Toad dreams of the open road. My spouse dreamt of the open road with a child on his lap. He sat with a child who woke from a bad dream. He took the cat who fell out the window to the vet at three o'clock in the morning. He still grows silent and hard to reach when something goes wrong. He drives too fast. He curses at cars that try to cut him off. He never asks directions. He never admits to pain. If something is wrong he grows quiet. When a child of ours was in the operating room he was silent for the entire five hours. He didn't want to hold my hand. I held on to his sleeve. I talked without pause, till my voice grew hoarse. He is different from me. Some of those differences are gender-related but none of these differences excluded him from playing games of Monopoly, from trips to the zoo, from bringing cupcakes to school for a child's birthday. He is a man but the magnet pulls him close.

He is not a rarity, not an oddball. I see them all over, fathers at the swimming pool, in the park, at the doctor's office, at the teacher's conference. Yes, there are absent fathers and abusing dads but they are not the only kind we produce.

My oldest daughter, then six years old, sits between us. We are at her favorite coffee shop. She sips her hot chocolate which spills around her saucer and has already stained the green-and-white-checked taffeta dress I bought for the occasion. We have been to family court. My new husband has adopted her. We are having a ceremonial snack. Her name has been legally changed, her birth certificate altered, the old one destroyed, or sealed away. My daughter has trouble sitting still, she is a child who does things her own way. Her long hair falls tangled down her back. She is not going to be easy and having a new father is not going to erase or change that. I am hopeful: too hopeful. My new husband admires his new daughter. "She's a wild thing," he says, but he doesn't seem to mind. Not yet. She crawls under the table and out into the aisle. She grabs a piece of bread from a nearby table. "It's all right," I say. I want a perfect home, a home that will make all the children happy ever after, stepchildren, new children, my daughter. I want it so badly I can feel the desire burning behind my eyes. I also feel that strange kind of tearfulness that appears at weddings, the kind that comes from knowing too much.

Many feminists have explained the traditional division of labor and the attendant powerlessness of women on the particular origins of human society. Survival in the Paleolithic era demanded that women nurse their infants, using their hands to gather food, while men hunted bison at a distance from the hearth. Other feminists have described the unequal division of power, man as king, woman as servant, as one imposed by male brute strength, its purpose to preserve male lineage, to satisfy the male need to know that the child is his, deserving of his protection and inheritance. Simone de Beauvoir says, "Since the oppression of women has its cause in the will to perpetuate the family and to keep patrimony intact, woman escapes complete dependence to the degree to which she escapes from the family." All these theories seem true enough but do not in themselves explain the misogyny that seems to flow naturally through most all cultures: the images of Medea, Lilith the demon bride of Adam, the omnipresent taboos about the menstruating woman, the exclusion of women from the priesthood, from the judiciary, the need to control women's minds, to exclude them from inner councils, from being witnesses, from studying sacred texts. The omnipresent fear of women is most strange and needs explanation.

This is what many psychoanalysts believe. Women take the rap for baby's fear of being alone. Mother becomes the target of the anger that follows the child's fear of abandonment.

Chodorow says, "The very fact of being mothered by a woman generates in men conflicts over masculinity, a psychology of male dominance, and a need to be superior to women." The fear of regressing to infancy is the fear of merging again into the mother and losing the hard-won edges of the self. The need to dominate women is the need to show that you don't need them, that you are separate and more powerful. The male chest puffed up reassures his always insecure self that he is not going to die if his mother should leave him. The mother of childhood needs to be rejected in order for the man to claim his place in the world. Of course, this drama mostly takes place in the ever rambling, thunderous waters of the unconscious. Boys still need and love their real mothers, grown men are usually kind if distant to their real mothers, but in the imagery that haunts the fetid, seething lower depths there lies divisive danger: there roils misogyny. In this view we always carry with us the resonances of our earliest moments. We continue as we grow to struggle for independence threatened by a great fear of disappearing, merging back into Mother Earth, losing our most precious selves.

Nancy Chodorow and Susan Contratto in a paper called "The Fantasy of the Perfect Mother" write, "One consequence of the fact that women are primary socializers for boys (who later become men) is what Horney calls 'the dread of women.'" They go on to say, "The mother initially has complete power over the child's satisfaction of need and first forbids instinctual activities." This they see as the beginning of the child's sadistic impulses. Anger at being interfered with is directed at the mother and the mother's body, and later in life at women in general.

De Beauvoir had earlier said, "The earth mother engulfs the bones of her children. Death is a woman. Woman is night in the entrails of the earth. Man is frightened of this night which threatens to swallow him up. Woman is fauna, flora, perfumed berry. Nothing lies deeper in the hearts of men than this animism. Man has magic feelings of disgust, awe, and fear of woman." Dinnerstein points out that it is between female piss and shit that we are born. She says, "The child's will then is poised, for dear life's sake, to confront and resist the will of women." De Beauvoir observed this too. She said, "Women know everything about man that attacks his pride and destroys his will." The threat to male autonomy from women is perceived as more primitively dangerous than any such threat by a man. John Donne wrote in his poem "Loves Alchymie," "Hope not for minde in woman: At their best / Sweetness and wit that are but of mummy possest." In other words, the woman is just a mother slightly disguised, and mother is a creature to be feared and despised because she would take you over, eat you up.

In harems and brothels women are kept captive by men in reality.

In fantasy many men hold in their heads an imagined group of women who are slaves to their wishes. This is a form of a childhood fantasy in which the mother can no longer roam the world and leave the child but must stay and do his bidding. In the harem James James Morrison Morrison's mother cannot get out the door much less go down to the end of town. Dinnerstein says that resentment and need are destined to form part of our permanent stance toward female authority. "Mothers are the targets of unjust blame for misfortunes that they have warned against — they bear the brunt of a profound, many-faceted early filial spite and they bear it alone." The results of our child rearing practices, Chodorow writes, "are disastrous. We are all prone to mother hating because we live in a society that says that mothers can and should do all for their children. The mother first forbids instinctual activities by encouraging the child's first sadistic impulses to be directed against her and her body. This creates enormous anxiety in the child." Everybody has seen children pull their mother's hair, bite at breasts when they are nursing, tease the mother with refusals to get dressed or pick something up. Everybody has seen a child punch, kick, lash out at a mother. Every mother has been through a bad moment or two when her own body has taken the brunt of the child's anger.

We go on all our lives asserting ourselves against the first parent with a vengeance. In their school years boys turn away from girls. Their disgust, their lack of interest, their exaggerated macho pose is caused by the memories that float at the back of their minds of babyhood, of dependence, of the dominion of their mothers. Girls turn to other girls in hopes of recreating the closeness that they felt to their mothers, but they spend much of their time creating little poison games of exclusion that express both the rivalry they also felt with their mothers and their fear of being left alone. Little girls are forever leaving someone out, changing best friends, forming exclusive clubs because there is so much pain in leaving mother and so much threat in hanging on. This, combined with the competitive issues between women which are always part of any human equation, means that the first love, the mother love, is always a fateful attraction and one impossible to surpass, surmount, or avoid.

I hear my two youngest girls come home from school. The door slams. They walk past my bedroom-office. They go into the kitchen. I hear them talking and laughing. I hear something about a meeting. They are both on the high school's underground newspaper which is edited in their room by a small committee of ragged chain-smoking intense types. I go to the kitchen and they stop talking. I say, "You want some cake?" They shake their heads. They gather their books up. They disappear into their room. I hear whispering as they go. They look back at me. Their faces are blank, cold. What have I done? I stand alone in the kitchen. The phone rings and is answered. It is for one of them. The afternoon light is soft on the countertops. I could have a cup of coffee. I have no one to drink it with. I knock on their door. "Get out," one calls. I stand in front of their door. "Is she still there?" one asks. "Probably," says the other, and they lower their voices. I know that this is the time of their lives when everything is a secret, when the emotional thermometer hits tropical peaks. I know I can't help, solve, soothe, remind, caution, protect, save. I can't follow them into their room, into their journals, into their days. I am full of self-pity. I feel wronged, innocent, awkward. Sometimes I am like a detective, lurking in their shadows, picking up matchbook covers to see where they've been and rifling drawers looking for signs of sex, drugs, love. I know I am not the only mother who keeps this vigil. That is small comfort. I feel like an exile in my own home.

The cycle spins. The more they need to push me away, the more I try to come close. I know better. I can't stop myself. I feel like a rejected lover. I behave like a shy child. I return to my office and put my head down on my desk. I have things to do, my own life is there, awaiting my attention. I'm not interested. I want to make a new house rule. You must talk to me, whatever your secret is, tell it to me. I'm your mother. But that's exactly why I'll never hear the secret. "Trust me," says my daughter. Those are the two most terrible words in the English language.

Sharon Olds writes a poem entitled "My Son the Man."

> Suddenly his shoulders get a lot wider:
> the Houdini would expand his body
> while people were putting him in chains. It seems
> no time since I would help him to put on his sleeper,
> guide his calves into the gold interior,
> zip him up and toss him up and
> catch his weight. I cannot imagine him
> no longer a child, and I know I must get ready,
> get over my fear of men now my son
> is going to be one. This was not
> what I had in mind when he pressed up through me like a
> sealed trunk through the ice of the Hudson,
> snapped the padlock, unsnaked the chains,
> and appeared in my arms, what I had always wanted,
> my son the baby. Now he looks at me
> the way Houdini studied a box
> to learn the way out, then smiled and let himself be manacled.

When women speak honestly among themselves, in literature, they talk of being left behind, of following after their children, of waiting for phone calls, for letters, for the return of the love that they gave which cannot be returned in kind, which does not come. As families now live, fathers are spared most of this drama. As mothers now live, they cannot escape it.

One of my daughters is in the second grade. She loves horses and jump rope. She plays jacks and some strange game with her sister that involves a lumpy doll named Bernie who is always causing trouble and getting knocked on the head. She has a best friend and the two of them are writing a novel. It is a kind of scroll. Page after page is put together with Scotch tape. This is true desktop publishing. At school there is trouble. My daughter refuses to touch her lunch. She doesn't like whatever the cafeteria is offering. Her teacher insists she eat. Her teacher stares at her. "You must." My daughter won't. Day after day she won't. Day after day the teacher insists. The battle lines are drawn. My daughter takes a bite or two and scrapes her plate onto the floor. The teacher sends notes home. "My god," I say, "this is the beginning of an eating disorder." I see my child rail thin attached by tubes to a hospital bed. I see her enormous, chins resting one on another. "My god," I cry, "what should we do?" "What," I ask, "have I done?" I am once again convinced that some bad thing has passed mysteriously from my psyche to hers, as if I am a pollutant, a Typhoid Mary of mental health. After all, I am her mother and nourishment is connected to the maternal breast. If she won't eat lunch then I must have incited rejection, rebellion. Then too I am embarrassed. Why is my child acting up in public over a few strained peas and a meatball?

Also I am angry at her. Only in the wilds of the Northwest woods is stubbornness a survival tool. In the heart of the city, accommodation, adjustment, is in order. Even in the woods defeated wolves know to stick their throats out in gestures of helplessness when their fight has been lost. My daughter doesn't offer her throat. She puts meatloaf in her pocket, carrots in her book, and stashes potatoes in the tops of her socks. Above everything else I want her to survive, do as she is told, get into college. The world is her oyster if only she will eat. She will not. It's about will, hers vs. mine, hers vs. the teacher's: at night I think I can hear the wind battering against her will, I hear no bending only loud banging. My own will has changed into a pleading thing, a pitiful insecure thing, love weakens my will, fear that something is wrong with my child reduces me to dust. I am furious at my daughter for reducing me to dust.

Why is everything about who controls whom? I ask around. Everyone shrugs. It just is, people say. Why is everyone so keen on independence? I ask. Everyone shrugs. Autonomy, I say, is less than it's cracked up to be. No one, including my daughter, believes me. Her fight against the school lunch is a do-or-die battle against a woman teacher who made the mistake of drawing the battle lines. It is a war over my daughter's right to say no. Any agreement would be regression, agreement would be merging, agreement would be a return to feeling helpless as a baby whose mother leaves the room. Anger rises. Even as they love them little girls hate their mothers who, like Ulysses' sirens, seem to be calling them back away from the open sea, away from the open road. A feminist theoretician Susan Rubin Suleiman wrote in *Signs,* "The child's feelings toward the mother are ambivalent, a conflicting mixture of tenderness, gratitude, and destructive rage." Every mother knows this is true. If only it weren't, how much lighter a load we would carry.

Is some form of this struggle built into all children raised by mothers? It seems so. Is there a resistance movement throughout childhood in which the dependent child frantically builds walls to keep out the mother, builds roads that lead away, plans escape long before the time is ripe, rejects this parent's wish for her child to play the violin and that parent's ambition that the child join the debate team? The first child wants to play soccer, the second stutters on and on. Is this drama the inevitable result of mothers singing lullabies to babies who cannot yet walk away or is there something we can alter so that childhood is less of a war zone and more of a level playing field for both genders? The terrible twos disappear into a facade of cooperation in most children, but the angers do not disappear, they simply go underground, appear tamed but bide their time. Melanie Klein, the Freudian analyst who dared put her head into the lion's mouth so she could examine his teeth, said, "Feelings both of a destructive and of a loving nature are experienced towards one and the same person and give rise to deep and disturbing conflicts in the child's mind." Easy to say in an academic paper delivered at the Freudian Society in civilized London, but not so easy to live with in the real world. One way around this rage of the child's against the mother might be to actually share the experience fully. If that were done the child would be as angry at father as at mother and half as angry at both. The dilution of rage toward either parent might seem like a small thing but it could change matters significantly.

It is hard for women to give up the special privilege of being mothers. The sanctity of motherhood, the respect it appears to get in our culture, the secret delicious pleasure of the thing is most important to us. If we share with men our momminess, we feel we might be exchanging what little turf we have in return for a handful of nothing. Makes sense. But we have our backs against the proverbial wall. That vaunted respect for mothers is hypocritical and followed quickly by contempt. Madonnas always get the short stick. The power of the womb, marvelous as it is, does not have enough wattage to light up a whole lifetime. And if we keep child rearing for ourselves we will pay for this exclusivity by creating men who are afraid of the dominion of women, afraid of human intimacy, and women who feel isolated from men. The fear of being swallowed, the fear of not being autonomous or being too autonomous will continue to fly right at the heads of women. At least we ought to be talking about this as frequently as we list male defects, male defections, male corruptibility. A fifty-fifty split of motherhood might make us feel better altogether. Certainly we would experience less guilt. Not just conscious guilt for the things we know we haven't done right but for the bad feelings that appear and disappear at the edge of our consciousness. Susan Rubin Suleiman puts it clearly: "If the mother did not somehow imagine herself as omnipotent in relation to her child, she would not need to feel guilty and murderous every time she turned away from the child to pursue other self absorptive goals." Men carry lots of heavy things. Let them take half our load of guilt in return for half the tender feelings we receive on a good day.

All this complicated theory about the development of woman hatred, of mother fear, lends support to an early practical feminist position. If the men would take a full share of the responsibility for child care, child raising, why then women would be freed from the onerous tasks, the necessity of staying home, and could fulfill a destiny in the world. They would contribute to the economic well-being of the family while being a woman in the world, not merely a mother. Chodorow and Dinnerstein have proposed that we change the paradigm of mother–child and give each infant two parents, two equally involved parents, two equally bossy, dominating, giving, merging, independence-fostering, loving parents, and in doing so they say we will undo the fear of women. We will create a new order in which the earth (Mother Nature) herself can be respected because men will not have to defile her in claiming their own ascendancy in order to escape the dominion of their mothers. Dinnerstein says, "The universal exploitation of woman is rooted in our attitudes toward very early parental figures and will go on until these figures are male as well as female." This makes sense to me.

This call for full and equal male participation was made originally without any psychoanalytic backup theory. It struck a lot of women as just and small numbers of men agreed. However, the call itself for Daddy, for men to learn how to clean the oven, for absent fathers to cut down on their work hours, for Daddy to enter in and do the scutwork, diaper changing, bottle giving, nursery school dropoffs, sick days, laundry, play dates, birthday parties, reading a story, getting the last glass of water, calling the pediatrician, remembering the list of allergies, cleaning the toilet, wiping the tub, the whole bag of obligations and pleasures in an equal way, was heard across the land but not adopted — not on a scale that would really test out the Dinnerstein theory. No matter how many movies patted good dads on the back the numbers of children raised by mothers alone rose year by year. No matter how often fathers were invited to parent–teacher conferences, fewer and fewer of them were in the home to receive the invitation. It seems as if there was a mass flight in America away from actual daddiness despite the continual cultural images of good daddies that we saw in movies and books.

It's not just Iron Johns running around in the woods banging on drums, it's the whole masculine sense of self that seems to back off, not from being a good daddy but from being a good mommy. That, given the interpretations of early childhood of Chodorow and Dinnerstein, is understandable. The home represents regression, the loss of self. Changing this meaning of home may take dynamiting the system; it will take tremendous concentrated effort. If male fear of becoming a woman, merging into Mother, is so deep that it creates a resistance to becoming more like a woman we are in a circular bind. Nothing will change just because we've raised a little consciousness about woman's potential. Remember how Huck Finn wanted to get away from Aunt Sally and venture out into the real world? Mark Twain saw it clearly. The woman was the apron strings, the tie to civilization and control, the boy was chafing at his leash, ready to make a dash for the great river. Remember Thurber's little man rounding the corner and seeing a looming figure of his wife, merged with the roof of his house, waiting for him with a scowl on her face? This is the dangerous, neurosis-breeding unlove between man and woman that we need to alter. To break the cycle we need a whole new revolution in how we act with our spouses and children, and it needs to be made clear to all who participate what a deeply revolutionary effort is being made.

It may be that the Dinnerstein–Chodorow analysis of the problem is somewhat utopian. Usually when you tinker with the human social system something else, something unexpected, untoward goes wrong and you have a whole new set of problems. The human tragedy seems built in, permanent, every action has unwanted side effects. That said, it still wouldn't hurt to see what we would be like if parenthood were not the primary responsibility of one sex. Even in the most liberated of homes today there tends to be some assumption that Mother will do it: stay home if the child is sick, ring the baby sitter in an emergency, remember the child's favorite color, etc. In our home my most liberated husband counts on me to remember our grown children's telephone numbers. They are too important to me ever to forget. He doesn't have to bother.

One wonders why a culture that took to the idea of woman in the workplace like ducks to water has continued to resist the more profound idea of mother as not exclusively female. To paraphrase Henry Higgins, why in fact can't a father be more like a mother? Why can't a father be a mother?

Instead of insisting, instead of focusing on men as caretakers, instead of making a whole political agenda, a whole revolution about fathers as mothers and mothers as fathers, we have sat around and cooed while Robin Williams cross-dresses in order to be a good father in *Mrs. Doubtfire* and all of America stays awake for Tom Hanks in *Sleepless in Seattle*. We yearn for the father-mother. We just haven't insisted on his arrival.

True, we are not absolutely sure that men can do it. Are they really capable of the day after day, two in the morning after two in the morning subjugation of their own egos and control of their own wills that mothering requires? Will men spiral into postpartum depressions by the millions? Will men desert their babies, abuse their babies? Will men if they become mothers be fathers still? That is to say, will men continue to be sexy in bed, protective of us, work hard for us, bring to their family the fruits of the harvest, the hunt? Will a man still be a man if he is a mother? Will human beings still be adventurers, go off to walk the moon, discover the cure for cancer, make things in factories, laboratories, build sky-scrapers? If men in families alter their emotional valences, will men still like baseball? Will they have to take hormone supplements at age twenty-five? This is not to say that men have not been good fathers all along or that men have been uninterested in acting like fathers. Certainly many have. Even in the dark days of the nineteen fifties men paid for their children, tenderly taught them to swim, play tennis, shoot baskets, fox trot, etc. But the average man of that era was a father from a safe distance. He arrived home late, excused from the visits to the pediatrician for shots, from the making of the Halloween costume. His job was to make the family financially secure. His manliness kept him at a certain remove from the child who was vomiting, from the child who was crying, from the child who was frightened of the dark. The loss of intimacy that so many women stuck in their houses complained of stretched over to the children whose real lives continued as if a glass wall separated man and child. It is that glass wall that needs to be cracked.

The feminist movement has been so busy blaming, chastising, attacking men that it has barely had a moment to catch its breath, change its signals, and call to men to come into the home and stay awhile. If we weren't always watching TV programs about incestuous dads and fathers who did us dirt by marrying wives younger than we are or abusing dwarfed twin sisters we could discuss father participation with more urgency. The feminist movement has pulled in two directions. One is away from men, away from their dominion. The other is trying to pull men in, to make fatherhood and motherhood a truly joint venture. These two directions have often been at cross-purposes. One thing for sure is that we can't have it both ways. We can't complain endlessly about their brutish nature, their incestuous sins, their predatory powers and at the same time encourage them to make nice to our babies. The women's movement has tilted now toward the complaint side, toward the blame side of the argument. We're shooting ourselves in the collective foot.

If we go back in time to the way it was for the first humans, for Lucy and her mate, we see that the sharpness of the biological division, the fact of womb and lactating breasts, bound the infant to the mother in the beginning. We see that what is male and what is female was once a combination of biology and necessity. But the great gift of humans is to imagine and invent, to control circumstance and change it. Once we needed women to stay with small children. Now we need people to stay with small children. Once we couldn't spare men from the task of struggling with tusked animals. Now women can join men in their economic hunter roles. So of course men can join women in their maternal work. This doesn't make man and woman the same creature. The biological difference, the hormonal baths we undergo, the high voice, the low voice, the hairy chest, the soft skin, the different musculature, the penis thrusting, the testes pumping, the vagina pulsing, the labia flushing, these are different givens and will make us different, still appealing to each other, but not necessarily in the old ways.

Mothering by women may have a different rhythm than mothering by men, but if we tell our boys that they are nurturers, insist to our girls that if they want to be mothers it's a good idea to be paired, to be two mothers instead of one alone, we might make stronger families. If the father-mother brings the sperm and the mother-mother brings the egg, well that's not the end of it, that's just the start. If the female-mother carries the baby in utero, the father-mother can do so immediately afterward. Love, which is an artifact of human survival (we have to believe our future rests with the squalling infant), may be expressed in different styles by different genders but there is every reason to believe that it would be a good idea to have daddy-mommies, mommy-daddies, fill the holy seats around the family dinner table, around the cradle. At least it's worth a try.

In the next years we might take the father-mother idea which has been creeping around in the backwoods of our culture for a while and bring it forth, put it in circulation, insist from every pulpit, every power center, that freedom from women means joining women in their daily, often grinding baby work. We have allowed men to be boys and drift off. How exactly did it become normal in certain poverty-level cultures in America for men to father babies and then just walk away, supporting their children with neither money nor affection? True, there are many economic factors that make such an arrangement plausible, but the drawbacks for mother and child, even for father, are obvious. The women's movement ought to be there, working its way into the head of every girl who is thinking of bearing a baby out of wedlock, raising it by herself. The women's movement ought not to sanctify the womb without simultaneously sanctifying the father's role. Why haven't we convinced fathers that their babies are their babies and that humans are not sperm-depositing animals? Fish ejaculate and swim on. Humans, whose offspring are born helpless and remain helpless for a long time, can't. Till we devolve back into gills and scales, men will be bound into the process not just of conception but of rearing. That's a biological fact that should produce pickets on the streets, have priests and ministers thundering from their pulpits, have presidents appointing commissions, offering medals of honor, campaigns.

If having a baby were thought of as a true partnership, a thing that is done by two parents, a responsibility held by two people, then the self-sacrificing involved would be halved for each and the child would be doubly strengthened. Consciousness raising was the way the feminist movement was spread. It ran like a brushfire throughout the culture as groups of women talked, as more joined in the conversation, as magazines and newspapers ran opinions and counteropinions, as cartoonists and radio show hosts talked for and against, as women wrote book after book which were read and reviewed, summarized in the press, carried in the diaper bags, handed from friend to friend. So too we could have raised and could still raise the issue of men — men at home, men with their children, men as nurturers, men as fathers — and say what we believe, what we expect, demand more, rumble against the going culture, fight back against the departing father, paint him with the letter *D* for desertion, let *People* magazine run articles on crazy mothers who have rented planes to skywrite their absent husbands' names against the heavens. If we could make a revolution about what women did, we can make a revolution about what men do, what families should be. It's just that we stopped halfway. It's true there is no commandment on the tablets that came down from Sinai that we should honor our children. We will have to write one.

It sounds like a hard sell. Why should a man want to take care of his child the way his mother took care of him? Maybe if we consider the man as a stiff-necked creature, the man of the suburbs with his alcohol and his lawn mower, his John Cheever days and his Norman Mailer nights, long commutes to and from homes that fade away as he approaches, we can see that he would be better off if his connection to his children were maternal. If we consider the middle-class man drinking through the weekend, wondering what has meaning, what has purpose, what keeps his molecules together, we see that to come closer into the home might be better than to drift off.

If we consider the man of the inner city, hanging out on the street corners with his own kind, running against the jagged edges of his limits, with no permanent partner to sweeten the days, to picnic with in the summer, to hold hands with through a movie, if becoming a caring father could cut his isolation, blunt his fear of the big world, make him protect instead of retreat, then he would stand to gain everything. We might convince him of that if women stopped calling him names, throwing brickbats at him from behind our university walls. Men like the idea of being fathers but it doesn't have the same hold on many of them it once did. Perhaps we can remind them, reconnect them, let Huck Finn and Tom Sawyer know that the biggest adventure of them all awaits at home.

One of my early memories: I am going for a walk with my father. I heard my parents fighting. She said he had to take me. He said he didn't want to. She won. I am walking along the street with my tall father. He walks fast. I fall behind. I stop to look at a dog. The owner lets me pet the dog. I look up and I don't see my father anymore. I run ahead and I see a tall man with legs encased in blue trousers just like my father's a few steps in front of me. I reach him and put my hand up for him to hold it. The man takes my hand. We walk together half a block. "Who are you, little girl?" the strange man says. I drop his hand. Shame grips me, fear also. The streets seem very long. I am not allowed to cross without an adult. I am near home but not so very near. My father is two blocks ahead. I point out his back to the stranger. He calls to my father and runs after him. I am found, but I know I was lost and possibly forgotten.

There is nothing in that story that needs to be repeated generation after generation.

PART IV

 END RUNS AROUND
THE NUCLEAR FAMILY

ONE MORNING when I was eight years old I was sitting on the edge of the bathtub watching my mother soak in a bubble bath. The room was hot and steamy. It smelled brutally of cold cream, nail polish remover, nicotine, a left-over pastrami sandwich, face and body powders. She was smoking a cigarette and the ashes were falling on the white foam. She had a bowl with ice cubes in it on the floor beside her and every few minutes she would ask me to hand her a piece of ice which she would rub across her swollen eyelids. She had cried the night before and her face was puffed and pinched. She asked me then if I would help her make a big decision. I would. She asked me should she get a divorce. The words went through me like an electric shock. No one I knew had divorced parents. "Don't do it," I begged her. She had handed me the key to release her from her prison and I dropped it out of cowardice. That's the simple version of this story. In the darkest fifties before all the fertility technology, when adoption was the deepest secret, before the rash of divorce, before the love that had no name took a name, we were bamboozled into thinking that there was only one way. Disgrace was always waiting for us in the wings. Now that I have been divorced and remarried, now that I have had stepdaughters and daughters, had a child adopted by my mate, I know that living within the traditional family can be murderous, but living outside it can be murderous too. It's not at all as easy as breathing. As a culture we are indeed winded.

The nuclear family survived the reports of its death in the nineteen sixties but today we live in many different kinds of homes. The issues around these family designs are of crucial importance to our mothering and while they concern our most personal intimate feelings they also highlight the hot spots of our political conflicts.

DIVORCE AND REMARRIAGE: HOW WE STUMBLED ON THE HAPPINESS PATH

Divorce is of interest to the state. It's about property, ownership, and intimate human relationships. We use the courts when we can't avoid it. Divorce, like marriage, is the most personal of matters yet it requires the public stage. The laws have been vastly changed. Ideas about lifetime alimony, property settlement, custody have altered because of the feminist movement. We are no longer vessels or vassals. But in the ensuing chaos some feminists are still screaming foul. Sometimes they are right, sometimes they are not. Sometimes their automatic favoring of the female creates trouble.

Divorce itself was an issue not quite counted on in the salad days of feminism. It was true that the earlier generation of feminists did indeed get divorces at what was then surely a shocking rate. Charlotte Perkins Gilman herself left a lout of a spouse as well as a child. Kate Chopin wrote a book about a woman whose intention to break out of her marriage led to her suicide. Our own stage of feminism was accompanied by a rash of divorces. Betty Friedan was among the most prominent women to leave her husband. All across the land the new aspirations of women were aggravating marital trouble, which often erupted in wide unhealable fissures. This left an unprecedented number of children living in homes that were split. It created a gold rush for divorce lawyers and vast legal changes in the habits of the courts which forced many women and children below the poverty line. Some women left their children behind as in *Kramer vs. Kramer* but most took them along for the tumultuous ride.

My two stepdaughters and my own daughter were all children of broken homes. This somewhat melodramatic expression does not quite cover the experience. One of my stepdaughters, now in her thirties, today speaks of her parents' divorce as the most shocking, saddening thing that ever happened to her. She says the divorce was the shaping, pivotal event in her life. She measures everything before and after. She was taken to live in another city, and while she visited her father and his second family every other weekend and summers, she felt always torn, in transition, not a full member of her father's household. She speaks bitterly. She speaks angrily. She now has a full life and a good home but the divorce spoilt her childhood and no one can give it back to her. She says so. She knows that her parents left each other for reasons that were not trivial. She knows that her father and I did everything that we could to give her stability, affection, a home. We had birthday parties in hotel rooms. We drove three hundred miles to see third grade plays. We succeeded in growing some cosmetic grass over the crack in her life but we know now that there was no undoing. Life was not *Kate and Allie,* with everyone bouncing along and joking about new marriages. When one of my stepdaughters was married she wanted both of her biological parents to stand up with her and walk her down the aisle. It was a kind of formal ritual undoing of the divorce, but of course it wasn't and her strong feelings about it remain.

My older stepdaughter wants to live with us. She has had terrible fights with her mother. Her mother throws her into the street in the middle of the night. We are many cities away. We hear them on the phone, screaming and threatening each other. She refuses to allow the girls to visit us in New York. Every other weekend we drive down to Washington with my daughter in tow. The visits are painful, stiff. The younger stepdaughter trembles when she sees her father. The older one is sullen. "You left me," she says. The younger one holds my hand as we walk down the street. We play with cutouts, with puppets, we furnish imaginary rooms in imaginary red flowered chintz. My own daughter cries. I am paying too much attention to the other one. My daughter is clumsy, impulsive, heavy boned, large for her age. My younger stepdaughter is petite, careful, watchful. She can spell every word in the English language. She is polite. She does complicated math problems in her head. My daughter will not sit still, pulls at the curtains, rolls on the floor. My older stepdaughter will not stay with her mother. The phone rings at all hours. Lawyers are called. My husband suggests boarding school. His ex-wife refuses. Late at night I watch my husband, pale and tense, talking to his older daughter or trying to calm her mother. My body is stiff. I have hitched my star to a broken wagon. Nevertheless I want to rescue the older child from the rage that surges around her. I want to be the good mother I do not think she has had. I want to make her welcome. I want her to know that I will always be there for her. I want her to know that she can always count on me. I am reeking of goodness. I am fairly stinking with good intentions. I want her to like me. I make conversation about things she is interested in, the Beatles, movie stars. I pick her up after school. I wait in the orthodontist's office. I admire her math ability. I admire her mind. I want to buy her new clothes, new records. I fix up her room with a quilt with daisies on it. She has told me her favorite flower is a daisy. She is thirteen years old. We leave her one night with my child. When we come home we find the six-year-old with a dark spreading bruise on her face. My stepdaughter had pushed her down the stairs. So what I thought would be easy was not so easy. Soon we realized that we couldn't leave them alone. It simply wasn't safe. I understood the anger of the older one. I understood the fear of the younger one. I understood the anxiety of the younger stepdaughter who developed mysterious stomach problems left at home in Washington with her mother. Her mother refused to let her visit us. We had to hire lawyers again. Pregnant, I flew down to Washington to identify the ex-wife to the subpoena server. I was ashamed. I felt as if I had become a walking tabloid but we didn't know what else to do. We couldn't abandon the child and continue to live our lives. Finally her mother agreed to allow her to visit us every other weekend, vacations. The financial cost was high. The emotional cost was higher. Her mother told the younger child that her father was cheating on his taxes. He wasn't.

Among the older children there was always the tension of who lived with whom and why. I sputtered, I stuttered, I pleaded, I calmed, I reasoned. I ignored. I hoped that time would help us. Time did not.

My oldest stepdaughter stole and pawned my jewelry (she apologized many years later). She asked us if she might have friends come by and shoot a movie they were doing for school. We were leaving for the weekend. She would never come with us. If we had stayed home she would have gone away. I supplied the refrigerator with Cokes for what I assumed would be a thirsty film crew. We opened the door Sunday night to a strange odor in the hall. In our bedroom I found the blankets and sheets on the floor, the windows wide open, and a deep long burn exposing the springs of the mattress, fabric charred and flaking, on my side of the bed. A lamp had started a fire. I stared at the hole and knew that it was no accident that it was my side of the bed that had gone up in flames.

I wrote an article in the *New York Times* in 1972 about the rebuilding of families, the potential wonders of the stepfamily. I was overly optimistic. After my piece was published, my oldest stepdaughter wrote a letter, which they printed, claiming she didn't want any part of my family. She was seventeen then. She meant it. I was embarrassed and angry. Actually she was right. I had been publicly tap-dancing on the grave of her childhood. I had not understood how hard it was for my stepdaughter, how little she would appreciate my desire to build a new home on the ashes of her old one. I had been naive and in my slapdash American way thought all endings could and should be happy.

Stepmothers are particular stories with their own mythology but I thought I could beat the rap. I thought I could redo, rescue, undo. I was wrong. Of course it wasn't just the divorce that made life hard for these children, and many others have survived in better spirits, but this business of bonding with stepmothers and stepfathers is not a simple matter and despite cute stories that appear in women's magazines from time to time, all is not well that apparently ends well. Dr. Judith Wallerstein and others who have studied the results of divorce are struck by the difficulty of the crisis, how long its effects last and how hard it is for children to stagger away from their parents' failed marriages with trust intact. This does not mean that many stepchildren do not make it through with flying colors or that many children of divorce do not grow up into strong and vibrant people, it only means that the road is steep and the obstacles fierce. Of course it makes me enormously sad to say this. I wanted the blended family to be a new form of home. I wanted my stepchildren and children to link tightly one to all. Perhaps like Julie Andrews in *The Sound of Music* I wanted to march with all my children over the hills to freedom. Some of my daughters were most certainly arrested at the border. Like nearly everyone else I wanted to make a family for my children that would be better than the one I came from. All I can say is it could have been worse. But my stepchildren's memories are not from Hallmark and I have grown fat from eating humble pie.

My oldest daughter, who spent the early years of her life without a father, has divisions in her self that come from early father loss. Substitute fathers are fine but memory lingers and wounds like that don't easily heal, and while I can't measure the damage I know it's there. It influenced her choices. It made her doubt her lovableness. It warped something. Divorce was not exactly an option. I did not do it to find myself or make myself happy although that was the result. I did it because my first marriage was so egregiously a mockery, the stage fell down, the scenery collapsed. In truth I don't know anyone whose divorce was hasty, opportunistic, selfish. They were almost all driven by extreme necessity. The anti-feminist vision of women running out of their homes and pursuing careers may have some echo of truth but I didn't see it. I saw women confused, unhappy, hoping to be better loved, to feel better, to do more, desperate and filled with shame at the failure of an endeavor that the most modern skeptic among us counts as sacred.

The contribution of feminism was to insist that one's own two feet were for standing on, and the outside world was waiting. Most women who left marriages were driven out, abandoned or trapped in situations that were tearing them apart. Most men who left marriages did not do so because a prettier, younger woman lured them away. Most of them were caught in some unhappy web of their own spinning and thought, correctly or incorrectly, that their lives depended on undoing the chokehold of that marriage. Nevertheless, whatever the whys, however great the necessity, it was a betrayal of the children. For many of us it was true: we had no choice but to leave, to stay would also have been a betrayal of the children. It was in the time of divorce that so many of my friends began a litany of complaint. Men were this and men were that. Men were always able to find younger and prettier partners while many women languished, faded wallflowers. Many women told their daughters things about their fathers that were not quite accurate. The legal wars between the sexes created casualties among the children. Freedom was anything but free.

MOM ALONE, DAD ALONE, MOM AND MOM, DAD AND DAD: THE MODERN FAMILY

When I was a single mother before the great wave of divorces that hit this country in the mid-seventies I took my baby with me to parties, on weekends with friends, on errands and on dates. I had a hard time keeping to schedules, making routines routine. I allowed her to meet all the coming and constantly going men in my life. Sometimes she met them at breakfast. It wasn't good for her to be so much a part of my adult life. (I didn't know that until my present husband told me on our second evening together but by then . . .) It also wasn't good for her to be without me. I didn't like being alone at the nursery school class meeting and I didn't feel strong enough to head a household. I had no choice. Sometimes I forgot to do ordinary things. The lights were turned off and we ate dinner in the dark. The gas was turned off and we went to the corner for pizza. I wanted to be a hippie and travel America in a multicolored van but I had a child and I needed to grow up. I did, more or less.

Working, raising children on their own or with the occasional help of a departed partner is not the way most women dreamed their lives would unfold but it happens. It happens through death and it happens through divorce and it happens because some women have not been able to find the ideal or even the less-than-ideal partner and have chosen to have babies on their own. Children with only one parent have a harder time separating from home. They are less certain of continued care, they do not have the advantage of the other pair of hands to read a story or take a trip to the zoo. They do not have the blend of interests and skills that two people can bring to the home. They do not have the money that double wage earners bring. Nevertheless, a good many children raised in single-parent homes become strong and contributing and loving adults. To assume that life without father or mother condemns a child to misery is to vastly underestimate the resiliency of children, the capacity to make do with something short of the ideal. Children can be well tended, connected, protected by one parent. It's better to be rich than poor, it's better to be American than Sudanese, it's better to be born of educated parents than uneducated parents. And yet children from poor backgrounds, children from immigrant homes, children with only one parent have all flourished and conquered over the more obviously advantaged. So the single-parent mother, burdened by knowing that her very singleness is not a good thing for her child, burdened economically, burdened with the necessity of being in many places at once, looking for some kind of emotional fulfillment for herself, can nevertheless create a family that supplies the essentials: consistency, support, physical and emotional care.

I am in the playground with my oldest daughter. The year is 1963. I am the only divorced mother around. The other women are kind to me, invite me to dinner, tell me about rhythm classes for small children at the local Y and bring extra washcloths and cookies and juice for my daughter because I frequently forget. This day I have my own friend with me, a former dorm mate at college who has been living in Spain writing for a liberal underground newspaper. She is passing through my city on her way to cover a South American insurgency. She watches me in the playground and listens to the talk of the women on the benches. "I don't believe it," she says to me as we leave the park. "You can't be happy doing this stuff. What's wrong with you?" But I was happy. I was happy with the way my daughter laughed when I read her books. I was happy to look at her face when she listened to records. I was happy picking up crayons that had fallen under the bedsheet. I was happy bathing her and washing her hair. I was happy when she was clean and in her pajamas and leaning against me in her favorite chair. I was happy looking at the night sky with her. I was happier than I had ever been in my life. This was strange and I didn't blame my old friend for wondering what had become of me. I was enthralled with my child and proud of the fact that, sloppy or not, I was able to take care of her. My old friend said, "I feel real bad for you. You used to be so interesting." "Don't waste your pity on me," I said. "I'm all right." I was. Of course I would have liked to go to South America too.

The nuclear family with two devoted parents who do not hate each other is a good thing we all agree, but the single-parent family is not the last stop on the express to hell that it has been labeled. It's the harder way but a thousand turns of fate lead to a harder way — handicaps, job loss, sourness of soul or minor depression, illnesses physical or mental, alcohol abuse by parents, constant arguments between parents, moving from place to place, etc. The harder way is deep within the nuclear family as well as far without. Most of us have had a taste of hard and made do with less than what we hoped for. So I'm tired of hearing the single mother attacked as if she were a blight upon the land. The single mother may be a mother between mates or she may be permanently alone. In the long run what matters to the family is her resiliency, her capacity to create strong children, her luck, her basic emotional fiber. Mommy and Daddy together bringing up baby is a good idea but no more than that. Cold fathers, angry mothers, fearful mothers, temper-ridden fathers, uncommunicative mothers, bullying fathers, bitter women, indifferent men cast their inhibiting gloom even when they remain under the same roof. There's no need to get carried away and assume that disaster will follow if the family is headed by one parent. It's just not true. Disaster, regrettably, doesn't play by the rules.

The lesbian or gay family certainly has to suffer the censure of certain Bible thumpers from coast to coast. It also has to endure the curiosity and titillation of even tolerant neighbors or teachers or co-workers. But this hardly seems a catastrophe. Society has always despised somebody and those somebodies have always refused to be despicable. Homosexuality while it does not have the easy political acceptance of being left-handed or musical or good at computers is simply another human way and the children living in these families learn how to cope with hostile views toward their parents' sexuality. They are most often wanted children, cherished and supported however they are conceived and whichever partner in the family conceived or adopted them. In this they are already among the most fortunate.

In the wake of the sexual revolution Americans have learned that gender identity is sometimes confused with social stereotypes. What you do in bed with whom is only part of your story. People with all their full individuality, humanity, oddness, warts and all are capable of the deep connections that a family requires no matter the gender they love. The same rotten things will go on in lesbian and gay homes as anywhere else. More's the pity.

If we define family as a bond, biological or chosen, which is dedicated to the caring for all, the raising of children, the economic survival of the home, the place of food and rest, of nurture and purpose, the most dangerous place in the world, then the genders of the adults will affect the style, the culture, the politics of that home, but no more. There is no threat to the survival of the species from loving parents of the same gender and there is no threat to the psychological sturdiness of children who are well loved. The questions that rise are interesting. We do not yet know what psychosexual differences it will make to a child to be raised by same-sex parents. What does the Oedipus triangle look like in these circumstances? What about separation fears, attitudes toward the absent sex, etc.? Preliminary studies seem to show that the sexual orientation of children brought up in gay or lesbian homes is no different from that of children raised in heterosexual homes. One thing for sure is that these children are less apt to be fearful of human variety, more likely to be open to all the experiences sometimes still kept off-limits to one gender or another. The one thing we know is that traditional families are already making many people crazed, sad, compulsive, obsessive, criminal, self-hating, sado-masochistic, impotent, frigid, lonely, and odd. If the gay and lesbian family does as badly as the rest of us we won't be able to blame the parents' sexual orientation. Where once the culture was rigid and excluding, now there is enough flexibility to allow for alternative choices. In part this is a feminist contribution. As we tossed the sexual stereotypes onto the bonfires of the fifties we made room for more people to care for children. This can't be bad.

I have considered carefully how I would feel if one of my daughters announced to me that she was gay. Uneasy I'm sure. I'm old enough to have been affected by social norms and to be afraid somewhere in my heart of society's condemnation. Her sexuality would mark her as contemptible to some and that would alarm me. I am conventional enough to want her to be like me, to live like me. I would be concerned about what she would lose by placing herself on the social margin. But most of all I would grieve if she were not to have children, not want to have children, not ever hold a child of her own. If she were to have children with a loving stable partner I would be calmed, infinitely grateful for the modern technology that could make that possible. I would feel that all was right in whatever heavens are looking down on us. I cannot defend this as reasonable. I do not think it is politically right or wrong. Still, I would want the blessing of children (never a pure blessing) for my daughters. I know that all my attitudes, all my deepest fears of gender confusion are creations of my time and place, my own sexuality, my prejudices and limits, my most unbounded and not necessarily good hopes.

WHOSE BABY IS IT? THE NUCLEAR FAMILY WITH SEVERAL NUCLEI

The new technologies came as a wondrous surprise to those of us who had already completed our families. My sex education came from a book about birds and bees that didn't include vaginas and penises and now we were in an era when you needed advanced biology to understand what was going on. Now the sperm could fertilize an egg in a petri dish and who owned what ever after was in question. My friends and I talked about what we would or wouldn't try if we needed to. We all agreed we would do what we had to, we would try whatever we could afford. I daydreamed about having another child. Perhaps the new technology could help me maintain a pregnancy although I was approaching fifty. I considered Sarah and Abraham and in vitro angels appeared in my dreams. Once I passed a newborn baby in a carriage and the sun shone on the carriage handle and the baby blinked and sneezed and I felt a peculiar surge in my breasts as if milk were again spilling forth. It wasn't hard to understand why a woman would be a surrogate or why she would change her mind and try to keep her own child.

Mary Beth Whitehead conceived a child with William Stern's sperm. She was originally doing this under contract for the Sterns. Elizabeth Stern had multiple sclerosis and was afraid of a pregnancy, which might make her disease worse. When Mary Beth Whitehead decided she wanted her baby back and the Sterns said no, and William Stern said with equal passion that he wanted his own child, all hell broke loose. Some feminists were signing petitions for Mary Beth. They said the sperm donor was incidental, the womb was all. They said that a woman's right to her own child cannot be abrogated by a contract or anything else. They said that Mary Beth was a victim of William Stern's patriarchal behavior. Katha Pollitt wrote in the May 1987 issue of *The Nation,* "Sarah suggested that Abraham impregnate Hagar in order 'that I may obtain children by her,' but Hagar was a slave. What's modern about this story is that once pregnant, Hagar, like Mary Beth Whitehead, seemed to think that the child was hers, no matter what anyone said."

This was true as far as it went, although perhaps it wasn't fair to compare Mary Beth who was not a slave to Hagar. (Mary Beth had her own complicated reasons for wishing to bear this child including getting back at a husband who had disappointed her and gaining a sense of power in a world that gave her too little.) The conception was entirely voluntary. The problem with Katha

Pollitt's analysis of this tragic tangle is not that she understood Mary Beth Whitehead's desire to keep her own child. So do I. It is that she had no sympathy for or understanding of William Stern's identical need. She especially had no concern for Elizabeth Stern, who wanted the experience of motherhood but not at the cost of risking her life. When a large number of prominent feminist women released a statement to the press on the steps of the Bergen County Courthouse urging the judge to decide in favor of Mary Beth and take the baby away from her biological father and would-be adoptive mother, a fateful turn was taken in our feminist politics. The inherent divisions in the feminist movement came to a head.

At a meeting of a women writers' group held in a loft on lower Broadway, after many passionate speeches that convinced me that if I had been born in Russia I would long ago have disappeared in the gulag mists, I refused to sign the petition. I was unmoved by the class analysis which made Mary Beth a working-class heroine opposed to the educated middle-class Sterns. I was untouched by the argument that the patriarchy (judge, lawyer, psychiatrist) was persecuting a helpless mother. Although I too was angry at the testimony of psychologists and child experts that made Mary Beth, on flimsy grounds, seem a less-than-ideal mother, that wasn't the point at all. True, it may have been the contrast with my own father that made me admire William Stern, but of such stuff are political positions taken.

Then too my oldest daughter had a father who had not wanted her, neither the financial nor the emotional responsibility. This was not entirely his fault. He had acquiesced in my desire to get pregnant. He had never fooled me about his inability to see himself as a father. We were sitting in a dark hotel bar on Madison Avenue when I asked him to take a part in his daughter's life or allow my present husband to adopt her. At the time he was gambling and drinking. His hands were shaking. His eyes were bloodshot. His last play had failed and he had stopped writing. He looked like a large raven with a broken wing nervously pacing the forest floor. He quickly agreed to give her up for adoption but I knew that he was sad, sad that he couldn't do better, sad that the demons that plagued him were disqualifying him from taking care of his child or so he thought. So I think today. There was between us, me eating the peanuts, he on his third drink, a pool of hopeless tenderness. He was the one who had not come when he promised. He was the one who had not written postcards when I had suggested that as a method for staying in touch. He was the one who had deserted his child. Nevertheless, because I knew him so well, I grieved for him. I was taking something away from him that he didn't want. Despite the irony I felt rotten. He smoked cigarettes with a long black silver-tipped holder. His upper-crust English accent swirled around me. I knew he vomited on the floor at four in the morning. I knew he was a kind of brilliant hustler, a man always smuggling goods back and forth across the borders of sanity. Tenderly I offered him the papers to sign. He asked me about my new mate. "His favorite author is Trollope," I said. "Ah," replied my first husband, and I will never forget the envy in his voice as he added, "He must be a very good man." So I knew that the signing of the adoption papers was a bitter act for him even as it was a bittersweet act for me. I know that father love is not incidental to our lives and if it is missing there is no way to overcome a fear of the dark.

In the Baby M drama here was the good father and here were the feminists jumping all over him in public. I didn't know who should get the child or how the case should be resolved or what exact legal precedents should be created, but I did know that the women's movement should not be perceived as taking an egg-over-sperm position. A glorification of the power of the womb seemed to me just the wrong message, just the way to keep men away. If biology was not a destiny that should keep us in the kitchen barefoot and pregnant, it should also not give us an advantage over the male when it came to custody issues. Having it both ways seemed to me dishonest. The mother is not necessarily the best parent and the father is not necessarily the best parent and the law which so likes generalizations must instead evaluate each of the human beings involved, including the best interests of the child. The nightmarish quality of custody cases lies in just this puzzle. The power of the womb is awesome, but without the sperm it is merely an organ that spills blood once a month.

Friendships were broken over this issue. Heated arguments among women crossed from dialogue about disagreement to cries of treason. The strong feelings, the hostility of women who signed the petition against those who didn't was quite remarkable. I didn't sign. I couldn't. I received angry telephone calls from old friends whom I have not seen since. I walked up to a group of women at a writers' meeting and there was a sudden terrible silence.

Some feminists have made much of the actual bearing and birthing of the child as if this was reason enough to give women greater rights and control over their offspring. Pregnancy and labor are indeed a woman's part and the male is not as active a participant in the pure biology of birth, but the baby is not an animal that survives without a social context and this social context does make the father an equal participant in all the nurturing of the infant. The psychological development of the child is not divinely given to a parent of one sex or the other.

I knew that history had given men property rights over females and their children and that this injustice fueled the contemporary feminist position. However, the answer to an injustice is never another one, and just because men had once designed the law in their favor is no reason in the twentieth century simply to invert the process. I knew that some feminists felt that Mary Beth should be given an edge under the law in the custody battle because she had carried the baby for nine months. This edge was supposed to nullify the general male edge of more money and power in the culture. The way to undo deep social inequities is not to create unjust laws or precedents of preference but to keep the law just, gender neutral, and work on creating a different social balance. If the mother, because of her nine-month relationship with the fetus, was generally considered the more valued parent it seemed to me we were sliding backwards, weakening our arguments for full male participation in child care.

Some feminists developed a hatred of the idea of surrogacy. It was claimed that having a child for someone else was a kind of bondage whether it was voluntary or not. The idea of doctors being involved in the process, which they had to be, fueled the already existing paranoia about males stealing women's eggs for their own profit, about male manipulation and control of female reproductive organs. I went to a book party given by a friend in the women's health movement for a new book claiming that male gynecologists were stealing eggs from anesthetized women whose surgery had nothing to do with reproduction and giving those eggs to other women for a price. A roomful of prominent women writers congratulated the author of the book, bought signed copies, and mingled with one another. That the book, with possible rare exceptions, was a paranoid fantasy went unmentioned. Caught in the social moment I shook the author's hand and wished her luck. Was I mad?

The case of Mary Beth Whitehead vs. William Stern occurred just as some women were deciding that male doctors were exploiting females by doing too many hysterectomies, by insisting on medicalizing births when they were better handled by midwives. The anti–male medical establishment feelings were running high. Women in the know politically had been since the early seventies examining themselves with mirrors and using yogurt to treat vaginal infections rather than going to physicians. The DES scandal had been exposed. Reproductive medicine was regarded as a male preserve and despised as such by some women within the feminist movement. The heat on this issue has died down. In the nineties the male physician is no longer a direct target. Women who need help in conceiving babies continue to go to fertility clinics. Women still go to doctors, male or female, when something is wrong with their ovaries, womb, or breasts. The emotional intensity behind the anti-male medical positions has faded away for most women. But it left behind a bitter divisive taste.

The feminist movement in the Mary Beth Whitehead publicity circus had taken a side that contradicts what most women need: fathers who desperately want to love their daughters and sons, husbands who want to be fathers, and men who treat their sperm not as meaningless seed one scatters across the land in blind hope of DNA longevity but as something precious, tender, personal, offered to the parade of humanity but tended at home, a home in which one stays. Katha Pollitt and the other feminists who signed the petition in Mary Beth's favor were deliberately and intentionally expressing contempt for the male contribution to the existence of their children.

This didn't seem so strange given all the angers swirling about in the air, the books about horrid husbands divorced in a moment of sudden revelation, horrid fathers seen now as repressive tyrants, bearers of the bully stick of the patriarchy. I wrote one of those books myself. So did a lot of women I knew. Each of us wrote from the injured heart. Most of us were right: we had been wronged. However, the result was a plethora of words on male evil. It was about time we told our stories. It should have cleared the air. It seems to have created smog instead.

Among our much-watched celebrities divorce is more common than the cold. We are all used to the high figures. We no longer scratch our heads and sigh when we see them printed in the papers. In place of yesterday's divorce scandal custody battles have begun to fascinate us. A biological father lays claim to his child given away at birth to adoptive parents and the case winds its way through the courts and we share in the drama of the child ripped in two. Custody battles have also changed with fathers taking children more often. Some feminists see this as a reversion to the time when children were patriarchal property and if a woman was exiled from her marriage she lost everything including the children. Others think that this is just what should happen if men are to feel that they have a franchise, that the responsibility is his as well as hers. Some feminists want women to win every case. Others of us feel that the children too are part of our feminist concern and that each case is singular and men are women's equal when it comes to raising and tending a child. The fight in the culture is about how far this father business is going. Will it end with women being robbed of the power they hold as bearers of the infant or will it end with women, off the maternal pedestals, free agents, able to take care of themselves?

Almost a decade ago when the surrogate issue first arose, so alarming in the Mary Beth Whitehead case, we hadn't imagined the common and regular use of the sperm bank and how that would affect us. In vitro fertilization is the other major weapon against infertility. The hundreds and thousands of children now so conceived and their grateful parents are among the foremost beneficiaries of modern science. Ironically enough, however, modern science has been pressed into the service of the most primitive of evolutionary instincts. Men have always been driven to have as many children as possible in order to protect the survival of their genes. At least that's the way it must have been in the caves and fields of early man struggling to stand upright, to add brain cells and shed body hair. The invention of the technology to artificially inseminate, to freeze sperm, was a great boon to the infertile couple, to the woman who wished to create a child but whose husband couldn't, to the unmarried or the lesbian woman who wished to be a biological mother. The science of insemination is fine and the gift of motherhood it may bring to a woman who has delayed childbirth too long or whose mate cannot offer her viable sperm is a blessing, a sacred blessing. But this wonderful technology has worked against our plans to make fatherhood a more permanent human endeavor. Men are donating sperm and doing so anonymously, motivated by altruism, egoism, a small fee, a sense of drama; they are, like male chimps, leaving parts of themselves in different banks around the country. The fact of sperm donation weakens the very connection some of us were trying to strengthen between father and child. It makes possible biological conception without personal responsibility. Sperm donation, which we welcome as a gift, has a dark side. It contributes to the notion of reproduction as a woman's thing, as a matter of technology not ethics, not emotions, without consequences for the male. Such clever technology is the result of our wonderful human minds and yet it reduces our humanity, making us more like rabbits than like gods. Maybe we are. The ironies are there for all to see.

The feminist theorist Sara Ruddick writes in a textbook called *Conflicts in Feminism,* "Women buy men's sperm but leave men out. This is rough justice. Rough justice is an improvement upon the misogynist and male dominated institutions in which women have had to give birth and undertake mothering." This attitude toward men is hardly encouraging and in an academic theoretician with status and power gives permission to students to nurse their anger, consider revenge, and deepen the already wide enough chasm between the sexes. Sara Ruddick speaks for many of her feminist peers when she quotes Gertrude Stein as having remarked that "fathers are depressing." Elaborating she adds, "If an absent father is depressingly disappointing, a present father can be dangerous to mothers and children." That is hardly the way I would describe fathers.

In his first marriage my husband and his first wife traveled with two young children to Europe. The girls were very picky eaters.

One wouldn't eat anything without mustard on it and the other wouldn't eat without ketchup. My husband packed bottles of both and all across France and Italy he would take out his daughters' condiments and put them on the table so they could eat. It was his way of watching over them. Perhaps their eating habits were somewhat depressing but as a father he certainly wasn't. I remember him with my oldest daughter on his lap, reading to her from the Bible, skipping the hard parts, skimming the long lists. I remember her head on his shirt and her hands fiddling with his tie. I see him now in the kitchen baking bread for his grandson who is also a picky eater and with a hearty appetite eats Grandpa's bread. I see him fishing with one of our daughters. His face red with excitement, pull, pull, he yells at her and she struggles with the heavy rod. The moment slips away and becomes buried and she may not remember how the water sparkled, how her father laughed as the fish thumped on the boat floor, but the measure of the thing goes on.

Complaints about male cruelties that don't include female cruelties send a message, hill to hill, campus to campus, *don't* trust the beasts, beware the male, stay with your own kind, beating the drums of anti-patriarchy feeling. Ruddick says that she prefers the use of "the word *mothering* over the word *parenting* because the abstract notion of parent obscures the pervasive injustices suffered by women-mothers and more generally, the myriad father problems that vex and divide feminists." In other words, let's get rid of the word that includes fathers because some of us really don't like them.

It is perhaps encouraging that two recent major custody battles were instigated by fathers who felt very passionately about raising the children they had sired. The battles were riveting to the public as the drama of a child ripped from the only parents she and he had ever known unfolded in the media. One's natural sympathy went to the adoptive parents who were about to lose a child with the same kind of finality that death brings. They were good people certainly. Both these babies had been given up by mothers who did not know that the fathers would want to take care of these children. When the fathers made their claim the adoptive parents thought they could fight it off. The decision of the courts reinforced father rights, father necessity, and as such was healthy for the community, painful and ghastly as the bitter experience was for all concerned. I know that for some feminists reinforcing father right is seen as an oppression of women, a treatment of the womb as if it were the property of the male. But if we ask men to be caring, then we have to respect their feelings in custody and divorce arguments. If the sperm counts, it counts always. If a child is a prize in a battle between parents, then both biological parents must count equally. This leads us to the slippery slope of abortion and whether or not men should be legally involved in this decision. The miseries of that are too terrible to contemplate though logic tells us if we want men in the home, men cannot be treated as irrelevant to conception, as passers-by, as rain to seed. If we want from men responsibility in contraception, in sexual behavior, we cannot treat them like spawning fish even when it's hard, even when this causes the social puzzles to grow more complicated.

ADOPTION

I am not a disinterested observer on the issue of adoption. I consider my relationship with my stepdaughters one that involved a kind of emotional adoption. Even though I have had to share them with a biological mother who is always more important to them than I am, I know that loving a child or being furious at a child is not about reproduction of genetic codes. I know that I was able to add to, to spice and flavor, to alter my stepdaughters' lives. I intended to love them perfectly. I loved them as best as circumstances would allow. The things that went wrong between us cannot simply be attributed to our different chromosomes.

My oldest daughter has a biological father she has not seen since she was two and a half and an adopted father who is pledged to her with all his beleaguered heart. For a while she would ask us, "Who do I look like?" She looked exactly like her biological father. I would tell her so. She would ask the question again and again as if the answer might change. Every time my youngest stepdaughter came to visit, as she did every other weekend and for long vacations, my older daughter would do something to make everyone mad. The footprints of our past walked all over our present. Once a family has been formed the question who is the best beloved becomes like the site of a neighborhood toxic dump. In families everyone is always competing and sniping and pushing and shoving. The adoption in our household was just an additional complication in an already complicated constellation. But it made me feel better that my child was legally within my spouse's arms. It gave me constant hope that one good human choice might erase a bad one. I was overly optimistic but moving in the right direction. In my family adoption was not caused by infertility but the issues are similar: Can you love someone who is not of your flesh even though shadow parents, the biological real ones, continue to play through your life, through their lives? I come to the question of adoption with no objectivity at all and a deep commitment to the possibilities it holds for children, for parents, for grandparents, for same-sex parents, for people of all colors and shapes mingling together.

If I had not been able to conceive children I would have adopted them, many of them. When I was a child the Catholic archdiocese owned a great old building on Madison Avenue in New York City. It had a cobblestone courtyard and in the courtyard there was a covered crèche with an empty cradle set in the center. My mother told me that poor girls who had done the unthinkable, unmarried girls who had done what must never be done and given birth, would put their babies in the crèche and ring the bell that was placed at the side. The nuns inside the building would wait a discreet amount of time, letting the sinner disappear back into the city streets, and then they would come out and take the baby, foundling that it was, and save its soul and body. As I rode the bus past the building I would stare at its ornate stone walls covered with carved grape leaves and small gargoyles. I wanted one of those babies for myself. I thought that maybe one night I would come downtown, hide in the shadows, and when I saw a mother leave her infant I would rush inside the open gates and snatch the child while the nuns were waiting behind their closed doors.

Never mind that this is not a story of a nice little girl wanting to practice being a mother but of a child who hoped to rescue her symbolic self from the cold. The point is that adoption, the taking of a baby that would not otherwise have a home, is a deep-seated and reasonable solution to the problem of infertility that has always been with us. We are used to the fact that money is distributed unequally in our society but so also is the capacity to take care of a child, to give nourishment and support, financial and emotional, to a child. When the imbalances leave the ones with the capacity without a child and the ones without the capacity with a child the rational solution is to remedy the situation. The adoptive parent is not a conditional parent, not a substitute parent, not a second-best parent but the real thing all the way. We know that because we know that real parenting is in the doing, the brushing the teeth, the washing the hair, the preparing of food, the reading the story, the turning out the light, the coming back with a drink of water, the looking under the bed for monsters, the meeting with the teacher, the throwing the ball, etc. Parenting is not a one-time body roll of sperm and egg. If it were, how much easier being a parent would be, we could drift off in the currents letting the waters flow through our gills, carefree evermore.

I am not such a romantic that I don't see the problems, the potential for special kinds of rejection both on the part of the parent and on the part of the child. I understand that sometimes adoption brings incompatible intelligences or temperaments together and everyone is harmed. Adoption gives a peculiar spin to the psychological hurdles that each child climbs. On the other hand, death, divorce, poverty, illness also create special climates where storms can breed. Nature deals out the cards without consideration of our feelings, and our own genes too can produce grief unlimited. Despite the battering that many adoptive parents have received I believe we are at our best, most human, when we love because the child is there, not because our genetic immortality awaits.

A feminist can be a supporter of adoption as well as a supporter of abortion rights. There is no contradiction here. Adoption, although it has its psychological complications, is the best solution for the parentless child and for the childless parent. Abortion is the solution to the unwanted early pregnancy or to pregnancy with a damaged fetus. A woman can desperately want a child at one time in her life and just as desperately not want a child at another. It is true that if abortion were outlawed more babies would be available for adoption, but that would serve only the purposes of the infertile woman not the woman who is carrying an unwanted child. Good social policy would make it as easy as possible for women who want to raise children to do so while at the same time making sure that children are wanted by the mothers who care for them. After abortion became legal, after the sexual revolution when contraception was more easily available and the shame of the unwed mother was replaced by the do your own thing attitude that swept the culture, babies were rare and I'm sure fewer and fewer were left in the archdiocese's crèche. Adoption became less of an act of rescue and more of a self-fulfilling goal for parents who couldn't have children.

Originally we had regarded adoption as a kind of cure for the population explosion. I shouldn't have my own, many of my friends were saying. We shouldn't add to the earth's burdens. This was politically sweet but proved untenable, tainted by the totalitarian Chinese regime checking on women's menstrual flow, and offensive to a people that hardly believes in the collective good at all. If we live in a culture that can't raise taxes for schools or bridges, for the poor or the young, we certainly can't ask sacrifice of people's reproductive urges for mankind's sake.

There is something poignant in the ads one reads today in the local newspaper: "Bill and Susan have love and financial resources to give to white newborn, call at any hour." Now along with the difficulty of adoption is the threat of instability in the adoption, difficulties stirred up by adoption's opponents. Starting with Betty Jean Lifton's bitter discussion of her own adoption and her search for her birth mother came a new knowledge that adoption itself is not the end of the story. Many adopted children need to discover their birth mothers and many are uncomfortable without biological roots. How many is questionable. Is this a story of some noisy few or is it a common experience of the adoptee? We don't yet know. Adoption is, however, a far more complicated situation for a child and for the adoptive parents than we had earlier understood. We've known for a half century that adoption ought not to be kept a secret. Secrets leak like carcinogens into a family, wreaking havoc. The new talk about discovery, searches for birth mothers, adds another potential for massive hurt at the end of the line. The opponents of adoption are fanatically certain that all children would be better off with their birth parents and that adoption is a kind of wound of the soul that cannot ever heal. This voice in our culture is one that contributes to our giving primacy to the womb and degrading motherhood to some kind of literal fundamentalist condition in which only the biological mother will do. This anti-adoption movement has over ten thousand active members and an umbrella organization deceptively called American Adoption Congress, which includes a militant subgroup called CUB, Concerned

United Birth Parents. These groups have been actively involved in recent custody cases on the side of the biological mother. They claim — and may be right — that the social work system did mothers and babies dirt by sealing records. They have begun to influence social work policy in favor of birth mothers, leading to decisions to leave crack babies with their mothers in dangerous situations. These groups set women against women. The one who had the child is now viewed as a victim and the one who adopted the child is viewed as a child stealer.

The anti-adoption forces have come up with some questionable statistics to argue that children of adoption are in a lifelong fury and do not adjust to their homes. Common sense, human experience tell us that adoption has its special knots, its places where it needs care; identity questions are complicated for every child and more so perhaps for the adopted child, but such a voice of fated doom is absurd. We all know happy adopted children. We all know good parents who couldn't give birth themselves. We know that it is one of the particularly remarkable acts of human imagination that people can, with their whole hearts, love their adopted offspring, suffer with them, abide with them, go through the thick and the thin of it all and the biology doesn't matter compared to the depth and color, the shadings of the relationship. Adoption is an important issue here because as we think about motherhood, how it might be better lived, we have to know that parenting is an act of identification, of empathy, of imaginative connection with a soul that is not one's own and may not even carry one's own genetic code.

We tell ourselves stories about wolves that have brought up human babies. We have Romulus and Remus, Mowgli the jungle boy, and others. We invent stories for ourselves about animals who cannot imagine their own death but can still care for babies who are not of their species. If that sort of adoption seems possible if only in fantasy, how much more so do we know, really know, that the mothering is in the doing. It is an act of mental connection not genetic connection. If it were not possible for other mothers to mother, fathers to father, then all our stepfamilies would be doomed to endless failure and the women who long for children of their own could never be satisfied. This cannot be a feminist position. It leaves too many women wanting. It is too reductionist and simplistic. It places an emphasis on biology, the same biology we resisted in the early days of feminism, and raises the importance of genetics in a way that is fascist in origin and anti-nurture. It denigrates the power of environment to change and to heal. In America most of us hold to the ideal of the created self, the one that the mind has made, that hard work has produced, that imagination has spurred. So adoption is not a ripping asunder, it is a putting together.

I suspect that nothing should be secret unless the mother giving up the child wishes it so. The secrecy that bound up the adoption files of other eras was connected to the shame of birth outside of marriage. We are hardly a culture today overwhelmed by shame at illegitimate births. Legitimacy itself no longer seems a suitable term for a child's entry into life. Nevertheless there are children who cannot be mothered by their own mothers and they should be placed for adoption. The aura of something illicit taking place that the anti-adoption forces have fostered is not simply cruel but stems from a code of justice characterized by inflexibility. It belongs to the womb worshipers who think women who need to adopt are not natural mothers. Their cadre may be small. They may be birth mothers, surrogate or not, who regret having given their children away. There are unhappy adoptees. Their voices are irrational but loud. They have affected the public discourse about adoption.

The racial question in this country further complicates matters. Back in the sixties plenty of couples adopted children of other races. It was their well-intentioned gesture toward undoing racial distinctions family by family. The black-white identity splintering that followed made these adoptees look more like children without a country than citizens of one world. The retreat to racial typing in adoption has been a boon only to bigots of all colors. It made adoption seem like a raid on another tribe. Pity the children who lost homes, pity the parents who lost children in these ideological wars.

Women were the ones to suffer — the women who had children they could not care for but tried because adoption was not possible for their babies as well as the women who wanted babies that were suddenly unavailable just as infertility rates were rising. The new technologies in infertility have saved many women from barrenness just in the nick of time, but others were not so lucky. The anti-adoption purists are another group in America who want to tell women what they should or shouldn't do with their own family life. When I was growing up in the forties and fifties the neighborhood, the community was full of do's and don'ts, limiting life and love. Conformity was enforced by social pressures too terrible to recall. Everywhere there were girdles of the mind. The anti-adoption forces, like the anti-abortion groups, are filled once again with their self-righteousness and are ready to tell other women what to do. How cruel they are.

THE ZERO CHILD CHOICE

My women writers' group is meeting. We are going around the room, each woman in turn talking about her current work, what's on her mind. Suddenly a woman who has recently been divorced for the second time announces that the most important thing in her life is her grandchildren, the wonder of them. She turns on a woman who had chosen not to have children and says to her, "I don't know how you can stand it. Your life must seem so pointless." There is a gasp in the room. The woman without children does not seem flustered. But the rest of us mutter and object and many voices rise to point out the good work, the happy relationship with her spouse, the countless remarkable successes that the childless woman has achieved. The arrogance of it, the cruelty of it. Why should one way be assumed the right way?

Later as we go down in the elevator the woman without children says to me, "I haven't had any nasty darlings throw up in my lap. I haven't had to curtail my ambitions, or worry about saving money for college tuitions. My life has been lived for my own benefit. No whining child with problems has come between my husband and myself. We are each other's children." She looks at me with a *poor you* expression on her face and I realize that her choice of adjectives when talking about children would not have been mine, but her view is not without merit. Maybe it's envy of the path not taken that makes women tend to prod one another with small slights meant to establish their own superiority. Maybe it's just too hard to admit the other person may have something you don't have. On the issue of having a child, that cuts both ways because it seems to me that you're worn to a frazzle if you have children and you are deprived of major loves if you do not and so each woman may just as well choose her own rough journey. It was a very depressing evening because if there is no space for women to make and experience the consequences of different choices within the feminist movement, what hope is there that America will ever let us breathe easy in our multiple roles?

The ultimate end run around the nuclear family is to leave the field. Those women who in the early seventies protested the pronatalism in the culture and who felt that they were being pushed into having children they may not have wanted did indeed have a point. The woman who then desired life without a child was really regarded as a cracked vase, a cracked pot, no longer useful for its purpose. One of the liberations of feminism was surely the freedom to insist on choice as a meaningful matter. If you don't want to have a child, well then don't. Women are not all nurturers any more than men are. Some women will always find the idea of child care, child responsibility, child ties unappealing. So will some men. Their reasons are multiple and personal and probably more conscious than most women's reasons to bear children. The pity is that even today they often feel besieged by the rest of the baby-hungry culture. They feel alienated from their peers who do have children. This is not the culture's fault. The culture simply reflects the majority view. The culture has a stake as the species has a stake in reproducing itself. However, it's important that the multiplicity of ways to be human includes the option not to have children, no social penalty attached. When we grow kinder as a society we will easily be able to handle the natural variety of ways of living that exist among us, without whispers, unwanted interpretations, or name-calling.

I always will have a twinge of regret that I did not become Amelia Earhart soaring in the skies. I know that most women who have not had children also sometimes feel regret. In the elevator I want to launch into a speech about what my children have given my life, I want to map out my inner landscape, my dearest memories. But I stop myself. There is no need to justify one's life by insisting it is better than someone else's. It probably isn't. It is the presence of our regrets that makes us intolerant, self-justifying, and sharp-edged on this subject and others.

Most of my not so nuclear family has gathered for a Thanksgiving dinner. The daughter at school in Chicago has arrived. My step-daughter, her husband, and her two boys are in the living room. Another daughter and her boyfriend are draining packages of frozen spinach in the kitchen. My oldest daughter is complaining that the youngest is dressed like a throwback to the sixties. The youngest is insulted. The two sisters closest to each other, my two youngest daughters, are having a terrible fight. I don't know exactly what the fight is about. I think the younger one praised someone who had been unfriendly to the older one. They had been eager to see each other. They speak almost every day for a long time on the phone. Now that they are under the same roof the tension is so thick I'm nearly nauseated. Chords of sullenness sound through the rooms of the house. The younger one is no longer humble and the older one, used to exercising an easy dominance, is disgruntled. My stepson-in-law doesn't like where we live. He prefers the mountains. My stepdaughter is mad at me. I can tell by the way she bites her lip and avoids my eye. Perhaps she thinks I have not paid enough attention to her children. But there is the meal to prepare and the other voices to listen to. My husband is happily stuffing the turkey. I want the two younger daughters to end their fight. The sharp sun hits the windows like a smack in the face. My stepson-in-law makes fun of my two younger daughters. They are not amused. My daughter's boyfriend talks to me about his latest project. Is he permanent or temporary? Both of us are wondering. If I were him I might make a quick exit. The smell of cranberry bread and pumpkin pie floats up the stairs where I am now sitting with the little boys who announce that they hate turkey and will eat nothing at dinner but Cheerios.

Later we sit down to the meal, the fights are over. Suddenly there is a general glow of mutual affection in the room. The day is darkening, shadows fall obscuring parts of the room, blurring the edges of tables and lamps. We light the candles. If you don't look in the corners, a person could even be happy at least for a while.

The patched-together nuclear family is not necessarily a good place to get out of the cold but where else would we go? My children will come home until they don't anymore. I wish I could edit their memories. My husband carves the bird. My stepdaughter smiles at me. My stepson-in-law tells me something interesting about his work. My younger daughters laugh together at some shared joke. My husband remembers not to make rude remarks about my stepson-in-law's favorite football team. My oldest daughter talks about the time she and my stepdaughter sold lemonade from a stand by the side of the road. Someday I will get used to the fact that families are like nature, implacable but all there is. The little boys meant what they said. They eat only Cheerios but that's all right.

PART V

THE REAL WORLD:
WHAT PRICE IS PAID

Maybe if the parenting of infants changed, the anguish that teen-agers experience and the anguish they bring to the home would also diminish. It generally isn't until the children enter their teen years that Oedipus demands full payment. Neither the mommy-and-daddy family nor the single-parent family makes the transition into adulthood a pure joy. The hostility built into the nuclear family erupts as the children prepare to separate from the home. In my house all hell broke loose.

My oldest daughter began to shout at me, "You hate me," when I tried to find out where she was and what she was doing. Soon enough I could feel her pulling far away from me, onto street corners, into places I couldn't imagine. She slept all day and stayed up all night. She left me apologetic poems on the windowsill. The window was open and she was out. The sweet round flesh of childhood was gone and in its place smoke and fury, whirl and run. "Help her," I said to another psychiatrist as he offered me his box of tissues. Autonomy was her desire, drug dependence her achieve-ment. I felt her reaching for me even as she was slipping away faster and faster. I saw her once on our corner, dark and lithe, eyes flashing, smoking a cigarette under a lamp. She was wearing some-thing yellow, tight, the tattoo on her shoulder showed, a fish skele-ton with a red eye. Her lips were painted dark red like my mother's. There were black circles under her eyes. She was beautiful but not good: a moth with golden wings headed right for the bright light. She was already singed. There were thick burn scars on her arm where she had leaned against the grill of a hot dog vendor's cart.

How does a mother let go? It certainly used to be true that women spent their twenties and early thirties in child rearing and by the time the children were off to college they were left behind professionally. They were vacant, limp, lacking training, and way behind in all the skills of dealing in the workplace. It used to be that these women were shelved matrons. That, we all know, was a disaster. It caused this awful empty nest syndrome, which really was a euphemism for a woman's empty head. Now of course the working woman, the creative woman, is supposed to regard her children's growth and departure from the house as a sort of welcome sign of a job well done, a kind of reward for years of buying food in bulk. Most women, however, still find the passage difficult. They do not clear out the children's room and sweep up the old beer cans left under the bed and go out and waltz the night away.

Now that the chips are played and my mother role has shrunk to what I can imagine, what I anticipate, a little conversation in the late night, moments of shoring up sinking egos, moments of harping, scolding, nagging (Please stop smoking, please gain a few pounds, please wear a warm coat, give your heart cautiously, don't be too careful. You need a haircut. Please don't cut your hair), I am grateful to have my work to fill my time. What if I were just staring out the window, just waiting for the phone to ring, what if I were out shopping for hats or playing cards, what if I had no further function but like a flower wilting in the vase just dried on my stem? There is no way to keep the illusion of daily usefulness the way it was when the children were home. Now there is only one's work, one's mind, one's enjoyment of one's own life for its own sake. Is that in fact enough? I'm not sure. I do know that it is better not to have the sum of one's worth in the bank of motherhood. The dividends are not so dependable and the coupon clipping not so dignified.

We go to my youngest daughter's college graduation. This will be our last. The total funds spent on higher education could have bought us a mansion by the sea or so I imagine. It rains on the outdoor ceremony. We sit on folding chairs, the umbrella raised, and listen to the speeches, not minding the sonorous tone, not minding the repetition of names, the endless applause. The lawyers, the doctors, the philosophers rise and at last the undergraduates throw their hats into the air like so many blackbirds that rise but do not soar. I see the other families all dressed up, some holding plastic bags over their heads to ward off the rain, flowers for their graduates clutched against their raincoats. I see the younger brothers and sisters running around in the aisles. I see the fathers in their best suits, mothers tucking away the program in their purses, saving it for the treasure box of first haircuts, baby pictures. There is mud around my feet as I raise my camera. She is impatient to be gone, to kiss her friends, to scream and shout and avoid questions of the shaky future, the unknown ahead. Reluctantly she poses for my camera. "Hurry up, hurry up," she says, "the robes have to be returned." The picture will show her irritation, her smile not quite real. "Wait, wait," I want to say. "Look back, look back, you won't turn to salt," I want to say. I intended not to cry, I cry, a good long nose-turning-red, eyes-puffy cry that has to do with time's indifference to my welfare. I see her with her friends. They are drinking champagne, taking swigs from a bottle they pass around. I know that they are not as happy as they seem and that I am happier than I seem.

I had a career when my children all began to move away. I was not left with only the photo albums and memories of a time when I was needed, my hands, my voice, my decisions. Like most of today's mothers I was glad to turn more of my attention to my work, glad not to have to spend so much time planning, watching, thinking about the children. However, the letting go was still hard. The switch from being the person at the center of their lives to being the last to know, the one that they moved behind, around, was hard, painful, and not a relief at all. If I had listened to the noise in my head at the time I would have heard a constant tearing, a ripping, searing sound as their lives became their own.

In the textbooks this all sounds easy. The psychologists who tell us about adolescence make it sound like a rational step along the path to maturity. They don't tell you about the six kinds of hell it really is, not all the time but enough of the time. They don't tell you how to make yourself composed when you are frightened, how to let them be and still hold them dear. The entire business of mothering simply doesn't stop because a child is eighteen, twenty-two, thirty-four, forty-two. We learn to be gracious. We learn to pay attention to our own interests. We learn not to listen for the telephone or wait for letters. But returning entirely into one's own skin the way one owned oneself before having children is virtually impossible. If amputees have feelings in their phantom limbs, think how mothers feel about their phantom children. Mothering as we do it in this society now is a lifetime habit, a kind of addiction that you never get free of, just as we speak of Catholics never being able to truly leave the church, just as Jews can only pretend indifference, so mothers even more carry on.

The social image of the middle-aged mother is no comfort. Feminism has not made the woman past her prime into an object of envy (Gloria Steinem excepted). She is still considered sexless, unlike the male of the same age, no longer beautiful, her powers dying on the vine. If she has succeeded in work she may take comfort in her position in the world, but her womanliness is not at high tide, regardless of how the juices may run in her imagination. She is a biological creature with no further biological potential. Despite what the feminist movement says, this affects her power in the world. You can't dismiss anatomy with a wave of a wand. We are creatures designed for evolution's purpose. Our social constructs include the biological imperatives. It's not what feminists would wish but it is so. The women's movement has done much to ease this condition. But something in the way we were mothers makes it impossible for us to regain the beauty of a freestanding human being: we are more like ghosts attending a feast after our death, haunting the happy guests. It is possible that if we shift the psychological experience of mothering to one of co-parenting, truly, in every aspect, this desexifying of the woman, this sense of endless connection to a child who is in fact moving off will shift. One would hope so.

At dusk when the grey light hits the ground like promises unkept I sometimes think:

One day one of my daughters is almost statistically bound to develop breast cancer. I think of them in the bath, little girls with soap foaming over their chests. Fear rises.

One day one of them may develop multiple sclerosis: Evil Eye look away. I remember my mother spitting, crossing the street, the tarot cards spread on the table. Being rational I have no defenses against the Evil Eye.

One day they may break up with the boyfriends or the husbands they now seem to love. Their lives will be turned upside down. They'll need courage to reweave their place.

I feel it like a chill on a damp day by the ocean. It sits in my heart chanting: loss, loss.

What if the men they love become depressed, alcoholic, crazed?

What if they are betrayed or if the men fail at their work? What if the men they love do not deserve their love? I could bear this for myself. I could not bear it for them. What if they can't have children?

What if they have children but something is terribly wrong. Autism. Retardation. Limb malformation. Heart trouble. Cystic fibrosis. Deafness. Blindness. The entire March of Dimes parades through my head. I hear the tree falling in the forest even though I am not there. "Not that," I would pray if it were my habit.

What if the ones who are not yet set economically do not find the way? What if no jobs exist for them? They will, they will. I reassure myself. What if they are robbed and killed on the subway late at night? What if the one who hasn't yet given up cigarettes develops lung cancer or emphysema? Deeply I breathe myself as if my lungs could help her.

What if a disaster strikes them that I cannot even imagine? I try to stop my imagination but under the crack in the door I have rushed to close slip shadows of foreboding.

One of my stepdaughters has graduated from medical school. My father would have gone pale with shock. Would my mother have believed it? My brother grumbles. He doesn't like the specialty she has picked. He knows I'm evening an old score. She complains. Is this what she really wanted? The achievement that seemed so far away in the fifties is now so routine that she can afford an identity crisis. I am puffed up, my side triumphant, my feminism no longer desire but fact. I want her to have power. To use her title, to put M.D. on her car, on her door, on her listing in the telephone book. She doesn't care at all. I have turned into an authoritarian type. I want her to have rank and to pull it. "Hah," I say to my brother, "move over," I say to him. I may even have said it aloud. It took me awhile but I got here. I feel smug like an immigrant mother whose son has become a doctor. I want to stand on the rooftop of my childhood home and shout out the news. This little girl with the big blue eyes and the tiny hands and feet, look what she has done. Victory is ours. Not quite mine but close enough. I can hug a member of the revolutionary cadre. Never mind that she doesn't see herself as a revolutionary. She is thinking about when to have children and where to buy a wedding dress. We are on different Ferris wheels and our cars pass each other in the sky. Mine is going down. We wave. Ah well. Yes, I know good feminists were not supposed to achieve vicariously. The point of the feminist consciousness raised was that each woman had a right to her own life, choices and all, and should achieve herself, not through her children's report cards. But it's not just that old habits die hard, it's that once you're invested in a child its life becomes imaginatively, powerfully fused with yours. This is what frightens them sometimes. They don't want the baggage. They don't want to carry a mother or a stepmother wherever they go and yet we're always jumping on their backs. Take us this way, take us that way.

The late years of motherhood are also a time of hard admissions. What is spilt milk is unrecoverable. Mistakes made cannot be undone. Time does not go backward except in the imagination. In a corner of my mind I've kept my fertility alive, only to sneak it out occasionally in dreams. It still is there. Even though at age fifty-four I had a hysterectomy and the capacity to bear children was then concretely gone. Grief was short. I thought I had long ago banished the wish for another pregnancy from my mind. I had other things to do besides mope about the inevitable direction of living creatures. But I found myself staring at the young Orthodox women who live in my neighborhood, who had four, five, six small children around them. The boys had velvet yarmulkes and on holidays they wore dark suits and the girls wore long dresses. Envy was what I felt for the fertility, for the bearing of the child, for the round pregnant bellies, for the strollers packed with doubles or children so close in age that neither could walk alone. Envy I felt for the broods that were still growing. I could still comment on life but I could no longer create it. Ah well. I knew that this envy that swept over me was sentimental in part, the women were exhausted, their bodies weary, their families fraught with all the tensions that afflict everyone else. I knew that as these children grew they would find sorrows, misunderstandings, conflict with parents and conflict with siblings, just like John Updike's families in white America, just like Alice Walker's families in the black South. The solution to our human woes is certainly not a population explosion. On the other hand, how grand they look, those women with their many children.

The point of feminist politics was always to give women fuller, better lives, a chance for equality with men and an opportunity to use all of their human potential. It's all very well in the abstract to speak of the virtues of motherhood like the flowers sent from across the country on Mother's Day, but up close, in the thick of it, we have to consider, is it worth it, what does it do to us, how exactly does it make us feel. Because the emotions good and bad of the common mother are the building blocks of our next political direction. Feminism, which was all about self-fulfillment, forgot that giving up some of the self, which is necessary for motherhood, is part of most women's self-fulfillment, another one of God's not so funny jokes.

Not have a child, not ever to have a child, the idea echoes down the corridors of my mind as if I were playing with fire, arsonist of my life. To conceive and bear a child alters, reframes, collapses the old self and sets all kinds of limits on the new. I can never know who I would have been had I not had my first, second, third child, or for that matter what would have become of me if I had not been a stepmother. If I'd had no children would I have written better books, would I have had a more adventurous life, would I have traveled to Tibet or seen the giraffes run on the African veldt, seen the sun set on the Parthenon? Would I be a better friend to my friends, would my love life have taken more curves, who would I know, what would I say or think? Would I be a politician, a talk show host, a lady with dogs or cats or clean upholstery? This is not a question that has an answer.

Some days it seems to me that I might have been more than I am if I had not become a self divided among others, one ear listening for a cry, one eye following the fate of another, one heart divided in many pieces, many times more vulnerable to fortune's turn, the sound of an ambulance five blocks away, the bad breaks and steep falls of a being that is as dear to you as yourself but is not yourself. Some days it certainly seems to me that I might have remembered to put lotion on my face, exercised daily, put money away in the bank if I had not had children. Other days I have no interest in those things and I think that without my children, whatever I might be, I would be less, diminished, reduced, imprisoned inside my own skin, a person who will not leave a forward trace, the trail would only wind back. Some days I think if I had not had my children I would surely have gone mad, paced the inside of my mind till I knew every cranny and crack and, like a flower plucked by its roots, thirst for the ground, dream of the soil, wilt in the sun. Sometimes I think that if I had not had children I would never have grown up, that I would always be watching my own bubbles as if I were a goldfish swimming in a bowl. It is true that having children is a sanding of the ego, a rubbing down of pride, a kind of placing in proportion one's ambitions, defusing the grandiose, cutting back the unreal. However, it may not always be a positive thing to grow up, to regard oneself as light on the way to being extinguished rather than as a comet shooting across the applauding night sky. Just because psychiatrists make such a fuss about maturity that does not mean that immaturity might not be, after all, the preferable condition. The truth is that I am not sure if having children is good or bad for one's happiness, good or bad for one's creativity, all I know is that conception brought to term or not is never forgotten, and congratulations to a new mother is something of an oversimplification.

IS MOTHERHOOD BAD FOR ART AND INVENTION?

Of course, just because you can have your own child doesn't mean you should. How does motherhood affect our creativity? Is there some devil's bargain here, give me a child and I will stop drawing, composing, writing? Is the fact that all the great women writers of the nineteenth century abstained from childbearing a mere coincidence or a significant clue? Certainly Jane Austen, George Eliot, the Brontës, America's Emily Dickinson and Edith Wharton were not weighed down with offspring. Virginia Woolf, the only writer in the twentieth century whose reputation stands up to James Joyce and Marcel Proust, did not have children either. Kate Chopin's heroine Daisy in *The Awakening* begins to draw, to respond to music, color, as she sends her sons away and decides that she has no interest in mothering them. The great Southern female literary voices that appeared in the postwar era included Eudora Welty, Carson McCullers, and Flannery O'Connor, all of them women without children. Mary McCarthy had a child but barely raised him. She declared openly her unmaternal nature.

Ellen Glasgow reports in her autobiography that when she consulted a doctor on some minor physical complaint he said, "The best advice I can give you is to stop writing and go back to the South and have some babies. The greatest woman is not the woman who has written the finest book, but the woman who has had the finest babies." Sexist, old-fashioned, and probably ridiculous as this remark now seems, the thought hangs around in our heads. It takes the form of either/or. It assumes that women are the ones most involved with the baby. No one would ever have said this to a man.

It is assumed that his reproductive life history is irrelevant to his creative work and no comparisons are needed or expected. It would be easy to ignore this as the prattle of dismissed generations. But women do pick up the prejudices against them in their culture and repeat them like so many performing parrots. I stopped working when my children were ill, not so much because I was needed every second by the bedside but because my concentration was gone, anxiety held me captive. At those times my work seemed unimportant. I know that when I dried my children with a towel, feeling their round limbs in my hands, I felt waves of contentment that no paragraph well done could bring me. As they got older I began to browse in bookstores, would they like this one or that one. I began to check the theater listings, this or that. I watched *Peter Pan* with them at my side. Wonder returned to me through their wonder. Better than writing, better than anything.

Isadora Duncan, a dancer who broke a few molds, had this to say about the first flames of feminism that were flickering across America's avant-garde. "Oh, women, what is the good of us learning to become lawyers, painters or sculptors, when this miracle [of birth] exists? Now I know this tremendous love, surpassing the love of men. I was stretched and bleeding, torn and helpless while the little being sucked and howled, life, life, life! Give me life. Oh where was my art, my art or any art? But what did I care for art! I felt I was a god, superior to any artist." Poor always overwrought Isadora Duncan whose children were drowned as the car they were riding in sank into the Seine, who herself was always larger than truth, emotions blown up with intensity if not purity. Isadora who did nothing because it was conventional uttered those conventional words when she gave birth.

An entire feminist movement has come to pass since Isadora wore her last toga, got into a sports car in Nice with an Italian boyfriend, and flipped her long scarf over her shoulder only to have it wind itself around the wheels and snap her neck as the car began to move. Some sixty years later in 1985 Mary Gordon writes in the *New York Times Book Review* as she is about to give birth to her second child, "It is impossible for me to believe that anything I write could have a fraction of the importance of this child growing inside of me or of the child who lies now her head on my belly with the sweet yet offhand stoicism of a sick child." No one asked Mary Gordon to measure her children against her books. It is a habit women come to naturally. Men don't.

This whole discussion makes me squirm. I know where the argument is leading. Either I should not have had children and made my books the object of my affections or I should have paid more attention to my children, had a few more of them, and let my work wait. Either way I feel coerced, not happy. Like Mary Gordon and Isadora Duncan I hold my children more important to me than any work I might accomplish. I know this is not the correct feminist position. And yet it seems so universal, so prevalent that I can't help believe that its truth lies in some biological force that won't be reasoned with, that has no agenda other than its own (species) survival, and there's no use fighting it because it comes back at you again and again if you try to avoid it. Even a feminist scholar at the University of Chicago, Virginia Held, has said, "Creating new human persons and new human personalities with new thoughts and attitudes is as creative an activity as humans are involved in anywhere."

Of course it may be that great art requires a kind of monomania, an absorption so intense that children would be interferences, beside the point. It may be that great art is made by men and women who are exempt from the pull of ordinariness. The artists we admire may all be half mad. I doubt they have any choice in the matter. Who would choose to be an artist when they could be just a man or a woman living an ordinary life? Most of us would prefer ordinary satisfactions along with ordinary pain. Possibly I say that because I'm a woman lacking in ambition. Possibly I say that because I have seen so many lives consumed in the pursuit of great art. That passion is not unconnected to alcoholism and madness and while great art comforts us all its creators are frequently moral freaks. Ambition is certainly not an exclusively male characteristic but in its extreme, a desire to challenge the gods, it may be a condition incompatible with child care.

This is why the "I'm just a mom" answer ("What do you do?") is so grating. I can answer that question with a proper professional I.D. but I know that in ways that really count I too am "just a mom." So is Mary Gordon and most of the other women I know. Even after our children are grown, even when we have grandchildren (I will show you the pictures of my step-grandchildren just the way the ladies around my mother's canasta table showed theirs), this sense of identity, of meaning, lies with our children.

However, it isn't a full-time occupation. It certainly doesn't fill all one's hours or days. It doesn't prevent all the other work one does. It never has. That child rearing may be the center of the soul does not mean that there isn't room for other things. There is time enough in one life to find many different kinds of satisfactions and satisfy many different kinds of necessities. It has done us no service to have work opposed to our child rearing. It has done us no service to make child rearing the mother's thing like some compensation, a bone tossed to keep the distaff side content, to keep the generations coming.

How nice if men would feel this child necessity too. How nice if they would experience some jarring of their most ambitious grandiose dreams with their desire to reproduce. They don't have swelling bellies or lactating breasts. They don't carry the fetus or expel the baby into the world. Nevertheless, the creation is theirs too. I resent work vs. child arguments because both are possible, both are necessary to most of us, both make the world turn round. Both gratify our always thirsty egos. Both require the most individual personal stamp of our souls. Having said that, having children is more important than anything else we humans do, primary even. Then we can go back to our nondomestic work.

Still, a voice inside keeps on asking: Does having children strain or drain the creative force, does it weaken ambition?

Sylvia Plath writes a poem called "Metaphors" in 1959. In it she plays with the clichés we have about pregnant women, the sense of a body turning large, uncomfortable, bestial, primal, fertile, a little sour like a green apple, ridiculous like a melon on its tendrils, natural and unnatural at the same time, and beyond everything else, "Boarded the train there's no getting off," too late to change your mind, the process is in control. Plath has lost hers.

Sylvia Plath was an artist who had a clinical depression before her children were born and told us about it in a novel, *The Bell Jar*. In this autobiographical story of her hospitalization and partial recovery she tells us how disgusting she finds birth to be. The fifties were a time in America when so much about the body was secret and dangerous that the facts of sex and birth did indeed seem unholy, frightening, and disgusting. The fear we all had that our menstrual blood might show, that nipples might peep through a sweater, that body hair or sweat might be apparent to a watching male was part of our self-dislike, our inability to come to terms with nature's intention for women. In a misogynist world this was reasonable. In the more vulnerable among us these body secrets became unbearable.

Sylvia Plath's children, like her poems which were also hers to tend, could not save her and depression returned. Pulled toward death she abandoned her children. In her depression she found her babies far too heavy to carry, and their needs, encroaching as they were on her needs, were not enough to stop her from ending her life and may perhaps have contributed to her final despair. This was a tragedy, not a totally rare one, as mothers of all sorts, mothers who don't write poetry, also fall prey to postnatal depressions or suffer from other mental illnesses. The interesting part of this story is that Sylvia Plath has become a heroine in the feminist movement.

The culture has shifted. The obvious neurosis-breeding attitudes toward the body that prevailed in the fifties (menstruation was referred to as the curse) have been sanitized for the nineties but it seems to me that Sylvia Plath, going mad from an illness then virtually nontreatable, is a sad soul, not a heroic one. To make so much of her life mocks the others who held on, who fought their way through for their children, who didn't die.

Depression is a disguise that rage wears. Susan Smith, who drowned her own two boys instead of killing herself, performed an act close to Sylvia Plath's, a demon cousin of the same. When a mother turns on her children the world shakes and screams. This is not patriarchy speaking. It is the child that cries. It is our memory of ourselves as children that spurs our indignation: How could she? The feminist movement eager for deifications made more of Sylvia Plath than I would have. It makes as much sense to me as glorifying Susan Smith, turning her into Kali and putting burnt offerings in front of her jail cell. Sylvia Plath's postmortem fame did not arise simply from the quality of her poetry, which is so enhanced by a political groupie aura that it becomes hard to judge the poems for themselves. If they were not attached to the romance of death, to the thought of a young poet fleeing her betrayer poet-husband, suffering from griefs caused by a lost daddy, overtones of Oedipal love and hate rising in the background, they might have dropped down the black hole which has sucked in many other poets. Her life and her poetry, resonant with foreshadowing of suicide, gas, ovens, grandiose references to the Holocaust and Hansel and Gretel, have become a myth, a feminist parable. If she had not become an emblem, a martyr to the stupidity of an indifferent world of husbands, fathers, psychiatrists which still confined women to secondary places, what would we think of the poems? If they were written by a woman whose suffering was less dramatic and whose story was less public would we still find them art and make a cult figure out of their author?

The sad fact is that Sylvia Plath is a heroine partially because she is a sufferer and because she can be seen as a victim. The fact that two babies were in the apartment in which she released the gas that killed her has not stopped some feminists from seeing her as a victim of male cruelty. For me, however, she will forever be a woman with an illness so horrendous that she couldn't see or care about the separate reality of the lives she had created. She got off the train she had boarded before it arrived at its final destination. To do so was not a victorious act, nor a courageous act, nor a sign of uncommon insight. It was rather the desperate flight of a wounded woman who couldn't or wouldn't go on. She is neither heroic nor romantic. She is pathetic. She allowed or couldn't help but allow her own inner life to deny the budding personhood of her small children. I wouldn't make such a point about this here except that some feminists, in their easy assumption that children are part of some patriarchal scheme to enslave, have allowed a woman who left her children through voluntary death to become a major moral force. Barely a word is said about what the children experienced, calling out to their mother in the early hours of the morning, echoes of silence where a parent should be. In the balancing act of self vs. child Sylvia Plath falls down, and while we can sympathize, understand, regret, we cannot forget that she, as an abdicating mother, hurt the innocent in ways we cannot admire. For a mother to leave her children even through self-destruction is shocking. Our commitment is to stay through thick and thin, to let the child's need take precedence over our own. Sylvia Plath may or may not be a remarkable poet. What she is not is a heroine. She had a tragic illness which itself may have led her toward her poetry, but she did not have the will to fight for her children's happiness. She quit, and that, while it can be understood, is not heroic.

We also have the poetry of Anne Sexton which rings with self-absorption, a loud outraged cry that her role as a wife and mother stifled her, and we have heard from her children how she used them emotionally and even sexually in an erratic roller coaster of love and hate, ending in her suicide. These poets (along with their male colleagues Lowell, Berryman, Schwartz) suffered from mental illness, better treated today with the modern pharmacopoeia but still occasionally lethal and always destructive of the mothering self, the she who would pick up, embrace, interrupt herself, turn away from inner thoughts, turn attention outward. It became a truism in the women's movement that being a mother was a bad thing for one's art. Motherhood consumed, it shifted focus, it demanded that the time spent alone be brief. Motherhood imposed on art and ate up the soul rather like the dragons who gobbled down ships that wandered off the ocean's edge on our earliest maps.

Tillie Olsen, who wrote one extraordinary book of stories including the classic "Tell Me a Riddle," then wrote a book called *Silences* in which she explained how her artistic drive, her needs had been chased away by the voices of her children, by the demands, and they are never minor, of domestic life. Many of us in the seventies thought that motherhood was probably not the way to artistic success. Men had always been fathers and artists too. They did not carry the primary responsibility for their offspring. They were never the primary psychological parent so their responsibility, financial and worldly, barely claimed their attention. The male writers of the fifties and sixties were with some exceptions always divorcing wives, leaving their progeny behind while they went on to the next woman, who would ofttimes both bear their next child and appear in their next novel. Unfair.

After my writer husband left I decided to try my own gift and write a novel. It doesn't take much courage to begin a novel when no one is looking at you. It's rather like testing out a recipe for a soufflé in your kitchen at midnight, no guests expected. I bought a notebook and began. I wrote when my baby was taking a nap. I wrote in the playground looking up from time to time to be sure she was still there and hadn't fallen off anything. I wrote waiting in line in the supermarket. I wrote at night with her sleeping in the bed beside me. She was afraid of the dark so we kept all the lights on all night. I was able to write despite having a child. However, that covers only the mechanics of the matter. How well I was able to write is another story. Would my first novel have been better if I had not had a child? That's one of those questions that can't be answered. What can be said is that many mothers have written books, poems, scripts. Women's voices are now participating in all forms of cultural dialogue and many of those women are mothers. What has to be admitted is that American writers of the fifties, sixties, seventies, eighties, and nineties, with the exception of black women, have not achieved as a group, even as individuals, the same level of genius as the men. Or does it just seem so? The males, Updike, Walker Percy, Cheever, Malamud, Roth, Bellow, Mailer, Heller, Barth, Styron, Doctorow, dominate the scene, as did the men in the generation before them, Fitzgerald, Hemingway, Steinbeck, Dos Passos, Faulkner, Saroyan, Sinclair Lewis.

Of course these fellows got all the awards and all the attention. Perhaps the appearance of male genius as weightier on the whole than the female's is an artifice, a result of the way we view things, not a reality at all. Perhaps the trouble with female genius is not that it is diverted to the womb but that it is overlooked when it appears. I prefer to think of women's creativity as a continuum. It starts with biology, it can result in a child, it can result in a book, or both. Women's literary work tends to be slimmer, plotted less like a Napoleonic campaign and more like a dinner party at which everyone drank too much or talked too much, more domestic in focus, but nonetheless electric. It hits like a lightning bolt when carefully aimed. Women's fiction may in fact be more suited to the modern novel, which finds its subject right under the ordinary, beneath the surface of spoken thought, in the resonances of our common condition. Think of Toni Morrison, Alice Munro, Margaret Atwood, Grace Paley, Jane Smiley, E. Annie Proulx, Pat Barker, A. S. Byatt.

Feminists looking on the art of other generations could say that the best women writers were like men, unencumbered by children. Their babies were sublimated and transformed into work on the printed page. Feminists who felt unfriendly toward motherhood could say that raising a child was an obstacle to achievement, an apron string that tied the spirit to the mundane and prevented imagination from finding its own way to Mount Olympus. If we knew this to be true we'd have to decide if it was the conditions of women in other times that made this so or if it was something in the biological condition of pregnancy, lactating, caring for a child that drained the female resources and would limit women's artistic gifts no matter how feminist the society around them.

Optimism brings us to the conclusion that once women and men participate equally in child care we will have women who become as extraordinary as Shakespeare and Dickens who are also mothers increasing our pool of genius, resources for us all. My anxious soul tells me otherwise. It may be true that the female biological story in some way limits the woman artist with children. It is not a matter of finding quiet time to do the work. That, difficult as it is, can be managed. The more serious problem is that she cannot close herself off. She cannot stop her heart from beating with her child's. Her attention is divided and her emotional energy, the soil of creation, is constantly depleted. Perhaps this puts an outer limit on her creation. Time will tell.

The only thing I know for sure is that I would rather have a child than a book. I would rather have a warm-blooded body to carry my message to the world than the most perfect of artistic creations issued in my name. I do not think this makes me anti-feminist or opposed to female achievement, it is just a statement of priorities, one that I have found rings true in every corner of my being. I know that no male writer would say that, at least not yet. Does that make their books better or worse? It could be my view because I was a child in the forties. It could be my view because I brought the fifties along with me into the rest of my life and consciousness rises only as high as the arms of the individual can lift it. It could be I am typical of most men and women who are destined not to change the cultural currents but simply to swim awkwardly in them.

Women writers are hardly the only ones who wonder if their creativity, if their drive to excel, will be weakened by child care. We all want to stay in the race whatever our worldly ambitions might be. Children should not be a limitation on half of us if they carry forward the humanity of all of us. But what if they truly are?

In the nineteen fifties the short story turned to the handwriting on the wall of suburban marriage. Again and again we read the story about the wandering man, the woman who fell in love with the tennis pro, the martini drinkers who pined away after each other's wives, dancing with them at the club. If one begins at the beginning of the fifties and reads through every issue of the *New Yorker* until yesterday, some forty-five years' worth, one's head would be full of the disappointment man causes woman and woman causes man. It is rare indeed to find fictional reports of that disappointment which is at least as common: child disappoints parent, in particular the mother. But surely writers know this tale well enough. The best writing seems to have it the other way around. Parent disappoints child. That we have in first novels. Again and again the sensitive kid watches parents create havoc, ruin marriages, drift off, abandon love, in Salinger and Roth, in Cormac McCarthy and Alice Walker. The pernicious footfall of the adults going about their business haunts our literary experiences. To see from the parent's point of view children fouling things up is rare. Which isn't to say that outside of fiction it doesn't happen all the time.

Surveys have been done that report that children are bad for marriage. Adolescent children present great obstacles to the parents' marriage. The sociological surveys seem to indicate that childless marriages that do survive produce more partners satisfied with themselves. Whatever questions were asked we know that this kind of survey is not a subtle instrument and cannot measure the inner experience of people who may be angry at a child one day and delighted the next, and the sum total of their emotional relationship cannot be given a number or quantified by a stranger. However, it seems reasonable to me that childless marriages would be steadier, less caught in panics, upheavals, reproaches, fears. Whether or not that amounts to a happier marriage is a more complicated question. By those standards happiest of all perhaps is the person who never marries, never leaves home, is without ambition in the outside world, and passes his or her days like the family dog, sleeping contentedly on the porch, flicking flies away with its tail.

There are things one learns through being a mother, things one has by being a mother that are not measurable on the charts. Here is Mary Gordon writing about nursing an infant: "Perfectly still, almost without volition, I nourish. A film of moisture covers my flesh and my son's. Both of us drift in and out of sleep. I could be any woman lying there. There is nothing original about me. I am ancient, repetitive. In a life devoted to originality I adore the animal's predictability. The pleasures of instinct are more real than any I would ever have known." This last sentence is not quite accurate because there are instincts that women know without bearing children. Sex, sleeping when tired, eating when hungry, screaming when mad, crying when sad are a few of them. What I think she means primarily is the melting of ego, the closeness to human process, the fact of being unoriginal, animal-like, is experienced as having entered a sacred spot and becomes one of those revelations that leaves behind altering perspectives. The bond of woman to child carries with it the potential bond of woman to humanity, of earthlings to space, of dust to dust. It has a hint of death in it. It is holy knowledge.

PRIDE AND FEAR: BEYOND THE BORDERS OF THE SELF

Then there is pride. My oldest daughter won a poetry contest for the entire school. She was eleven. Her poem was a strange, sad poem about death and trees on a Vermont mountain. I read it over and over. I put it in my library. I put it by my bed. I brought her Emily Dickinson. I brought her Langston Hughes. For every writer there is a wall, the wall is just in a different place for each of us. The wall is placed at the far border of one's own gift. It can't be climbed. It's a wall that blocks the vision, that stops language short, that makes you repeat yourself, find clumsy metaphors, stumble. I thought my daughter had climbed over my wall. There she is on the other side waving at me. I was proud. I felt like a poor woman whose daughter has married a rich man. The journey though hard was worth it. The next generation would arrive.

Then there is shame. On the day of her high school graduation where she is to receive the English prize we stand on the steps before the ceremony and a friend of hers comes by. The friend asks a question. It's about the quality of the drugs used the night before. I am ashamed. I am afraid. I know this means that promises have been broken but I don't know what to do. Suddenly the white graduation dress is not so beautiful, the clear air stifles. I use my camera but I forget to develop the pictures and eventually the film is lost. I remember the day well enough.

I do develop the film though when my youngest daughter enters the local horse show that summer we spend in Connecticut. There she is, a black velvet hat on her head, strap under her chin, on a large animal, jumping over a fence. Her face is tense, intent. Her small body controlled, determined, leaning forward just right. Both her grandfathers arrived in this country steerage class. I see her now in someone else's America, rancher, animal lover, reins held just so. She is not born to horses and our subculture regards this sport with an old class antagonism that does not disappear in a mere generation or two. Nevertheless the possibilities open. Any place under the big sky could be hers. I watch the fence, it seems too high. I want to call out, don't do it. She does it. The watching crowd applauds. The smell of hay, of horse, of sweat comes through the air. Huge black flies buzz around. I see her hands clutching her blue ribbon and her eyes burning from deep within. God, I am happy. So happy I can't imagine that the feeling won't last a lifetime through, so happy I can't remember ever being less than happy. Later that summer when she falls off a horse and we are in a small-town hospital waiting for the report of the X rays (does she have a concussion?), I think that riding is for fools and Cossacks. As I sit there waiting for the doctor my fear turns me to stone, grey granite, dull. I hardly breathe. I am fed up with breathing. How would I count my life's condition that Connecticut summer? Acute would be the answer. But acute is not a measurement.

Things I have been proud of in my two younger children:

The way they worked at a food pantry, Friday after Friday, through their high school years.

The way they argued with me. The cartload of paintings, jewelry, clayworks they gave me. The plays they were in at school. The plays they put on at home. The inventions, creations, costumes.

The way they protested their school's investments in apartheid South Africa.

The way they loved their friends.

The way they always wanted to do things by themselves.

The way they understand technology: answering machines, VCRs, computers.

The technical languages they speak, graduate school
   signifiers, Foucault, Lacan, Derrida.
The way they dance, as if they were possessed, natives of a
   land I never even visited.
The way they love, intensely, with heartbreak, without
   caution.

Things my two younger children have done that frightened me:

Stayed out at night without telling me where they were.
Smoked: Camel cigarette packs found under the cushions.
Had trouble recovering from a broken relationship.
Threatened to take a year off from college and travel around
   America on a motorcycle.
While in high school threatened to go to Nicaragua with a
   priest who had designed a peace program and work in a
   village in an area where the contras were active.
Not eaten enough and grown alarmingly thin.

Always I am wondering, are they strong, will they make the right
decisions about this course of study, that boyfriend? Now I am like
a foolish mother in a Jane Austen novel. I can only watch and
fumble with my sewing as they travel out in the wide world. What
will the plot bring? Could I bear anything less than happily ever
after? Since I know there is no happily ever after I am prepared for
the worst, or so I tell myself. Of course my self-satisfaction factor
measured by the sociologists' yardstick is inevitably going to sink
under sea level. If I had no children I might love myself better but
what would the furnishing of my mind be?

I go to the East Village to hear my oldest daughter give a reading
of her short pieces in a local bar. I am old in this room, so old that I
am both conspicuous and invisible. There is a crowd at all the
tables. People are standing against the wall. The room is dark, still I
notice the black leather, the earring through the nose, the strained

faces, the frayed sweaters, the too blond, pitch black, too short, razor-sliced hair, the mark of would-be filmmakers, painters, poets, sallow skinned, the scotch and pot, the nicotine and urine smell of bohemian nights and days in the welfare line. I see my daughter in a strapless dress with fishnet stockings. I see her blue veins under her white skin, I see the bones of her body as if she were a broken bird. I see the gash of bright red lipstick, the heavy eye makeup. I sigh. The spotlight shines on my oldest daughter, she throws down a drink and begins her poems. They are poems that are not quite poems about the terrors of subways, the strangeness of light, the oddness of breathing.

I had wanted everything without artifice. I had thrown out girdles and garters, painting my face and dyeing my hair. I had wanted to be natural as home-baked bread. In my bohemia women wore plain faces and black leotards. In hers they wear chains and metal studs. They court the images of perversity. I had sought innocence. I had raised my own reaction. My daughter looks like a woman of the nineteen forties, or a parody of a woman of the nineteen forties. Her voice is strong, commanding, witty, lyric. The room is silent, frozen as if in a headlight's glare by an unseen emergency. Her power flows. Her hips are set forward, her torso sways, her feet are firmly planted on the small raised platform. The smoke rises and falls through the dark room. There is not enough air. I think of Billie Holiday, of squirrels and raccoons caught by rushing wheels and flattened on the highway, their fur matted in blood and bone. I stare and stare. When the performance is over and she has walked back into the crowd toward the bar where another drink awaits her my heartbeat returns to a normal rhythm. I am blessed with an Icarus of a child who dares to fly toward the sun. She is magnificent in flight. I anticipate the fall.

It is almost impossible to understand what mothering must have been like in other centuries. If approximately one in five babies died before its third birthday, then how could a mother allow herself the passion, the investment, the connection we know is necessary for the psychological growth of the child? That the physical part, hard work as it is, could be done is understandable, but how could you comprehend a universe which took away so many babies? How could you love when each child seemed so temporary, so like a chimera, so soon to go? No wonder in Europe the upper classes farmed their babies out to wet nurses. Who would not spare themselves the agony of child love followed by child loss if they could? Yes, religion must have helped. A belief in a hereafter would have been comforting. A sense of children as angels would have made death seem more palatable. Still, it must have been hard when every cold could take a child, when appendicitis, flu, earaches, skinned knees, TB, diphtheria, typhus, dysentery could all kill a small child, as well as scarlet fever, smallpox, measles, mumps, and the other plagues of childhood we now can vaccinate against.

Common wisdom has it that nothing is more terrible for today's mother than the death of her child. We have heard some reports. Child death is fortunately rare enough these days to be the subject of memoir, movie, play. We are fascinated because we are rehearsing. How would it be? Could one survive it? To hear a story about a child that died is like running your fingers quickly through the flame of a candle. You are not burned. You have beaten it. You are practicing to escape. Most of us do not experience the death of a child but the threat is shadow enough over our days. Everything raveled would come unraveled. There is no possible solace for that. I hear it in the voice of my stepdaughter as she reminds her spouse to lock the gate to the swimming pool. I hear it as she relates the story of a friend whose child has contracted a rare and damaging virus. I look in her eyes and see they cannot blink away the fright. I see it in my own face, a tightening around the mouth, a pallor on the skin.

My oldest daughter is in the airport waiting for a plane to Minnesota. She has told us that she is addicted to alcohol and heroin. We have arranged for her to go to a recovery hospital there. She is wearing a tight leather halter and a skirt with leopards printed on it. She has no luggage. It had been left behind somewhere in the East Village. She holds her black leather jacket. She says she is afraid of planes. Why is she afraid of planes and not of empty streets at four in the morning? We buy her magazines to distract her. Her hands are shaking. Only a few hours we say and you'll be there. Love and fury rise like bile in the mouth as I see the needle marks on her bare arms. Beneath the dark red lipstick, the heavy rouge, I see that her skin is grey and her teeth are stained. Erich Fromm said in *The Art of Loving*, "Motherly love is by its nature unconditional. Mother loves the newborn infant because it is her child not because it has fulfilled any specific conditions or lived up to any specific expectation." He was right and he was wrong.

She has trouble believing in a greater power. So do I. "Just believe," I beg her over the phone. This is no time for intellectual argument. She recovers. I go out to see her and walk the hospital campus with her in paths that wind around the tall northern fir trees. Everyone is hugging and telling each other what great persons they are. Everyone has a list of the good things about themselves that they keep in their pockets and add to from time to time. Suddenly she seems brave to me, adventurous, warm, alive. She is wearing jeans and a T-shirt and her skin is clean, her black hair shines. She takes me to the twelve-step bookstore. Shelf after shelf telling you how to shake addictions to men and food, to booze and gambling. There are free pamphlets at the door. I don't want any. I ride back to the airport in the hospital van. In the back is a young man with a leather jacket that says "Death lives" in pink neon. He wears black leather bracelets with silver spikes extended. His unkempt beard has crumbs in it. If I saw him on a deserted street I would prepare for the worst. He talks to me about whales. He is very interested in whales. He tells me he is a vegetarian. It turns out

I am the nasty carnivore and he is the tenderhearted veggie. I have hope for my daughter.

I tell my friends about my daughter's addiction. I tell them that she is in Hazelden getting well. I call people I haven't seen for months and have lunch with them, I call long distance. I am not interested in secrets. I feel too old for secrets. I want to hear their consoling voices. I want them to say, "It's not your fault." Some of them do. Others gasp and change the subject. They are embarrassed. Why not. I feel as if I had tumbled off the high wire mid-act. I am my own audience. I cover my eyes. It wasn't supposed to happen though the possibility was always there. I am startled at how unsurprised I am. I go over everything in slow motion. I tell myself stories of how it might have turned out differently. Then I stop. My daughter's biological father is an alcoholic. I married him that way. I hardly knew the word when we first met. I thought it applied to bums who slept in flophouses in the Bowery, begging for change on the rundown corners of Chinatown and Little Italy. Genes provide an excuse, a kind of half-assed alibi, but they don't issue free tickets to mayhem and disaster. They play their part but aren't the whole story. For a while I hold on to the image of genetic programming as if it were a life raft that would keep me afloat in a sea of guilt until a rescue helicopter arrived. I wait treading water.

I assume my friends are talking behind my back. Why shouldn't they? Gossip is the true story of our lives and it provides far more than entertainment. It's our equivalent of cautionary tales, morality plays, sermons from the pulpit. Gossip offers information, it's a trail map of reality. I talk about other people and the disasters that are befalling them, why should I not expect to be talked about in turn? A friend called, a member of my group of women writers. "Is it true that — " she asked. "What are the details?" she asked. Do I really believe that secrets harm us or am I whistling in the dark? I whistle. I want a friend to tell me that everything will be all right. I want a friend to lie to me. I would be irritated by any friend who tried. I become like the Ancient Mariner, I tug at sleeves: "My daughter, my albatross," I say. My love for her stuffs my head, stirred by my fury, becomes spilled ink forming a shifting Rorschach of evil creatures devouring their young or of mothers bending over beds, tucking in the covers, smoothing sheets.

I am not responsible. I am not alone responsible. Who is responsible is not the most important question. It will lead us nowhere. God forgives, but God is elusive and it's easy to imagine Him forgiving when He does not. Also I do not forgive God, which makes for an awkwardness. Furthermore I don't believe in Him.

Later when she tells me that she has tested HIV positive. Later still when she begins to get fevers. I tell myself that in other times loss of a child was commonplace. Motherhood was always a risk. I knew that going in.

My raised consciousness tells me that this is not my fault. It tells me that I live in a social-historical context and what we suffer family by family is a social ill. It tells me that I am a mother at the end of the century and something is still wrong with the way we raise our children, something is wrong with what feminism has left us with. If the personal is truly political then we had better look to our politics, take out our tarot cards, redesign everything.

In the first months when I was pregnant, before it was obvious to the casual observer, I had walked around wrapped in my body, satisfied, amazed, special, marked out among others, sanctified. Now I felt as if the same awe, the same mark, a secret behind my ordinary appearance affected my every move. But now the secret was not a baby that would arrive on schedule but an illness that could claim a young life. I could not grasp it. Sometimes I could not admit it. Sometimes I thought about it all the time. But days, months went by and I did not let myself imagine it, play it forward in my mind. When I imagined how she must feel, trying to cheerlead with the shortened baton of her life, I felt stunned, stilled, numbed. What else I feel I do not yet know. What else I know I do not yet know. Her spirit is tough and she cracks jokes into the existential void. She fights back, she writes stories. She performs at readings. She loves the man she has recently married, she loves us all. At her wedding the two of us danced together, she a graceful, glamorous figure, wild and fierce, irreverent and brave, me a plump grey-haired lady, shaking to the music as if there were nothing else in the world but the moment, but the music, but the sweetness of our dance. She blazes like a lighted match against her own darkness. She lights up mine.

Sometimes I'm so angry at her for having harmed herself that I could kill her. Always I feel helpless. My love for her burns on.

I struggled for a long time with guilt. I have just about wrestled it to the ground. Now she is showing me how courageous she is, how many people love her, how she can knit herself into life under the most difficult circumstances. I watch while she brushes her red-haired cat. I sit with her in a jazz spot and watch her eyes shine and her fingers drum on with the music. She used to lie to me all the time. She probably still does but it doesn't matter anymore. The lies are her way of making a long story out of her life. I like listening to the story. I would have wished other plots. Her lies protect us both from too much reality. Some days I feel as if I had accomplished nothing in this world. Other days I feel buoyant, expansive, confident. Nevertheless, I know what hurts her. It hurts me too.

I have included this part of the family story in this book because I know that it has affected how I write and see the world although I do not know exactly in what ways. My words and my mood, my writing and my living are suffused with it. How could it be otherwise?

PART VI

FAMILY VALUES
AND FEMINIST VISIONS

In 1940 only 8.6 percent of mothers with children under eighteen were in the labor force and now most are. I see my stepdaughter, one eye following her children, the other absorbed in her professional journals. Good, I think, very good, but I know she wants to be home more with the children. I know it hurts her not to be there all the time. "You're lucky," she says to me, a hint of generational reproach in her tone, "your work let you stay home." And that is true. Each generation has its woes.

My stepdaughter and other young women now regret that they will not be there for the morning nap, for the diaper change after lunch. They complain that no one told them that they would want to stay home all day. What is this interruption, this new necessity to be at a job? The irony rings loud. In 1956 when I was twenty my mother thought I was an old maid. Now women marry so late that some may not be able to have children at all. Now they must work and education is their royal road to survival. The independence we fought for can seem like a burden. Of course, the alternative was certainly a burden. How will they ever manage?

One of my daughters publishes a book. I hold it in my hand. I turn it over. There on the back is a picture of her. Her hair curls, disobedient thick locks, her eyes glare back at the photographer. What do I see? I see sass, energy, womanliness, but not the kind I was taught. I don't see helplessness, pretense, fear. I see clarity, brightness, and sexuality, her own, bold and strong, right there on the back cover of her book. I turn pink, so pleased am I. I think my daughter's point of view is bold, humane, and right. My daughter is a critic of the revolution in which I was a foot soldier and she was a beneficiary. I agree with her criticism.

I remind myself that this is her book, not mine. I must not blur the lines. I must not be too pleased. I am too pleased. For weeks and weeks I leave her book out on my table and hold it in my hands, staring again and again at the pages, reading them aloud. "I am her mother," I want to say to passersby in the bookstore. The phrase whispers through my mind day after day.

I want to warn her of this and that. I try. She pays no attention to me. I want to follow her around, remind her to eat well, to sleep enough. I try. She smiles at me. I know that I should pay attention to my own waiting work. This was the point of feminism, that I had my own self to watch in the firmament. My cup runneth over, but it is full with reflections of her life. I am a mother feminist. I ask myself is that a contradiction and this book begins.

Now I see my daughters worried about what to do with their lives that will guarantee them economic solvency. I see them burdened with the old problems, am I good enough, am I beautiful? I see them dieting, painting their toenails red just like my mother. I see them make faces at themselves in the mirror as if the reflection were imperfect. Must our reflections always be imperfect? Is it the fashion magazines that make it so or is it some old and inoperable human dissatisfaction that makes so many women feel not altogether whole, suspect that they could never find their way on their own out of the forest? I told my daughters that Marcia Brady was a rerun has-been. I told them that smoking was bad for them. I told them that domestic life was not enough. Still, so many of their friends are on Prozac. At their parties nicotine dominates the air. I hear stories of Ecstasy and vodka, of friends too fat, too thin.

Sometimes their relationships go sour and their hearts seem broken, not in girlish play but in honest-to-God grief. One friend stalks men who don't want her and another is in love with a man who sleeps with her best friends. Is that because sex comes to them earlier and without taboos? Where I was virginal and terrified they were already women of the world. Where I was married and divorced with a child they are pursuing graduate degrees. They seem so young when I thought I was so old. Sometimes they sound like Dorothy Parker or Jean Rhys. Sometimes they sound like Golda Meir or Margaret Thatcher. Sometimes they sound like William Burroughs's wife who let her stoned husband attempt to shoot an apple from on top of her head. He killed her. Sometimes they sound like William Burroughs. Do they believe that they could empty a canoe filled with water? I'm not sure. What do they see when they look in the mirror?

I suppose I shouldn't be surprised that we're still pursuing happiness and hardly gaining ground. Sexism is not the only problem. I'm afraid it's something else, something harder to erase. The female body with its mysterious and uncontrollable menstrual cycles, with its inner power to create, with its hormonal surges toward love, toward children is not a seaworthy vessel sailing out into the new world. Biology will not be banished by epigram. It still takes its toll. Maybe it's something else in our society that rocks the confidence of girls and boys, maybe it's the way they need to be aggressive and alluring at the same time. Understanding may remain the task of poets and novelists, madmen and prophets.

It may be that nothing, no human arrangement is just right and that each way we go runs us into the thorn bush of eros and ambivalence. We are still creatures driven by impulse, instinct, afraid of death, pursued by our own bad conscience even as we E-mail our way into cyberspace. The revolution that I was proud to be a part of has changed everything and yet not enough. Definitely not enough.

I was never the mother I wanted to be, calm, secure, rational, present, always empathetic, graceful. Good things and bad things have happened to my children. I can't really take credit for the good if I don't also take blame for the bad. In some corner of my mind a voice is always whispering, *it's your fault.* But I know genetics played its part. The siren calls of a fracturing culture also had their effects on my children's decisions, herding them toward their individual fates. Some days I cannot shake off the feeling that I am a cat running through an alley with a string of tin cans tied to my tail. The more I try to shake off the cans, the more they rattle and the faster I run. Nevertheless I remain a mother: a hovering presence, a protective arm around a shoulder, a radar warning system, a darkly moving shape shifter of memories, perhaps an umbrella opened against the too hot sun. Some days I'm a nuisance, I know it. I can't help it. "Sometimes you are annoying," says my youngest daughter. I am.

I have my own politics now forged out of those years, a feminist family politics.

In 1991 Susan Faludi called all this interest in motherhood a part of the backlash. She berated women for wanting "little nuclear sanctuaries." She saw the movies of the late eighties — *Parenthood, Baby Boom, Three Men and a Baby* — the TV sitcoms all pushing us toward reproduction in order to stop the women's movement, to send women back into the nursery. This was a reprise of the Ellen Peck position in *The Baby Trap.* The women's movement was running in circles. In fact these entertainments that set Faludi's teeth to grinding were echoing, reflecting real issues as both women and men tried to figure out their relationship to children, different from what it had been a generation before but still powerful, deep but no longer prescribed in traditional patterns.

Susan Faludi goes on the prowl through movies and TV searching for allusions to the desire to have children. She ferrets out images that show the pleasure and pull of nursing children or imply real connection to the child. She looks for these pro-child moments with all the zeal of a McCarthyite peeking under cinematic rocks for traces of communism. She waves her lists in the air. She finds that the media are overflowing with images that present child care in a positive light. This makes her angry. She thinks this is all a sign of a retrogressive force, drawing us back into the preliberated dark ages, a subversion of the liberated life. Actually the media reflect our concerns. They do not, in a democracy, direct our behavior, they reveal it. When the mother on *Thirtysomething* wants to nurse her baby, or the single woman character on that show feels lonely, or the cold, efficient female executive in *The Baby Boom* gives up her career in order to take care of a baby and falls in love with a sweet veterinarian, Susan Faludi smells a conspiratorial rat. The rest of us think that the scriptwriters have been talking to their friends.

It is true that media images of children do not reveal the reality. They do glorify it. They omit the daily grind, the hard parts. But that is the media. They also glorify work, romance, sex, doctors, lawyers, cops, etc. That the media images of child raising are incomplete is no reason to assume that there's a conspiracy to force us back into the home.

These dramas or comedies reveal rather than create those desires for children, for raising children, for being with children which are quite naturally, unprompted by TV, a part of most of us. No one manipulates the desire of a woman to be with her child, to open her arms to baby's first steps, to hear the first words, to touch the hair, to smell the folds at the back of the neck, to buy a child an ice cream in the park, to read a story after lunch. No one has faked the pleasure in the nursing breast, the sight, smell, softness of a newborn.

Women have real needs that include being near and with their children. The effort to deny these needs is as cruel as the prefeminist effort to deny women their minds. It is in fact the same maneuver, just turned inside out.

What we see now is a troubling truth. Motherhood and work life are not like glove in hand. They are more like dog and cat, in conflict, and when one is missing from their lives women yearn for the other. Most women need both.

The idea that the culture is rife with evidence of a conspiracy to make women bear children is a kind of politics-cum-paranoia that seizes even the best of minds in times of social upheaval. When this idea first appeared in the nineteen seventies the anti-child cry came from inside the belly of the domestic beast, the traditional American family. It was a thumb at the nose or a collective raspberry aimed at the culture that had raised its girls to push baby carriages while its boys could conquer the worlds of finance, art, law, medicine, industry. That original anti-baby spouting off was an understandable response to the unfairness of it all, the sense of having been culturally cheated, of being perceived as less than you are.

Today's anti-baby posturing is something else again. It repels most women. It makes it possible for us to avoid serious questions and issues about child care. It allows anti-abortionists to point fingers and position themselves as the protectors of the child. It has serious implications for today's politics as the women's movement is still perceived by many in America as anti-family. This label is a crock, it's a false label. It was created in part by those early anti-child drums accompanying the feminist parade and is echoed today by the popular feminists who may appear as our spokespersons on talk shows but who don't understand our real lives, which do, most often by eager deliberate choice, include the whole complicated warm messy frustrating dear and dreadful business of raising children.

The desire to have a child, to have it grow within oneself if possible, to do the backbreaking, wrenching daily grinding caring for a child was part of so many of our primary visions that we had no intention of giving up our roles as mothers, our chance for this ambivalent, dangerous, risky, painful, extraordinary, potentially tragic, usually conflictual, contradictory life unto death, love. The need for Faludi's "little sanctuary" is really the need for human intimacy, to expose oneself warts and all behind a closed door. The domestic weave has its own harsh demands and its own bitter heartbreaks but to avoid it is like staying home because planes sometimes crash and trains run late.

Early feminists like Germaine Greer did not give sufficient weight to the falling in love with the baby that was a part of most women's experience. They overlooked the ferocity of the mother's passion for her child. They wrote about exhaustion, demand, demeaning routine, loss of self accurately enough, but they forgot about pride, about contentment, about the expansion of self as it poured into the child. That stuff seemed corny. It was the blather of women's magazines. But it had its power. It had its truth. Jane Lazarre's report of the first years of her child's life left out the heat that forges the bonds, the affection that overwhelms, the reasons why so many women kept on having children, trying everything possible when fertility was compromised, adopting from the ends of the earth. This is important now because the right in America, which is truly anti-feminist, which would push back the clock if it could, seems to have preempted the pro-family agenda.

FEMINIST FAMILY POLITICS VS. FAMILY VALUES

Norman Mailer understood how the matter of babies enters our political discussions and turns all arguments on their heads. Dreadful old chauvinist that he is, sometimes he called it right. In *The Prisoner of Sex* he wrote, "It was here that all discussion of women as a class would terminate before the mysterious advantage and burden of her womb." If we look at feminism today we see that the womb is very much at the heart of the unresolved matter. If we look at the political right we see in clear focus the attitudes in America which divide us and unite us. The Christian Coalition, the religious right, all the Pats and Jerrys, the Ralph Reeds and their colleagues have very firm ideas about the family. They are not wishy-washy, undecided, bothered by second thoughts like the rest of us. They don't simply want to convince you that their way of life is the only path to Jesus, they want to take you on a forced march in their direction. They are not speaking right now directly about feminism, but it slips out, it comes into their talk radio, into their sermons. They don't like it. They want their Total Women at home, bearing children and washing things. That's what the Bible tells them to do. Rush Limbaugh talks about feminazis, as if it weren't lunatic to link Nazi brutality to feminist ideals for women. The abortion issue, real as it is in its own terms, has also become a code way of attacking feminists and feminist ideals. Alas, feminism in its emphasis on freeing the woman from domesticity appears to have created a political vacuum where the home should be.

Feminists have allowed themselves to get painted into a corner. If the Christian right stands for family values, then we, the feminist cutting edge, must stand for the destruction of the family. It's a subtle smear but a clever one. If family values are marriage and child rearing, if they are church and abstinence, if they are anti-abortion and pro-life, then what are we? The answer is obvious: Godless, promiscuous baby murderers and pro-death.

Look at the difference between what we offer our supporters and what they offer theirs. The big prize on their trophy table is life after death. We can't compete there. The second prize is order, security, a clear sense of right and wrong, a conviction of personal virtue, a way of preventing or avoiding social disorder. The Christian Coalition also offers up distinct people to abhor: homosexuals, sexual experimenters of all kinds, abortion doctors and their supporters, secular humanists, intellectuals, the anti-gun lobby, etc. It makes a person feel safe to have a clearly defined enemy named, out there. That makes it easier to avoid looking within, to catch oneself in compromising positions. A feminism that speaks of tolerance for sexual choice, self-fulfillment, economic independence for women is associated with social chaos, divorce, disobedience to the authority of the state or the authority of religion, worse yet free love.

That's old news. It matters now because these fundamentalist forces have organized brilliantly. Other groups tend to accept many of their ideas. They have strong allies among other religions and in all regions of the United States. They are wealthy and in certain areas of the country powerful. They are numerous enough to make the Republican party alter its platform, alter its direction. They have managed to get equal rights for homosexuals repealed in several states and have initiated nasty campaigns in others. Sanctimony gets votes. The religious right is close enough to real legislative power so that it is possible to imagine that the cacophony of American voices may one day be stilled in a tidal wave of righteousness. It is this righteousness that produced McCarthyism once and could again. The censorious public pressure, the blacklists, the fear that followed McCarthy waving his names at the TV camera could always return. It is not so easy to put a stake through the heart of conformism even after it consumed a good deal of blood and curled up for a long nap. Then the issue was anti-communism, now it is family values. It's all the same when it comes to forbidding diversity, sneaking totalitarian conformity in through the American back door.

This popular song about traditional family values comes from the communal gut, not unrelated to my stepdaughter's sadness about her parents' divorce. The uprooted American family, the alcoholic American family, the ever dissolving and re-forming, drug-abusing family leaves many confused and wounded. The tremendous popular acceptance of the AA model and its twelve-step holding pattern could not have occurred if we were not a country in which families could no longer support their members and people were not crashing on the road in huge pileups. The days of students running off to orange-robed gurus and hippies living in buses that crisscross the highways and drugs that are pushed by Harvard professors is over, not because these things don't happen anymore but because drugs have become old news and no longer need love beads to advertise themselves, and odd religions are as common among rural right wingers like the Branch Davidians as among suburban youth. The sixties used to act like Crazy Eddy trying to sell you a toaster. Now it has transformed itself into the Mall of America, with a parking lot big enough for everyone. The self-help section in any bookstore in any town in this country is brimming over with both books and needy customers. Everyone wants to live in a strong, happy family. Very few do. The difference between a feminist position and that of the religious right lies not in the goal of family happiness but in the map one would use to get there.

Feminists believe that the goodness of a family is not decided or dictated by its form, certainly not by the number or gender of the adults in charge. The traditionalists accept only one kind of family unit. Feminists see many possibilities. But every kind of family requires order, requires discipline, members must give up some individuality, some self-will for the good of the whole or else everyone suffers. Feminists do not see this discipline as divine law or as father-ordained. They do see it as regulating the impulses of family members. They know discipline is necessary. It takes a large measure of self-discipline for both men and women to deal day in and day out with children, with putting food on the table, with cleanliness, with illness, with the expected and unexpected while still keeping one's heart open to the flow of family feelings, the sometimes turbulent, sometimes ecstatic currents. The traditional family of the religious right tries to rule by fiat, by repression, by the stick, by the threat of damnation. The feminist family has its own forms of control, its own sacrifices of the good of the one for the whole. It makes its members feel guilty too, especially when things go wrong, but its methods are less arbitrary, its decisions are less stereotyped, and more variety is permitted and even expected. Sacrifice is sometimes needed, a job promotion turned down because of a sick child, a delay of a few years in a graduate program, no more time for golf, no money for a vacation because of a child's medical or social needs. Feminists just want an equal opportunity to have and to sacrifice for the family. Most of us are not looking for a life without limits because such a life would be a lonely affair indeed.

Feminists want families in which children can sharpen their minds, express their ideas, ask big and little questions, feel loved and secure. They want homes that protect the vulnerable, in which the adults can feel sexually alive and understood, in which pleasure is not constant but comes often enough to sustain well-being. They want to feel economically secure and when that is not possible, as it often isn't, to feel bound together in a place where they are safe, where the burdens are shared. They don't want men carrying all the heavy load. They don't want women limiting their intelligence or gifts. These too are family concerns and should be recognized as such.

Early in my second marriage I allowed my husband to do all the worrying about money. It sometimes made him miserable, remote, and silent. Then I would get mad at his distance from me. I thought he was a miser. He thought I was spoiled. He also thought he was responsible for all our practical concerns. I was more than willing to let him carry the burden. I thought his worries were phantom carryovers from the depression era that blighted his childhood. It took us a long time and some bruises to figure out that we were in this together, that I could handle checks and we could stare at reality better if we did our staring together. This did not improve the bank balance but it did wonders for our trust of each other. This was most surely a feminist family issue.

In all the emphasis on self-fulfillment perhaps the feminists have not asked enough of women. We should be caring for others. It should be part of the feminist vision that we do extend our tenderness toward our own mates and partners, children, relatives, as should the men we marry, have sex with, procreate with. The Christian right tends to be suspicious of the school system, of the government, because they think it is hostile to their way of life. They think that sexual material and religious doubts will enter their children's heads if they are exposed to the general world. Feminists need to make that general world even more inclusive, affectionate, caring. Violence in the streets, the abandoned mentally ill, drug addicts nodding under bridges, criminals pouncing on their prey, these are threats to us all. The less nuclear we conceive the family to be and the more extended into the community it becomes, the stronger the nuclear family will be. The family need not be a fortress surrounded by an alligator-filled moat. It can be a tent pitched on the communal green. Good day care, adequate medical care, support for the single mother, access to education, good schools, these are all things that nourish the family, not government interventions that will destroy it. A physician friend of mine had two small boys, one still in diapers, when her husband developed heart disease and died. She looked to her friends to fill in the father role with her children, to help the family by being there for her boys. Her friends disappointed. They were nuclear family types. Their responsibility and love did not cross over the threshold of their own doorways. We can do better than that. We can expect more of ourselves.

The image of the stiff-backed traditional Ma and Pa out on the prairie is not so romantic anymore. Now when the wind blows harshly and the Sioux are attacking and disease strikes and locusts threaten the crop, it is time for the neighbors to rally round. If this sounds socialist or worse so be it. Feminists need to be saying this loud and clear.

I can understand how alarmed some Americans must have been by the sexual revolution, by the apparent anti-authoritarian forces let loose in the sixties, flag burning, drug taking, wife swapping, bathhouses, etc. I can understand how the cold shivers went down the spine when children spoke back to their parents, Abbie Hoffman, Stokely Carmichael, blacks demanding seats in the front of the bus, Jews in the government and in the law firms. I can understand how important it must have seemed to assert that a way of life that appeared threatened was the right way of life even if you had to get ugly to be heard. Even if living that way of life sometimes brought you to the edge of despair and beyond.

The entire country has not become Bible-thumping followers of the Christian right. They have found no lost utopia and everyone knows it. Their men may sing hymns on Sunday and still punch their wives on Saturday night. Susan Smith's stepfather, Beverly Russell, abused her when she was fifteen years old. He was a leader in the local Christian Coalition. Snobbisms, adultery, alcoholism, corruption, theft, child abuse, loneliness, depression, not to mention swindles, tax evasion, corruption are not removed by waving the flag, by praying to Jesus to forgive. The human beast and what is foul in his heart is not altered by the life the Christian right proposes. We know that. What does happen is that people become rigid, limited, reactionary, hypocritical, watched and watchful, and motels still do a good business. Liquor stores do not close early. Teenagers misbehave and pay the consequences with the rest of their lives. Disgrace and shame are the rod of social control. Turning off the TV, keeping *NYPD Blue* and David Letterman out does not rout the snake from the garden. In too many homes God's love is the only love there is. This fascism of good deeds cleans out the library of books that might enlighten the mind but it leaves dirty thoughts, dirty actions beyond reach. Even if it enforces a kind of behavioral conformity on some, it creates in its wake a howl of sorrow, old human sorrow, the same as always, the same as everywhere else. This does not seem to feminists the way to value the family.

The authoritarianism implicit in this worldview is heavy-handed and afraid of questions. Inquiry, irony, cultural criticism — these are all anathema to the good people of the Good Book. For them sexuality is not something that enhances life but rather a temptation, don't spill seed, don't have sex out of marriage, don't allow Satan to gain ahold of your heart or you will burn. Their authority offers carrot and stick, threat and reward. But be careful what you say.

Joycelyn Elders lost her job as Surgeon General because she mentioned masturbation, something that surely seventy-five years after Freud should not cause the downfall of a public health official. The religious right doesn't want to hear the word in public discourse. If we don't talk about it maybe it won't exist. The speed with which all politicians agreed that she had to go speaks to the power of the religious right to shape the public culture. A word, a recommendation to help youngsters channel their sexuality in less dangerous ways than intercourse seemed to the Bible Belt as if Joycelyn Elders had picked up her skirt on national TV and demonstrated the act. The rest of us were never permitted to discuss the merits of her idea. In this way the secrecy of sex, the repression common to parts of the country determined the political fate of a representative of all of us.

The sexual issues that absorb the religious right are promiscuity, abortion, homosexuality, pornography, and premarital intercourse.

Feminist sexual issues are rape, abortion, incest, wife beating, male sexual harassment, and pornography.

Both sides gather emotion by roiling up the sexy sexual issues. Neither side has happy families. Neither side has stopped the drug trade. Neither side has stopped young mothers from having babies they can't take care of. Young women at Christian academies are eating too much or too little; so are their cosmopolitan sisters. Neither side has made men love women in a better fashion or women love men in a better way. Neither side has made the country more racially just, more economically equal, a better place for the elderly or the poor. Not my side, not their side. The feminist side might yet make some improvements. The religious right with their status quo view, with their dependence on repression and isolation and authoritarian control will never move us toward a fuller humanity, will always be hawking something they call values that have proved ineffective over a three-hundred-year trial. They haven't time for society's needs, so busy are they pointing fingers at others, painting scarlet letters on their neighbors.

We too have our absolutes and have sometimes gotten carried away with a party line, a doctrinaire self-righteousness. We have focused on male sin and ignored the way that women harm themselves and sometimes harm men and often harm children. In expending so much energy in sexual areas we have ignored day care issues, economic issues, family matters such as health care. But our intellectual system is open. We can catch our mistakes. We can make ourselves stronger.

Nobody thinks of abortion as a cause for celebration. Nevertheless, until birth control is perfected and everyone is using it properly all the time, abortion will remain a necessary protection against more human suffering. Legal abortion is a way to make sure that a child is wanted. A family of wanted children starts well, or at least better than one where the children came unbidden. Every child needs a receiving blanket woven of hope and anticipation. To avoid premarital sex, to avoid sex unless one wants to have a child, is hardly a beautiful or realistic choice and would not necessarily make families stronger or safer places to live. Sex is not so easy to banish, and when one does, other kinds of distortions and crippling occur.

Abortion choice is a feminist position but that doesn't mean that feminists do not have a sense of the sacredness, the awesomeness, the holiness of birth. We need to communicate that again. We need to feel it again. It is not true that all feminists are indifferent to babies or children. We hold them so sacred that we want each to be cared for by a parent who is capable, eager, and loving. The flame of life is so important that we don't want to create babies destined for neglect, rejection, pain, handicapped physically or socially. As the feminist movement connects itself more firmly through its actions and its language to the well-being of living children, our own moral power will light up the political landscape. Feminists want good families too. They don't want to live in dry dead places where the held hand, the shared joke, the unexpected touch never occurs.

My single-mother years were the hardest of my life because I felt vulnerable myself and I suspect my own trembling affected my child. I could have used more help. I felt, as I suspect most single mothers do, fearful that I was harming my child, hurt with her hurt. Sad when I saw another father lift his child up on his shoulders. Ashamed I had not done better. Convinced I had broken some unspoken promise. I was heavy with failure. But I have seen so many children come out of single-parent homes with loving souls and bright minds and I have seen so many children from two-parent homes flounder that I know that while two parents are best, best in the same house, loving each other, that is hardly the end of the story.

Family, whatever its form, however shaky, however disappointing, however many false hopes and illusions it must carry, however many nasty instincts it must attempt to suppress, whatever dark things appear under the conjugal bed, remains the common way to root ourselves into the earth, to protect ourselves against too terrifying isolation. To really make life better, not just creating access in the workplace, in graduate school, but to really transform our human experience we need to adjust our feminism so that it doesn't present itself as a flight from, a slap in the face to, an avoidance of male affection, attention, responsibility.

The "I'm more moral than thou" feminist ideologies don't help us. The emphasis on predatory male sexual behavior is out of proportion to actual male behavior or feelings. Of course we are anti-rape, -harassment, -brutality. But have we made it clear what we are for when it comes to men? Have we driven away a generation of young women by appearing silly in our sexual passions, which are not theirs at all?

If American women over the age of eighteen are concerned, like women everywhere from time beginning, with finding a mate, procreating, finding a job, finding a way to take care of their children, finding emotional support and sexual fulfillment, then what are we saying to them? "Beware of men, male the enemy, male the perpetual beast is trying to sneak his hand up your skirt" does not seem to be the most relevant message. It is as if we were telling them not to drink the local water, not to eat the local food, and not to sleep in the local beds. Of course they will not and cannot listen. This tactic is just as ineffective as the religious right's attempts to keep sex at bay. We should be pushing for justice for men in the divorce courts, in the sperm banks, in the custody decisions that ripple round the country. If we are going to change the family into one in which the gender roles are not so differentiated then we have to do more than just reverse past wrongs, which merely inverts the problem. We have to create a gender-neutral family justice.

If this were to work women would have to give up some of their mysterious, mythologized power over child rearing and men would have to move over, jump in, change their ways also. A feminist family agenda could not work if it were exclusively for a family of highly educated types each making a huge salary. Many such feminist families already exist and have not produced vast social change. To be truly revolutionary such a program would have to reach out across the nation and appeal to people of all kinds who could see some personal advantage if they adopted all or some of the feminist family style. Is this pure dreaming? Is this utopian thinking, useless in the real world?

When I was in sixth grade I wrote a poem about a poison smoke that leaked through the cracks in a house and the parents and the children died. My teacher thought I was expressing fear of nuclear attack. The early stages of the cold war had many afraid of imminent disaster. The principal of the school read my poem at a teachers' conference on how children were responding to the threat of apocalypse from the newly minted hydrogen bomb. It was true that we were practicing hiding under our desks in case atomic winter were to suddenly arrive but my poem was not about atoms fissioning, though eventually I was too embarrassed to say so and then ashamed I hadn't said so. It was about the unhappiness of man and woman, clashing with each other night after night. It was about how the children grow up bent and uncertain when the home is chaotic, deceitful, dangerous, and the anger of the adults boils on and on. I suppose I'm still trying to explain the real meaning of my poem but I know that family is a place where adventure lies, where character, strength, will, determination are tested. It is also the place where you can get poisoned.

Nevertheless, the world can only repair itself family by family, house by house. How desperately we need each other, how important a parent is to a child, how important the work that seems so dull, day after day: brush your teeth, change into your pajamas, another bedtime story, another drink of water, and yet there lies the frontier of human possibility.

In the Talmud there is a strange story about an eagle and her three babies who are living in the top of a tree on an island in a great body of water. A terrible storm raises the winds and the waters and the eagle must carry her chicks to safety across the turbulent seas. She picks up the first chick and halfway across the water she says to it, "When I am old and you are a strong eagle, will you take care of me as I am taking care of you?" and the chick replies, "I will, I will." The mother eagle drops the baby into the sea. She picks up the second chick and the story is repeated with the baby saying, "I will, I will," and the mother eagle again opening her claws and dropping the baby into the sea. She picks up the third chick and halfway across the water asks the chick if he will promise to take care of her as she has taken care of him and he says, "I cannot promise that. But I do promise you that I will take care of my own chicks as you have taken care of me." This is the bird that makes it to dry land and continues the eagle family into the future.

It's a tough story, baby birds falling through the sky, wings desperately flapping against the wind and torrential rains. But the point I suppose is that we are not meant to reap a reward from what we give our children except in an evolutionary sense. Our grandchildren become our path into the future as we become irrelevant. The story also tells us that there is some survival value in honesty, in avoiding the sentimental pieties and calling it like it is. From this point of view the mother eagle is performing some kind of triage among her children to find the one who sees without hypocrisy and is willing to risk the consequences.

I am on the phone with my younger daughter, who is in graduate school. She is becoming an American historian. She is being helpful. She gives me the names of some books that discuss the historical origins of some argument I am making in a column. I've never heard of them. She gives me the names of some theoreticians who have published on the subject. I've never heard of them either. Once upon a time I read her stories and found books for her and now she finds them for me. As she talks I have to ask her to explain certain words to me. "Oh," I say and hope that the information will remain in my mind. Once I knew more than my mother who never had a higher education, now my daughter knows more than I do. I feel simultaneously diminished and expanded. I am being left behind but that is as it should be. I am extraordinarily content for a woman who has just discovered that her ignorance is as deep as the ocean.

So what would I do if I could?

Change the focus of our concern from the sexual issues to the practical ones.

Bring men into the home.

Create decent, small, nonbureaucratic day care.

Change the emphasis from my child to our child, make the community care.

Stop carrying on about male evil and female virtue.

Make ordinary women and men and their children the subject of my politics.

Look at what men experience, not just at what women experience.

Create laws that treat men and women equally in matters of surrogacy, custody, divorce.

(I learned about making lists from my oldest daughter. It is a common twelve-step technique that clears the mind of its usual cloudy weather.)

There are several ways to attend to the child rearing problem and we probably need all of them. Men testing the warmth of bottles on their wrists, men holding babies on their shoulders while they scream their colicky cries, men in the laundry room might make a different home, one more hospitable to the male, who would be a primary architect of his own family, not a friendly bystander but a full participant. This idea is so old I am almost embarrassed to repeat it here. But we know it has not been adopted by the vast majority of men, at least not all the way, at least not completely. I believe that a women's movement that could so radically alter the way we live in just a decade or two would, if it put its heart to the wheel, be able to make this revolution complete, take it out of the upper classes and make it work in Harlem, in Watts, in rural Montana and the cattle towns of Texas. Every boy in every American corner should know that he is needed, that he is necessary, that the baby is not the mother's property, that it is his to nurture. The male as nurturer should not be some charming fairy tale on the local screen but should be absolutely routine, assumed. We can do this if we have the will, just as we changed the image of the doctor from male to male and female so we can change the image of the father from outside to inside, from an onlooker to a full partner especially for very young infants. Why not? It's worth a try. We know what the power of consciousness raised can do. We haven't yet tried fully to bring men into child care. At the moment when the feminist movement might have moved in that direction we turned instead toward the sexy sexual issues, leaving the need to nurture in the dust.

Of course it is not economically feasible to keep both parents home from work for months on end or years on end. It would be a fine idea if everyone had a trust fund and the spoons in the house were all silver but in reality parental leaves are brutally short and mostly taken now by women. And even if men were to stay at home for a few months after the birth of a child, the result would not necessarily be good for their career or the ultimate family income. Something else needs to change before men can become equal partners in the home. We need to solve the child care issue. This cannot be number twenty-five on our agenda. It is the issue of the day, the only one that will unite American women in a fight for a better life. There is no reason except traditional American individualism that we do not have decent, cheap, available day care for everyone. If small countries like Israel and Sweden can do it, so can we if we put our minds and pocketbooks to it. In response to a growing mumble of political concerns about child care, in December 1971 Richard Nixon said, "Neither the immediate need nor the desirability of the national child development program of this character has been demonstrated. For the Federal government to plunge headlong financially into supporting this program would be foolish." The government in America tends to do everything badly. Child care that ran like the motor vehicle bureaus in most states would indeed be a nightmare. All our children would be victims of friendly fire. But good, small child care centers, professionalized, with communal commitment to quality might be possible. Without society's participation many women will not be able to leave their homes until their children are grown, too late for equal opportunity, and backwards we would slide into the world that Philip Wylie knew.

Good day care might alter the patterns of poverty. Children taught and attended to from their earliest moments might have a better chance to learn language, compete with others, escape the crime and drugs of their streets. We don't need endless studies of Head Start. It makes perfect common sense that children who are not left to the TV, who can depend on the order of the school day, who will be cared for tenderly will be more alert, readier to learn than others left to the care of single women, worn, irritable, themselves underloved or overburdened. This is a feminist issue of primary importance. The motherhood of many of us needs rescuing, supporting, educating. For the next decade the politics of feminism ought to be the politics of day care.

This story was reported by Thomas Laqueur in an article in a feminist textbook. An Algonquin chief was confronted by a Jesuit missionary in the seventeenth century with the standard European argument against women's promiscuity (How else would you know the child is yours?). The chief replied that he found it puzzling that whites could apparently love only "their" children. Is it then individual ownership that promotes caring and affection among us? A feminist vision would have the social environment also protect and care for a child so that individual parents could function as they economically must in this world, both of them in the world, while the child is protected, enveloped in a social envelope, a day care center, other mothers and fathers, a neighborhood association, a group formed to care for preschool children. I am not some sentimentalist about Native American life. They knew some things we don't but we certainly know some things they didn't. However, the idea of getting the community involved in child care seems to me a proper feminist family issue right now. If day care were ideal it would support the parents in many ways, providing them with necessary medical, employment, housing information, allowing them choices of parenting styles, helping them to head off difficulties, bedwetting, fears of loud noises, sleep problems, eating problems. Parents could belong to councils that discussed issues that were relevant to their children's lives. This would soon provide community for parents, who would be less isolated, less nuclear but more comfortable. If one parent falls into drugs another can step in, if death or divorce creates a trauma for the child other parents can offer themselves as caretakers. If the world were truly feminist then the circle would be expandable. Our affections would not be taken in at night behind our closed doors. Feminists know the value of support groups. We made a revolution out of them. It could be done again if the will were there. As it now rests it appears as if feminists are exclusively concerned with individual choice rather than family life. This muddies our position and makes it possible for a conversation about family values to exclude us, as if we don't count because we don't care.

Divorce, then, in feminist values should be regarded as the solution of last resort. It is anyway. But it's possible that if more husbands and wives understood how high the stakes were for their children they might make even more of an effort to stay together. Romantic love is a fine thing in its place but it clearly isn't enough. A feminist view of this would be not to jump in on the side of the woman vs. the man but to make sure our communities provide help for families, make sure that men and women understand that the source of their unhappiness may not be altered with a change of partner. Feminism needs to be pro-marriage because that is the best way to make most men, women, and their children happy. If Christian fundamentalists are running around the country touting something called secondary virginity, feminists can be pro-remarriage. They can be pro-stepfamilies that need special support. The fact is that most feminists are fiercely pro-family. What they want most is for the home to be a hearth and available to as many as possible. I wish all those psychologists measuring adolescent self-esteem would turn their attention instead to what goes wrong between men and women who begin loving each other and end each with a divorce lawyer drawing up documents. We need to know a lot more about marital choice, about marriage as a lifetime arrangement.

Unlike the proponents of family values, feminists are truly prosex. This does not mean that they are pro-pornography, pedophilia, incest, rape, or teenage pregnancy. It means that they are for sexual knowledge for everyone and believe in the possible fulfillment of a biological sexual life. This does not mean that men and women in a civilized society can have sex as they might wish like cats in the alleyway. That idea was tried in our sexual revolution and it resulted in such massive misery that it was dropped. It does mean that sexual impulses are not evil, even though they may have to be controlled, sometimes ignored, subject to discipline, and subsumed by other issues such as loyalty, stability, dignity, health. Feminists look on ignorance as a far greater evil than lust. They believe in telling every child the facts of life. Fear and secrets do not lead to happiness.

Feminists hope each man and each woman will learn to enjoy sex with love attached. This is quite obviously far easier to say than to achieve but it is a starting point nevertheless. Those few feminists who have made such a fuss about pornography or male lust are out of step with most of us who do not want sex to disappear again, fenced in with rules and buried in silence. Feminism is not for keeping anything secret, not for repression. In this it is very different from family values à la Pat Robertson. Feminism is not for double standards. But if that is so it must learn to respect the humanity of most men as well as the humanity of women. If it is all right for Lorena Bobbitt to slash her spouse then it is also all right for men to arouse themselves sexually by harming women. Or both instances are examples of cruelty gone erotic and should be condemned.

Premarital sex is not the problem. People were miserable when sex outside of marriage was always a forbidden sin. There was sex anyway. Lack of knowledge about contraception is a problem but not the only problem. So many young girls are having their babies without permanent partners because their neediness is so deep, their hopes for themselves so narrow. We see girls having babies because they don't understand the consequences of being without fathers or education. It is not the sex that caused the disaster. It is the lack of opportunity in life, the lack of worth a girl suffers that she would think of such a solution to her loneliness. This is an emergency feminist issue that we can bring all our resources to address. Many feminists are white and middle class and we hesitate to rush in uninvited. We now view the settlement movement of the early years of this century with a certain disdain. We don't want to be accused of racism or intended genocide, and yet the lives of young women, the health and well-being of real children are at stake. Children need education, not babies. That is a family position. It is not enough just to discourage teenage pregnancy. We have to offer real alternatives so that every young woman has an opportunity to lead a better life. We changed the culture from a fifties model to a nineties model. We eliminated the locked-up housewife. Surely we can eliminate teenage motherhood if we try harder.

We need to fix our timing too. It was a mistake to encourage women to wait to have their children until their professional reputations were solid and their training was completed. It was a reasonable idea in the abstract but in reality it ran counter to our biological imperatives. Every year after thirty-five the woman produces fewer and less viable eggs. Fertility problems are frequent, and it has become clear that the female body was not intended for late childbirth. Too many women have found themselves infertile at the end of their thirties and they regret their loss bitterly. The newfound fertility techniques help some, but others have missed their opportunity to have a baby of their own. This makes them sad. Of course many women have babies into their mid-forties but the statistical curve drops way down. To encourage women to delay conception till the last minute may be a good idea for gathering troops to storm the glass ceiling but it is a bad idea for human happiness and its pursuit. As widespread as it is today infertility becomes a social grief. Adoption is not easy and not always possible. Older parents have an even harder time. Biological clocks need attention. Preferably children should be conceived before the mother reaches her mid-thirties. The techniques of amniocentesis and sonogram viewing are miraculous but better still would be the easier and more likely healthy births to the mother between twenty and thirty-five. There is no reason why we can't encourage women and men to take a few years off from their training. Why can't they do whatever balancing act they must do when they are younger? This would depend, of course, on our changing the workplace and changing what is expected within the culture at large. If the man were involved fully perhaps it wouldn't matter what stage of career development the would-be parents had reached. After all, in the nineteen fifties many fathers were in their twenties. We can find a way again to allow young people to work and have a family.

At the very least, more feminists should be screaming about the fertility problems that seem so common today. This is a public health problem that has been affected by feminism and needs to be addressed by feminism.

AFTER POLITICS: THE REAL WORLD

When I have lunch these days with a friend we first talk about our children. Where are they now? What are they doing? Who is married, who has children of their own. Who has become what. Mostly the news is good. That's because we are careful about what we say.

Nevertheless, I know some things about other people's children that demonstrate the collective price we've paid for our ambitions. Not because we weren't at home but because, a generation in transition, we couldn't prevent the chaos from seeping over us.

Stories of children of people I know:

Suicide.

Joined religious cults, some came out, some did not.

Lost to drugs, overdose accidental and intended.

Unable to find mates, long periods of loneliness.

Women and men infertile.

Severe mental illness, hospitalized, isolated lives.

Unable to decide what they wanted to do with themselves so drifting from badly paid job to badly paid job.

Unable to complete their education.

Fired from jobs and unable to find another in chosen field.

Economic failure.

Lost to alcohol, in rehab facilities, but too late to find professions.

Trying to enter arts, actor, actress, writer, dancer, but not able to find a place in the field, working at minimum-wage jobs into their late thirties.

One doctor's daughter hiding under assumed name because of dangerous jealous Gypsy husband.

Children marrying spouses of other faiths or races when this especially painfully violated family expectations.

Children choosing professions other than the parent would have wished. Doctors' children rejecting medicine, lawyers' children rejecting law, becoming potters, carpenters, mimes.

The traditional families of the religious right have done no better. Our families are not strong enough, extended enough, to fight off the dangers within and without. The nuclear family with all its potential for protection, support, love is also a swamp, a cesspool, a breeding ground for the worst pain, love unanswered, isolation multiplied, expectations dashed. Guilt grows like mushrooms in the dark. American individualism is our crowning glory. It is also the thorn in our side.

Feminist writers such as Charlotte Perkins Gilman and Germaine Greer have proposed communal solutions. In the real world these have never worked. Communities can turn oppressive in the bat of an eye. Children need specific parents for better or worse and the fact that it is so often for worse doesn't alter the need. So unhappy families, so children who cannot cope, so Electra and Oedipus, Cain and Abel will always be coming to Thanksgiving dinner and there's not very much we can do about it. Our politics are always broadsides, cannonballs fired at the rain of ordinary life.

If I were to tell the story of my life it wouldn't be about the conflict between being a mother and a feminist but about being a feminist mother and a mother feminist. It seems that the clash between feminism and motherhood is an artificial one. Mom is not a dowdy harpy perched on the roof of her house, glaring at her departing children. But it would be nice if the world outside her house gave a little bit of a damn about what went on inside. Real family life seems to me a birthright, not to be sold for a mess of pottage, not a luxury, not an attribute of the lucky, but something that resides in the human condition, or at least it ought. All we can do at the moment is recognize our limitations, consider our flaws, watch our backs. Try, child by child, home by home, for a little human happiness.

Some days I wonder if the way I love my children is not a burden for them. I know that I would do it again but I would like less guilt, more community, fewer expectations of success, more reality, more joy, no teenagers at all, at least not the way it is now, with all the tugging and pulling, separating and coming back, dancing on the edge of danger, sinking into babyhood, playing loud music in the dark. I would like to have spared my children the pain they experienced growing up American at the end of this century. I would like to have spared myself the pain I felt watching them grow up. Will the next generation be better? Will my daughters' feminism find a way to alter the community so that their motherhood can be glory-filled, multicolored, fine as human nature will allow?

When we watch movies in which a baby is born and the camera keeps a respectful distance and the music swells as the mother reaches out her arms for her newborn, we become choked, predictable tears flow, not for the family journey that lies ahead for those we are watching. After all, for them happiness appears at hand. The tears are for ourselves because we the audience know that implacable fate is pulling strings: things are not all as certain as they seem. Also at those tender moments longings flood, breaking reason's dam. These are a mixture of memory and hope, a cry of need, for another chance, for a new beginning, for the touch of a mother, father, child that we have lost to time, to age, to the real conflicts that shadow us through the days of our lives. Our unmet desires for tenderness, our edgy complicated loves, our hope for refuge and acceptance, our sense of purpose in the continuity of life are all aroused by even the most blatantly sentimental images. Our family feelings reside inside of us like so many raw nerves ready to respond to the slightest tremor.

When some politicians speak of family values they send a coded message to that part of ourselves that urgently needs the warm circle, where we can take our proper place in the line of generations. We want to be children protected from evil. We want our children to be protected from evil. Let the universe be vast, let the sky hang over our heads as indifferently as it pleases if only our homes were true sanctuaries against our own bestiality. Those who recognize family as the source of pain as well as the source of hope focus attention on ways for each family to fulfill its goals without suppression and harshness, without delusion and false unity. If there is such a thing as a feminist family it will be found in the doing, in the everydayness of every day.

We do not know for sure if the female's closeness to the young child is an immutable part of our biological makeup, our genetic history, or if it can be changed enough for men to take on the full intimacy, the hard work, the particular intensity that so many women experience. We haven't pushed this far enough to know where the limits are, or if there are any limits at all to male caring. In America we haven't tried communal solutions at all. We haven't created a good system of child care to support parents. Our failure on both these fronts is clearly driving women mad and leaving many children unprotected.

I am walking along the street with my stepgrandchild. He is seven. We are on the way to see the replica of the orca whale, a killer whale that resides in the bowels of the Museum of Natural History. We have been there many times. He can tell me the creature's vital statistics and does so as we go up the stone steps, past the imposing but politically incorrect statue of the general on a horse and the noble Indian by his side. "Can I have an ice cream?" he asks. This will be his third of the afternoon. "Sure," I say, "why not?" His mother and father would not approve of my largesse but they are working and can't see me spoil his dinner. We sit together on the bench outside the museum as the ice cream is consumed. He asks me, "Why don't I call you Grandma?" "Because," I explain, "you have two grandmothers, one is your father's mother and one is your mother's mother. I am the stepmother of your mother, your stepgrandmother, and so you call me Anne." He thinks a moment and then says, "You are my real Anne, aren't you?" "The one and only," I reply. So real is a matter of opinion, of deed, not merely biology. So motherhood which has been so exhausting, so complicated for me has also brought me this realness.